T0340124

VOLUME THREE

HANDBOOK OF MOBILITY
DATA MINING

VOLUME THREE

HANDBOOK OF MOBILITY
DATA MINING
MOBILITY DATA-DRIVEN APPLICATIONS

Edited by

HAORAN ZHANG
*School of Urban Planning and Design, Peking University,
Shenzhen, China*

ELSEVIER

Elsevier
Radarweg 29, PO Box 211, 1000 AE Amsterdam, Netherlands
The Boulevard, Langford Lane, Kidlington, Oxford OX5 1GB, United Kingdom
50 Hampshire Street, 5th Floor, Cambridge, MA 02139, United States

Notices
Knowledge and best practice in this field are constantly changing. As new research and experience broaden our understanding, changes in research methods, professional practices, or medical treatment may become necessary.

Practitioners and researchers must always rely on their own experience and knowledge in evaluating and using any information, methods, compounds, or experiments described herein. In using such information or methods they should be mindful of their own safety and the safety of others, including parties for whom they have a professional responsibility.

To the fullest extent of the law, neither the Publisher nor the authors, contributors, or editors, assume any liability for any injury and/or damage to persons or property as a matter of products liability, negligence or otherwise, or from any use or operation of any methods, products, instructions, or ideas contained in the material herein.

ISBN: 978-0-323-95892-9

For information on all Elsevier publications visit our website at https://www.elsevier.com/books-and-journals

Publisher: Joseph P. Hayton
Acquisitions Editor: Kathryn Eryilmaz
Editorial Project Manager: Ali Afzal-Khan
Production Project Manager: Swapna Srinivasan
Cover Designer: Greg Harris

Typeset by TNQ Technologies

Working together
to grow libraries in
developing countries

www.elsevier.com • www.bookaid.org

Contents

List of contributors

Jinyu Chen
Center for Spatial Information Science, The University of Tokyo, Kashiwa-shi, Chiba, Japan

Jinyu Chen
School of Urban Planning and Design, Peking University, Beijing, China

Wenxiao Jiang
Center for Spatial Information Science, The University of Tokyo, Kashiwa-shi, Chiba, Japan

Yanxiu Jin
Center for Spatial Information Science, The University of Tokyo, Kashiwa-shi, Chiba, Japan

Wenjing Li
Center for Spatial Information Science, The University of Tokyo, Kashiwa-shi, Chiba, Japan

Zhuochao Li
National Engineering Laboratory for Pipeline Safety/MOE Key Laboratory of Petroleum Engineering/Beijing Key Laboratory of Urban Oil and Gas Distribution Technology, China University of Petroleum-Beijing, Beijing, China

Yongtu Liang
National Engineering Laboratory for Pipeline Safety/MOE Key Laboratory of Petroleum Engineering/Beijing Key Laboratory of Urban Oil and Gas Distribution Technology, China University of Petroleum-Beijing, Beijing, China

Youyi Liang
National Engineering Laboratory for Pipeline Safety/MOE Key Laboratory of Petroleum Engineering/Beijing Key Laboratory of Urban Oil and Gas Distribution Technology, China University of Petroleum-Beijing, Beijing, China

Guixu Lin
Center for Spatial Information Science, The University of Tokyo, Kashiwa-shi, Chiba, Japan

Shikun Qi
National Engineering Laboratory for Pipeline Safety/MOE Key Laboratory of Petroleum Engineering/Beijing Key Laboratory of Urban Oil and Gas Distribution Technology, China University of Petroleum-Beijing, Beijing, China

Ryosuke Shibasaki
Center for Spatial Information Science, The University of Tokyo, Kashiwa-shi, Chiba, Japan

Xuan Song
SUSTech-UTokyo Joint Research Center on Super Smart City, Department of Computer Science and Engineering, Southern University of Science and Technology (SUSTech), Shenzhen, China

Lu Wenyi
Center for Spatial Information Science, The University of Tokyo, Kashiwa-shi, Chiba, Japan

Qing Yu
Department of Computer Science and Engineering, Southern University of Science and Technology, Shenzhen, China; The Key Laboratory of Road and Traffic Engineering, Ministry of Education, Tongji University, College of Transportation Engineering, Shanghai, People's Republic of China

Meng Yuan
Department of Planning, Aalborg University, Aalborg, Denmark

Haoran Zhang
School of Urban Planning and Design, Peking University, Shenzhen, China

Chen Zhiheng
Center for Spatial Information Science, The University of Tokyo, Kashiwa-shi, Chiba, Japan

Hao Zhou
National Engineering Laboratory for Pipeline Safety/MOE Key Laboratory of Petroleum Engineering/Beijing Key Laboratory of Urban Oil and Gas Distribution Technology, China University of Petroleum-Beijing, Beijing, China

Preface

In recent times, the smartphone is becoming more and more potent in both computing and storage aspects. The data generated by the smartphone provide a means to get new knowledge about various aspects like usage, movement of the user, etc. Increasingly, application and service providers collect data through sensors embedded in smartphones, such as GPS receivers, while mobile operators collect them through the cellular infrastructure. This information is precious for marketing applications and has an incredible potential to benefit society.

Mobility Data Mining (MDM) is a novel research and business field supported by the growth in smartphone use. MDM can help breed new digital, data-driven services that use several technological capabilities associated with intelligent mobility innovation. It relies on building an ecosystem of stakeholders that agree to manage the supply and demand of the services that travelers want, such as intelligent transportation systems, smart emergency management, sustainability development innovates, etc.

MDM is an emerging topic both in academic and industrial aspects. Currently, all studies about mobile big data mining are fragmented. Few works have summarized the systemic knowledge on this field. Specifically, there is no book focusing on introducing how to screen and process the potential value from "deluge" of unverified, noisy, and sometimes incomplete information of mobile big data. Also, few works comprehensively summarized frontier applications of MDM technologies. However, the above knowledge is significant for stakeholders, such as researchers, engineers, operators, company administrators, and policymakers in related fields, to comprehensively understand current technologies' infra-knowledge structure and limitations. Therefore, we planned to write a series of books mainly focusing on these issues.

The readers of this book can find the knowledge of how to preprocess mobile big data, visualize urban mobility, simulate and predict human travel behavior, and assess the urban mobility characteristics and their matching performance as conditions and constraints in transport, emergency management, and sustainability development systems that are undergoing automation and are highly dependent on software, navigation systems, and connectivity. Further, this book will focus on introducing how to design MDM platforms that adapt to the evolving mobility environment, new types of transportation, and users based on an integrated solution that utilizes the sensing and communication capabilities to tackle the significant challenges that the MDM field faces.

The handbook includes three volumes:

Volume 1: *Data Preprocessing and Visualization* focuses on how to efficiently preprocess mobility big data to extract and utilize critical feature information of high-dimensional city people flow. It first provides a conceptual theory and framework, then goes on to discuss data sources, trajectory map matching, noise filtering, trajectory data segmentation, data quality assessment, and more. It concludes with a chapter on mobility big data visualization.

Volume 2: *Mobility Analytics and Prediction* provides a basis for how to simulate and predict mobility data. After an introductory theory chapter, it then covers crucial topics such as long-term mobility pattern analytics, mobility data generators, user information inference, grid-based population density prediction, and more. It concludes with a chapter on graph-based mobility data analytics.

Volume 3: *Mobility Data-driven Applications* looks at various case studies to illustrate and explore the methods introduced in the first two volumes. It begins with a set of chapters on intelligent transportation management, using cases of bicycle-sharing, ride-hailing, travel time prediction, railway usage analysis, mobility data-driven service, and dynamic road pricing. It concludes with chapters on urban sustainability development, including road emission and living environment inequity analysis.

To help to utilize book outcomes by fellow researchers and developers, all book outcomes will be offered as Open Source Code. Please see the open project, OpenMob, https://github.com/openmob/openmob.

Acknowledgments

I want to thank all lab team members: Zhiling Guo, Dou Huang, Xiaodan Shi, Peiran Li, Jinyu Chen, Yuhao Yao, Qing Yu, Wenjing Li, Zhiheng Chen, Xudong Shen, Wenyi Lu, and Ning Xu, for their efforts, and would also like to thank lab leaders Prof. Ryosuke Shibasaki and Prof. Xuan Song for their support for this book.

CHAPTER ONE

Mobility data in bike-sharing systems

Youyi Liang[1], Meng Yuan[2], Zhuochao Li[1], Hao Zhou[1], Haoran Zhang[3], Qing Yu[4,5], Yongtu Liang[1]

[1]National Engineering Laboratory for Pipeline Safety/MOE Key Laboratory of Petroleum Engineering/ Beijing Key Laboratory of Urban Oil and Gas Distribution Technology, China University of Petroleum-Beijing, Beijing, China
[2]Department of Planning, Aalborg University, Aalborg, Denmark
[3]School of Urban Planning and Design, Peking University, Shenzhen, China
[4]Department of Computer Science and Engineering, Southern University of Science and Technology, Shenzhen, China
[5]The Key Laboratory of Road and Traffic Engineering, Ministry of Education, Tongji University, College of Transportation Engineering, Shanghai, People's Republic of China

1. Introduction

Urban transportation systems are under increasing pressure with urbanization, and bicycle-sharing systems (BSS) are becoming an important transportation mode to promoting urban sustainability [1]. BSS has received much attention in recent years due to its convenience, flexibility, and low travel costs, which helps to solve the "first/last mile" problem of public transportation [2]. Meanwhile, from a social perspective, by reducing traffic congestion and noise pollution, BSS can improve the image of cities. In addition, they can serve as an eco-friendly way to travel, reduce greenhouse gas emissions, and mitigate the effects of climate change. BSS has undergone an evolution from the first generation to the current fourth generation. The first generation of the BSS originated in 1965 in Amsterdam, Netherlands, and was originally known as the "White Bike" which has no fixed return point [3]. Development to date, the fourth generation enables real-time tracking of bikes, which allows users to see when and where they have available bikes on their phones [4]. The new generation of bicycles may also introduce types of bicycles, such as electric bicycles and bicycle redistribution systems [5].

However, with the rapidly growing of BSS, some underlying problems have emerged. For example, the layout of the BSS is commonly divided purely by administrative areas and does not user needs take into account,

Handbook of Mobility Data Mining, Volume 3
ISBN: 978-0-323-95892-9
https://doi.org/10.1016/B978-0-323-95892-9.00008-5

1

which leads to problems of imbalance between supply and demand as well as tedious rebalancing work. For the optimization of the BSS, it is particularly vital to accurately mine user data. Mobility data is a collective of movement tracks, which is an ordered record of time and location. Mobility data includes not only data continuously sampled with the global positioning system (GPS), but also data such as mobile social network check-in data, operator log data, and data collected by traffic smart cards. It has been used in a variety of areas, such as analyzing travel patterns, investigating traffic routes, and managing traffic layouts. The mode of transportation is a basic ingredient in understanding mobility within a transportation system [6]. Using mobility data mining gives several advantages for optimizing BSS: (1) The detailed understanding of mobility patterns provided by mobility data mining technology can yield a density distribution of bike-sharing users which informs the planning of BSS to facilitate the development of a more user-demand oriented regional distribution plan to make the best use of things and prevent waste [7]. (2) Based on user data, the number of cross-regional users can also be identified, and penalties can be instituted without affecting the overall system, which can guide the rebalancing plan for each region, making rebalancing easier. (3) The spatiotemporal location and movement trajectory of people can be provided by mobility data mining technology. By analyzing the potential market of the BSS through trajectory data, the layout of the BSS can be optimized more thoroughly.

In recent years, many studies on BSS have been conducted, such as understanding the usage of bicycle sharing to overcome management problems, developing novel method to optimize the layout and operation to improve the efficiency, and investigating the impact of bicycle sharing on climate change mitigation and fitness enhancement. Most of them cannot be achieved without the most basic data mining techniques.

The remaining sections are composed as follows: Section 2 reviews the update to date studies related. Section 3, provides three examples of the optimization of mobility data mining for BSS. Section 4 concludes the whole paper.

2. Literature review

Research on BSS relies on a large amount of data on smart card transactions (mobility data). The data provided by mobility data have many advantages over data collected through traditional methods. For example, the data collection is more objective and independent of the observer; the recorded sample is large, and almost the entire whole data can be collected, thus avoiding sample bias; and mobility data collection is a more cost-effective method compared to traditional data acquisition methods; and the data is more accurate due to the developed positioning technology [7].

Studies on BSS that are based on mobility data mining can be roughly categorized into three types: (1) the rebalancing problem of BSS; (2) the optimal management of BSS; and (3) studies on the environmental benefits derived from BSS.

It goes without saying that user flow can alter the spatial and temporal distribution of bicycle availability, and BSS operators need to precisely plan rebalancing to address the supply demand balance of the BSS to improve the efficiency of BSS. The rebalancing can be accomplished by either a user with an incentive program or by a rebalancing truck driver who balances a certain number of bikes between areas based on the reposi-tioned bikes. And the rebalancing can be divided into static rebalancing and dynamic rebalancing, or a conjunction of both. Static rebalancing is usually done at night when user activity is not disturbed, while dynamic rebalancing is done during the day when users are free to borrow and return [8]. As described in the literature [9], used real movement data of shared bicycles to tackle the problem of rebalancing shared bicycles at minimum cost using a set of powered vehicles using mixed-integer linear programming. Using bike-share data from Barcelona and Serbia, Spain, Faghih-Imani et al. [10] estimated the bicycle infrastructure using a mixed linear model and identi-fied rebalancing periods using a binary logit model, resulting in modeling templates for examining bicycle rebalancing in different contexts to improve rebalancing system management. Using the BSS data of NYC, Lin et al. [11] proposed a graph convolutional neural network with a data-driven graph filter model for predicting station-level hourly demand in a large-scale bike-sharing network, which contributes to accurate demand predic-tion and dynamic rebalancing of station-level bike-sharing. Sohrabi et al. [12] developed a generalized extreme value counting model using real-time system status data from bicycle stations, which can provide users with more reliable usage information and provide BSS operators with solid data for predicting future demand and optimizing rebalancing plans Luo et al. [13]. used data from a dockless BSS in Xiamen, China, and data retrieved using GPS devices mounted on bicycles to construct an optimiza-tion model for bicycle rebalancing and used a life cycle assessment model to quantify the greenhouse gas emission rate of the system to obtain an optimal bicycle fleet size and a rebalancing strategy that minimizes greenhouse gas emissions Neumann-Saavedra et al. [14] analyzed recorded data from three North American BSS and proposed a rule-based procedure to determine the value and limitations of stochastic programming for bike-sharing redistribution, facilitating the adjustment of redistribution decisions when the number of station-loaded bicycles differs from the number of optimally considered settings. To manage the supply demand imbalance in the free-floating BSS, Mahmoodian et al. [8] used real-time GPS location information of bicycles to construct dynamic hubs and hybrid rebalancing and solved the problem by a novel multi-objective simulation-optimization approach. Lu et al. [15] divided management subregions based on GPS shared bicycle usage data and road network data in Shanghai and used cluster analysis algorithms and heuristic algorithms to generate rebalancing schemes to decrease the number of rebalanced vehicles in use and distance traveled.

Optimizing management systems as well as fulfilling user needs are pivotal factors in the operation of BSS. Zhang et al. [16] explored the travel behavior of bike-sharing users using smart card formation data of Zhongshan City to provide a reference for BSS operators to optimize their management. Lu et al. [17] collected shared bicycle data streams in real-time to provide a novel data-informed model for the design and development of free-floating shared bicycle systems. From the extensive GPS records of bike-sharing, Yang et al. [18] captured the spatiotemporal variation of bicycle demand across the city and constructed a spatiotemporally more accurate coverage model to optimize bike station locations. Using smart card data and dockless bicycle sharing data, Ma et al. [19] discussed the relationship between bicycle-sharing usage and its determinants in the spatio-temporal dimension, providing insights and suggestions for improving the performance of docking and dockless BSS. Using 5 years of smart card data from Nanjing, Chen et al. [20] used longitudinal analysis to track the annual dynamics of commuter behavior to inform operational plan development and transportation planning. In order to learn about the factors that cause bike-sharing to be more competitive than buses, Christian et al. [21] developed a logistic regression model using empirical analysis of traffic smart cards and bike-sharing GPS data collected in Seoul. After analyzing real data from Beijing's Mobike BSS and New York's Citibike BSS, Zheng et al. [22] constructed an origin–destination spatial network of bike-sharing traffic flows to study the imbalance characteristics in the system, which can help develop more effective management methods. Oliveira et al. [23] conducted an interactive visualization study using data provided by the operator to provide an exploratory view of bike-sharing usage data and a deeper understanding of system dynamics, which provided a better reference for operational efforts.

The environmental friendliness of BSS is one of the crucial factors in its popularity. Many scholars have studied the environmental benefits based on mobility data mining techniques. For example, Zhang and Mi [24] used the data provided by Mobike to evaluate the impact of bike-sharing on energy use, carbon dioxide, and nitrogen oxide emissions in Shanghai from a spatial and temporal perspective. It is derived that bike-sharing has a great possibility of decreasing energy consumption and emissions. Based on Beijing Mobike data, Cao and Shen [25] constructed a CO_2 reduction and economic efficiency model that contributes to the healthy development of bike-sharing and environmental protection. To quantify the environmental benefits of bike-share trips, Kou et al. [26] proposed a bike-share emission reduction estimation model using bike-share trip data. Using data from New York City's bike-sharing services, Chen et al. [27] evaluated the environmental benefits of bike-sharing in New York City from a spatial and temporal perspective and used big data to analyze the energy consumption of bike-sharing use, resulting in the conclusion that the use of bicycles as a means of commuting can dramatically reduce urban pollutants.

3. Case study

Three cases are summarized in this paper to briefly illustrate the approach and results of BSS optimization based on mobility data mining techniques.

3.1 Case 1: Market-oriented subarea division

The first case aims to use GPS data to divide the sub area covered by the BSS according to market orientation [28]. The management model of existing BSS is mostly segmented by administrative regions, which can lead to problems such as supply demand imbalance and rebalancing challenges. Here, Yu et al. [28] proposed a market-oriented subregional division, which can effectively represent the actual mobility boundary. Modeling cities into subregions can reduce the model size and increase model solvability, which helps with system designing, supply-demand balance, and rebalancing planning.

The framework of the methodology is illustrated in Fig. 1.1, where cell phone GPS data are employed to analyze the latent demand for bike-sharing and divide the management subregions according to the spatial interactivity

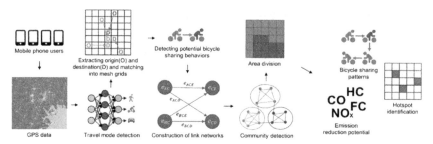

Figure 1.1 Framework of methods introduced for market-oriented subarea division.

of the potential bike-sharing demand. Specifically, in the first step, the travel mode is first detected from the mobile phone GPS data according to data mining techniques. After getting the information of origin (O) and destination (D) of walking, bicycle, and short-distance car trips, the network is matched and aggregated to form. In the second step, a linked grid is generated based on the potential bike-sharing behaviors detected in OD formation, and the linked communities are tested with community detection methods to complete the detailed segmentation of the coverage area due to the principle of dividing subservice areas in the layout of the BSS is to find subregions with strong connectivity within each area and relatively weak connectivity between areas, and community detection is the perfect solution to this problem. Finally, based on the results of subregional segmentation, three aspects of shared behavior patterns, hot spots, and subregional emission potential are analyzed.

GPS data used in this case is retrieved from the "Konzatsu-Tokei(R)" GPS dataset collected by NTT DOCOMO INC. "Konzatsu-Tokei(R)" data refers to foot traffic data, which is collected from personal location data sent from users' cell phones with their consent. This data is sent about once every 5 min and does not include information such as the gender and age of the individual, but only raw location (latitude, longitude) data. In this study, only short walks, bicycle, and car trips of 1—3 km were extracted as our study subjects since bicycle usually covers short trips of 1—3 km. Fig. 1.2 shows the spatial distribution of the trajectory data within 1 month, which includes 34,181,231 trajectories, including 19,821,894 walking trips, 11,994,279 bicycle trips, and 2,365,058 car trips. By mining the dataset, a total of 47,666,836 potential bike-sharing trips were matched, resulting in the construction of a linked network with 587,606 nodes and 9,425,875 edges.

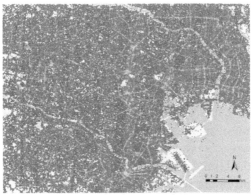

"Konzatsu-Tokei (r)" (c) ZENRIN DataCom CO., LTD.

(a)

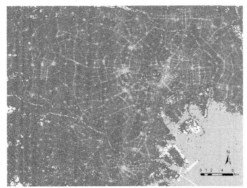

"Konzatsu-Tokei (r)" (c) ZENRIN DataCom CO., LTD.

(b)

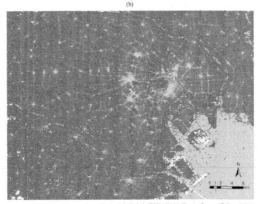

"Konzatsu-Tokei (r)" (c) ZENRIN DataCom CO., LTD.

(c)

Figure 1.2 Spatial distribution of trajectory dataset in 1 month. (A) Car trajectories, (B) bicycle trajectories, (C) walk trajectories.

The results of community detection on the link graph are shown in Fig. 1.3, where each link community contains an average of 27,948 links. It can be seen from Fig. 1.3 that the bike-sharing organization pattern is mainly radial in suburban areas to connect neighboring areas and local centers, while in urban areas, it is a high-density mesh distributed throughout the area. Using the precise mobility data, the results are based on linked communities in the subarea map shown in Fig. 1.4, which generate 21 subareas. The division of subregions is mainly influenced by physical geographies, such as rivers and mountains. For some subregions, subregions 6, 7, 14, 16, and 19, the boundaries are consistent with administrative divisions. These areas are mainly in suburban areas. Sub-districts 1, 2, 3, 4, 5, and 8 differ significantly from the administrative division of the city center. Small isolated areas with a high density of short trips were also identified, including Subdistrict 17 (Tokyo Disney Resort), Subdistrict 20 (Odaiba: an artificial island), and Subdistrict 21 (Haneda Airport). This result suggests that segmenting the bike-sharing market by administrative area would be inconsistent with users' bike-sharing patterns.

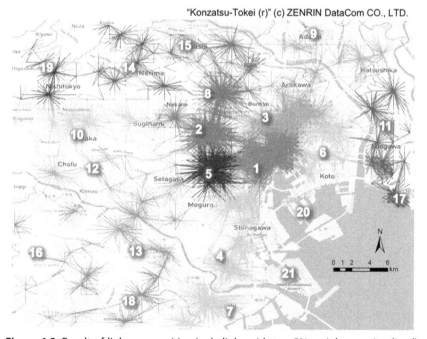

"Konzatsu-Tokei (r)" (c) ZENRIN DataCom CO., LTD.

Figure 1.3 Result of link communities (only links with top 5% weight are visualized).

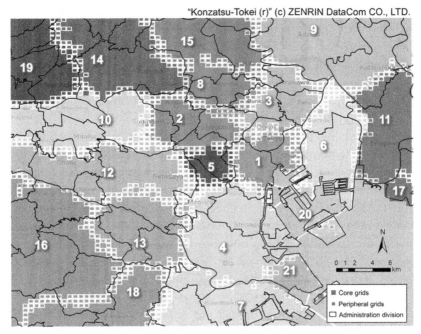

Figure 1.4 Division of subareas based on the link communities.

3.2 Case 2: Layout optimization

To demonstrate the key role played by mobility data mining techniques in BSS layout optimization, we provide an example derived from Ref. [29]. The BSS layout design is closely related to the performance of the system implementation. In recent years, problems regarding abandoned and uncoordinated rationing of shared bicycles have been commonplace. The main reason for these problems is the improper layout of the BSS. Pragmatic and performance-oriented layout optimization will be necessary for the healthy development of BSS.

However, performance-oriented layout optimization is a very complicated problem [30]. The first difficulty is demand forecasting. Typically, bike docking stations are colocated with hotspot areas, which include subway stations, universities, and shopping centers [31]. Determining the required bicycle spaces and capacity for each docking station requires estimating the potential bicycle rental demand by calculating the population density of each hotspot area [32]. This approach has several limitations, firstly as the method does not detect individual travel patterns, which leads to inaccurate demand forecasts, and secondly the lack of OD information to guide public bicycle rationing. The second difficulty is the uncertainty of site-specific construction conditions [33]. This is because it is difficult to collect reliable information on all available station locations during the layout phase. The theoretical best location is not necessarily the best location in practice. Under the condition of lack of key information, the layout design is more challenging [34]. Therefore, there is considerable uncertainty in optimizing the layout of shared bikes.

Zhang et al. [29] presented a relatively general computational framework and implementation method, which uses mobile phone GPS data to optimize the layout of BSS. The method consists of four parts (as shown in Fig. 1.5): (a) using the user's ID, latitude, longitude, and time in the cell phone GPS data to obtain information such as trajectory and travel mode. (b) A geometry-based probabilistic model is proposed to solve the uncertainty of the candidate bicycle docking station locations and construction conditions. This model is solved by using the OD information obtained in step 1 and an improved particle swarm optimization method. Although the optimal layout of bike-sharing stations can be obtained through a geometry-based probabilistic model and improved PSO, detailed design scale information (e.g., how many docking facilities need to be provided at each station, how many bikes need to be delivered to the sharing system, or even how much energy will be consumed when rebalancing the number of bikes across the system) is still not available. Thus, (c) a multiscenario integer linear programming model is proposed for the optimal scheduling of rebalancing operations with demand uncertainty. (d) The emission reduction effect of using bicycles for travel is evident, but the total emission potential may be attenuated by emissions associated with bicycle production and operation, such as those from rebalancing work trucks, which are influenced by truck type, truck fuel choice, and truck loading capacity. Therefore, based on the results of the layout and rebalancing, this study evaluates the emission reduction potential of a BSS.

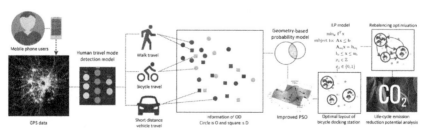

Figure 1.5 Framework of model utilizing mobile phone GPS data.

To validate this method in practice, this case used the GPS trajectories of Setagaya-ku, Tokyo for the year of 2012. As described in the previous case study, GPS data were extracted from the "Konzatsu-Tokei(R)" GPS dataset collected by NTT DOCOMO INC. Using the method described above, the GPS trajectories were classified into different modes of transportation (walking, bicycle, and car), and the dataset contained 3,659,703 trajectories, of which 2,904,820, 481,660, and 273,223 trips were made by walking, bicycle, and car modes, respectively. The OD information of these trajectories is shown in Fig. 1.6.

The optimal layout of the BSS is shown in Fig. 1.7 (the number of stations is set to N = 30, 50, 70, and 90, respectively). The blue circles represent the probability areas where the bike-sharing stations are installed, and the circle size is proportional to the probability area. The results show that most stations are located in locations with high OD information density and along major roads. Meanwhile, if the stations are set in locations with

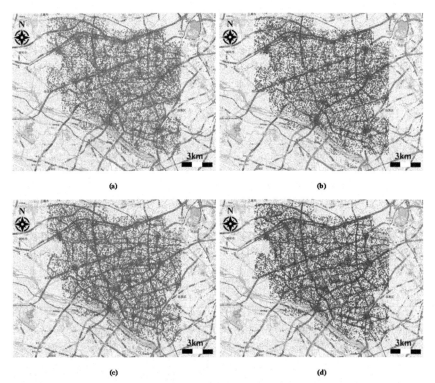

Figure 1.6 OD information for different travel modes. (A) O for walk, (B) D for walk, (C) O for bicycle, (D) D for bicycle.

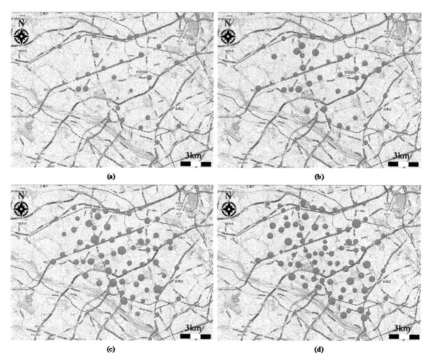

Figure 1.7 Optimal layout of bicycle-sharing system. With *N*= (A) 30, (B) 50, (C) 70, and (D) 90 docking stations.

high OD density, the probability area will be small. When N increases, some alternative stations will be divided into two or three neighboring stations. To avoid competing with each other, the probability area of these more finely divided stations will be small.

Fig. 1.8 shows the distance traveled by shared bicycle alternative for each mode of transportation with an optimized layout and operation of the shared bicycle system. The results show that the use of shared bicycles reduces vehicle trips, especially during weekday commuting peak hours and weekend afternoons.

3.3 Case 3: System design optimization

In this case, Yuan et al. [35] used human mobility data for the system optimiztaion of BSS. Bikes, rental stations, and a control center (depot) consist of a complete BSS. One can rent a bike at one station and return it to another. The control center is responsible for bicycle storage, maintenance, and dispatch. A complete BSS plan should consider all three aspects at the same time.

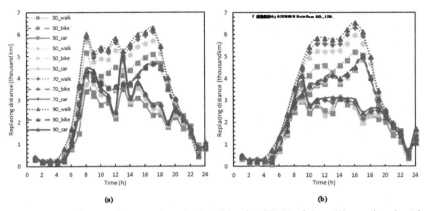

Figure 1.8 Replacing distance by sharing bicycle. (A) Weekday, (B) weekend with 30—90 bicycle-sharing stations.

However, planning a BSS is not a easy task. First, planning a BSS involves choosing the number and location of bicycle stations. Operators need to have enough stations to ensure that they can meet the various travel needs of users, and it is especially important to have bicycle stations close to public transportation stations. Second, the capacity of bike stations needs to vary with the density of users, and more docking units should be installed in hotspots than in other areas. Then, the design solution of BSS and the operation solution are interactive, and the location of the bike station affects the users' usage as well as the rebalancing plan, so a proper rebalancing plan is another hardpoint. Finally, the demand for BSS is a random demand, which is affected by weather, season, and working days. Considering the above difficulties, this study proposes a unified mixed linear integer programming approach based on human mobility data to address the determination of bicycle station locations and capacities, depot locations, and rebalancing and maintenance schedules.

The central area of Changping District in Beijing is used as a case study, which uses passenger flow from survey results as well as operational data from the Changping District Public Bicycle Management Service Center. Fig. 1.9 shows a map of the study area, which is a square with a side length of about 3.75 km. Representative areas like residential areas, offices, parks, hospitals, and schools have been marked on the map with different colors. Major transportation hubs such as train, bus, and subway stations, as well as landmarks such as shopping centers, are also indicated with different symbols. Major roads and bicycle paths are also denoted. We divided the study

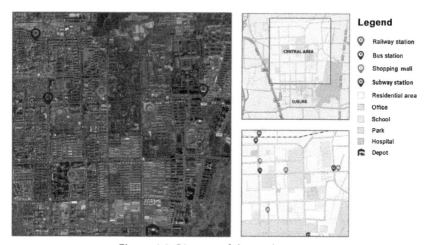

Figure 1.9 Diagram of the study area.

area into 10×10 blocks, with each block having an edge length of 375 m. Fig. 1.10 shows the average patronage of each block during some representative time windows in the study area on a given day. The brighter the color of the block in the figure, the more active the bicycle use.

Seventy potential bicycle stations and one depot are selected in the region (as shown in Fig. 1.11). The criteria for selecting potential stations are: (1) Stations should be within 300−500 m of major transportation hubs and close to major intersections. (2) Sites should be close to large residential areas, government offices, businesses, commercial areas, schools,

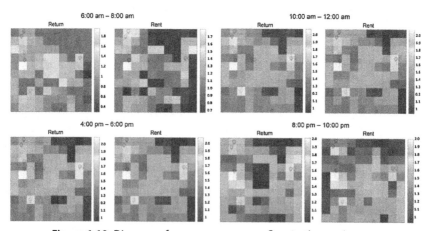

Figure 1.10 Diagram of average passenger flow in the study area.

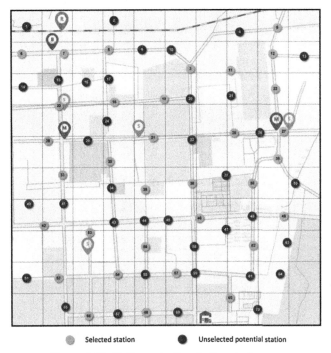

Figure 1.11 Station selection in the study area.

hospitals, and tourist attractions. (3) Stations should avoid being located on busy motorways and intersection entrances. After model optimization, Fig. 1.11 shows the site locations of the BSS. The yellow dots represent the selected sites and the blue dots are other potential sites. The results show that 32 bicycle stations are selected from the 70 potential stations. In addition, the size of the bicycle fleet deployed in the system is 934 bicycles and the number of docking units is 1586. Based on the station locations, all stations are categorized into eight types–namely, R for residential areas; T for transit stations (meaning train or subway stations); H for hospitals; S for schools; G for government agencies; SM for shopping/commercial areas; P for parks; and O for office buildings. Table 1.1 gives the types of selected bicycle stations, the number of docking units, and the initial inventory. Also, since the area served by a station may have multiple attributes, a station may have multiple types. As can be seen from the table, residential areas are the most critical areas with about 47%, followed by schools (28%); office buildings (19%); parks (12.5%); and transit stations, shopping centers, and government agencies (10%). Because of the low number of hospitals in Changping

Table 1.1 Information on the selected bicycle stations.

No.	1	2	3	4	5	6	7	8	9	10	11	12	13	14	15	16
Selected station	3	5	6	7	8	11	12	18	19	22	23	25	27	28	30	31
Type	S/R	R	R	T	H	S	T/R	G/S	S	R	SM	R	T/R	G	P	S/SM
Number of docking units	42	30	50	55	52	37	38	29	56	57	44	56	37	59	55	39
Initial inventory	21	15	25	28	26	19	19	15	28	29	22	28	19	30	28	20
No.	17	18	19	20	21	22	23	24	25	26	27	28	29	30	31	32
Selected station	33	35	36	38	39	42	46	49	52	53	54	56	57	60	66	68
Type	P	R/S	S/R	R	R	P	S	R/P	O	SM	O	R/S	R/O	O/R	O	O/G
Number of docking units	56	55	56	53	49	43	60	58	55	59	49	55	51	49	59	43
Initial inventory	28	28	28	27	25	22	30	29	28	30	25	28	26	25	30	22

Note: The stations are divided into eight types–R, residential area; T, transit station; H, hospital; S, school; G, government agency; SM, shopping/commercial area; P, park; and O, office building.

District, it is evident that hospitals have the lowest percentage. The results of our planning for the BSS were able to cover most of the areas that people visit in their daily lives.

Fig. 1.12 shows the rebalancing operations for the 32 selected bicycle stations in extreme cases, i.e., (a) 0.55 average passenger flow (APF) is small and

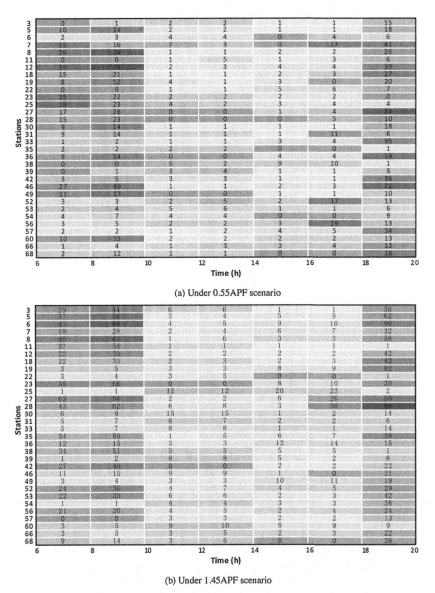

(a) Under 0.55APF scenario

(b) Under 1.45APF scenario

Figure 1.12 Rebalancing operation for selected stations in the study area.

(b) 1.45 APF is large. The horizontal axis represents the period of the rebalancing operation on a given day, and the vertical axis indicates the sequence number of the selected bike stations. The blue grid represents bikes being shipped in, the green grid represents bikes being shipped out, and the gray grid means that no rebalancing operation occurred. The darker the color, the higher the number of bikes that were rebalanced. In addition, the number of reassigned bikes has been marked on the grid. Fig. 1.12 reflects some extent the travel trajectory of users in Changping District throughout the day. The early morning peak of users' travel is from 6 to 8 a.m., and the users from 6 to 7 a.m. are mainly those going to work in the city. Because of the high cost of living in Beijing, most people live in suburban areas like Changping District to save money, so they need to get up early to rush from their residential areas to the subway or bus station to go to work in the city by subway or bus. Meanwhile, the users from 7 to 8 p.m. are mainly people who work in the area and students. The evening peak occurs between 7 and 9 p.m., when people are returning home from work and students are out of school. We can also see from Fig. 1.12 that the rebalancing activity occurs mainly from 6 to 10 a.m. and from 4 to 10 p.m., as there is a significant demand imbalance during these times.

The Changping BSS has been relocated several times because of the unreasonable initial design. For example, the black circle "R" in Fig. 1.13A is the former station, which was removed in 2018 and later replaced by stations 40 and 13 marked as red circles. Fig. 1.13B shows the BSS plan obtained by solving the proposed mixed-integer linear programming model based on

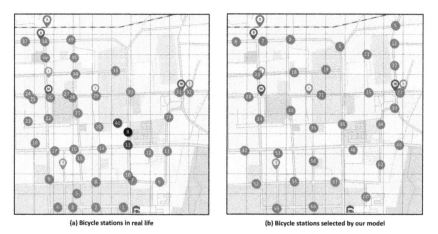

(a) Bicycle stations in real life   (b) Bicycle stations selected by our model

Figure 1.13 Comparison with BSS in real life.

human mobility data. It can be seen that the optimized central area is uniformly covered by the BSS without too much concentration or excessive looseness. This plan uses 1586 docking units, which is more economical than the real-life 1640 units. And the 24—28 stations, 7 and 10 stations, and 21 and 32 stations in Fig. 1.13A were combined. This helps to reduce the number of stations and lower the cost, while the even coverage of stations improves the convenience of service. If BSS can have a reasonable planning at the beginning, it can reduce the waste of resources and environmental damage caused by station changes afterward, and also reduce the difficulty of rebalancing. Therefore, it is important to plan the BSS from a comprehensive and long-term perspective as well as by using mobility data. A good BSS planning can increase the frequency of bicycle use in commuting, bring many benefits to the environment, economy, and public health, and also can achieve a balance between operator costs and user satisfaction, thus making BSS operations more successful and long-lasting, as done in this case.

4. Conclusion

There is a noticeable trend of using mobility data to analyze BSS problems, and more and more scholars are aware of the fact that the mobility data can offer a more credible and comprehensive information base for research. However, it is difficult for researchers to have an all-around insight into the application, development, and frontier works of mobility data mining technology in BSS research problems due to the lack of knowledge. Therefore, this paper summarizes the current research on BSS based on mobility data mining technology.

Since urbanization has led to increasing population density and complex transportation systems, one of the most appropriate and ideal approaches to better integrate BSS into urban transportation systems and to more rationally relieve the pressure on urban transportation systems by capturing user needs accurately is to use a large amount of authentic mobility data as the database for BSS research. The mobility data mainly comes from mobile phone GPS, traffic smart cards, etc. It is mainly applied to the research of BSS rebalancing problems, the research of optimal management problems, and the research of economic benefits brought by BSS. The objective and accurate mobility data are used to mine users' demand and users' spatial flow trajectory for bicycle sharing demand prediction, which improves the practicality and credibility of the research. The more accurate the demand prediction, the more reasonable the BSS layout, the simpler the rebalancing problem will be, the more obvious the optimization effect will be, and the environmental benefits will be improved.

With the rapid development and spread of positioning technology, mobile social network, and IoT technology, the variety and scale of mobility data are increasing fast, and the superiority of using mobility data for BSS research will become more and more pronounced.

References

[1] T. Mátrai, J. Tóth, Comparative assessment of public bike sharing systems. Transportation research procedia, Transport Research Arena TRA2016 14 (2016) 2344–2351, https://doi.org/10.1016/j.trpro.2016.05.261.

[2] Q. Chen, X. Pan, F. Liu, Y. Xiong, Z. Li, J. Tang, Reposition optimization in free-floating bike-sharing system: a case study in Shenzhen City, Physica A: Statistical Mechanics and Its Applications 593 (2022) 126925, https://doi.org/10.1016/j.physa.2022.126925.

[3] S.A. Shaheen, S. Guzman, H. Zhang, Bikesharing in Europe, the Americas, and Asia: past, present, and future, Transportation Research Record 2143 (2010) 159–167, https://doi.org/10.3141/2143-20.

[4] J. Zhang, M. Meng, P.P. Koh, Y.D. Wong, Life duration of bike sharing systems, Case Studies on Transport Policy 9 (2021) 674–680, https://doi.org/10.1016/j.cstp.2021.03.005.

[5] J. Zhou, Y. Guo, J. Sun, E. Yu, R. Wang, Review of bike-sharing system studies using bibliometrics method, Journal of Traffic and Transportation Engineering (English Edition) 9 (4) (August 2022) 608–630, https://doi.org/10.1016/j.jtte.2021.08.003.

[6] P. Sadeghian, X. Zhao, A. Golshan, J. Håkansson, A stepwise methodology for transport mode detection in GPS tracking data, Travel Behaviour and Society 26 (2022) 159–167, https://doi.org/10.1016/j.tbs.2021.10.004.

[7] M. Bordagaray, L. dell'Olio, A. Fonzone, Á. Ibeas, Capturing the conditions that introduce systematic variation in bike-sharing travel behavior using data mining techniques, Transportation Research Part C: Emerging Technologies 71 (2016) 231–248, https://doi.org/10.1016/j.trc.2016.07.009.

[8] V. Mahmoodian, Y. Zhang, H. Charkhgard, Hybrid rebalancing with dynamic hubbing for free-floating bike sharing systems, International Journal of Transportation Science and Technology 11 (3) (September 2022) 636–652, https://doi.org/10.1016/j.ijtst.2021.08.002.

[9] M. Dell'Amico, E. Hadjicostantinou, M. Iori, S. Novellani, The bike sharing rebalancing problem: mathematical formulations and benchmark instances, Omega 45 (2014) 7–19, https://doi.org/10.1016/j.omega.2013.12.001.

[10] A. Faghih-Imani, R. Hampshire, L. Marla, N. Eluru, An empirical analysis of bike sharing usage and rebalancing: Evidence from Barcelona and Seville, Transportation Research Part A: Policy and Practice 97 (2017) 177–191, https://doi.org/10.1016/j.tra.2016.12.007.

[11] L. Lin, Z. He, S. Peeta, Predicting station-level hourly demand in a large-scale bike-sharing network: a graph convolutional neural network approach, Transportation Research Part C: Emerging Technologies 97 (2018) 258–276, https://doi.org/10.1016/j.trc.2018.10.011.

[12] S. Sohrabi, R. Paleti, L. Balan, M. Cetin, Real-time prediction of public bike sharing system demand using generalized extreme value count model, Transportation

Research Part A: Policy and Practice 133 (2020) 325–336, https://doi.org/10.1016/j.tra.2020.02.001.

[13] H. Luo, F. Zhao, W.-Q. Chen, H. Cai, Optimizing bike sharing systems from the life cycle greenhouse gas emissions perspective, Transportation Research Part C: Emerging Technologies 117 (2020) 102705, https://doi.org/10.1016/j.trc.2020.102705.

[14] B.A. Neumann-Saavedra, D.C. Mattfeld, M. Hewitt, Assessing the operational impact of tactical planning models for bike-sharing redistribution, Transportation Research Part A: Policy and Practice 150 (2021) 216–235, https://doi.org/10.1016/j.tra.2021.06.003.

[15] C. Lu, L. Gao, Y. Huang, Exploring travel patterns and static rebalancing strategies for dockless bike-sharing systems from multi-source data: a framework and case study, Transportation Letters (2022), https://doi.org/10.1080/19427867.2022.2051798.

[16] Y. Zhang, M.J.G. Brussel, T. Thomas, M.F.A.M. van Maarseveen, Mining bike-sharing travel behavior data: an investigation into trip chains and transition activities, Computers, Environment and Urban Systems 69 (2018) 39–50, https://doi.org/10.1016/j.compenvurbsys.2017.12.004.

[17] M. Lu, K. An, S.-C. Hsu, R. Zhu, Considering user behavior in free-floating bike sharing system design: a data-informed spatial agent-based model, Sustainable Cities and Society 49 (2019) 101567, https://doi.org/10.1016/j.scs.2019.101567.

[18] L. Yang, F. Zhang, M.-P. Kwan, K. Wang, Z. Zuo, S. Xia, Z. Zhang, X. Zhao, Space-time demand cube for spatial-temporal coverage optimization model of shared bicycle system: a study using big bike GPS data, Journal of Transport Geography 88 (2020) 102861, https://doi.org/10.1016/j.jtrangeo.2020.102861.

[19] X. Ma, Y. Ji, Y. Yuan, N. Van Oort, Y. Jin, S. Hoogendoorn, A comparison in travel patterns and determinants of user demand between docked and dockless bike-sharing systems using multi-sourced data, Transportation Research Part A: Policy and Practice 139 (2020) 148–173, https://doi.org/10.1016/j.tra.2020.06.022.

[20] W. Chen, X. Liu, X. Chen, L. Cheng, K. Wang, J. Chen, Exploring year-to-year changes in station-based bike sharing commuter behaviors with smart card data, Travel Behaviour and Society 28 (2022) 75–89, https://doi.org/10.1016/j.tbs.2022.02.005.

[21] K. Christian, K. Seung-Young, K. Dong-Kyu, C. Shin-Hyung, Modeling the competitiveness of a bike-sharing system using bicycle GPS and transit smartcard data, Transportation Letters 14 (4) (May 2022) 347–351, https://doi.org/10.1080/19427867.2020.1758389.

[22] Z. Zheng, Y. Chen, D. Zhu, H. Sun, J. Wu, X. Pan, D. Li, Extreme unbalanced mobility network in bike sharing system, Physica A: Statistical Mechanics and Its Applications 563 (2021) 125444, https://doi.org/10.1016/j.physa.2020.125444.

[23] G.N. Oliveira, J.L. Sotomayor, R.P. Torchelsen, C.T. Silva, J.L.D. Comba, Visual analysis of bike-sharing systems, Computers & Graphics 60 (2016) 119–129, https://doi.org/10.1016/j.cag.2016.08.005.

[24] Y. Zhang, Z. Mi, Environmental benefits of bike sharing: a big data-based analysis, Applied Energy 220 (2018) 296–301, https://doi.org/10.1016/j.apenergy.2018.03.101.

[25] Y. Cao, D. Shen, Contribution of shared bikes to carbon dioxide emission reduction and the economy in Beijing, Sustainable Cities and Society 51 (2019) 101749, https://doi.org/10.1016/j.scs.2019.101749.

[26] Z. Kou, X. Wang, S.F. Chiu,) Anthony, H. Cai, Quantifying greenhouse gas emissions reduction from bike share systems: a model considering real-world trips and transportation mode choice patterns, Resources, Conservation and Recycling 153 (2020) 104534, https://doi.org/10.1016/j.resconrec.2019.104534.

[27] Y. Chen, Y. Zhang, D. Coffman, Z. Mi, An environmental benefit analysis of bike sharing in New York City, Cities 121 (2022) 103475, https://doi.org/10.1016/j.cities.2021.103475.

[28] Q. Yu, H. Zhang, W. Li, Y. Sui, X. Song, D. Yang, R. Shibasaki, W. Jiang, Mobile phone data in urban bicycle-sharing: market-oriented sub-area division and spatial analysis on emission reduction potentials, Journal of Cleaner Production 254 (2020) 119974, https://doi.org/10.1016/j.jclepro.2020.119974.

[29] H. Zhang, X. Song, Y. Long, T. Xia, K. Fang, J. Zheng, D. Huang, R. Shibasaki, Y. Liang, Mobile phone GPS data in urban bicycle-sharing: layout optimization and emissions reduction analysis, Applied Energy 242 (2019) 138–147, https://doi.org/10.1016/j.apenergy.2019.03.119.

[30] G. Erdoğan, M. Battarra, R. Wolfler Calvo, An exact algorithm for the static rebalancing problem arising in bicycle sharing systems, European Journal of Operational Research 245 (2015) 667–679, https://doi.org/10.1016/j.ejor.2015.03.043.

[31] C. Kloimüllner, G.R. Raidl, Full-load route planning for balancing bike sharing systems by logic-based benders decomposition, Networks 69 (2017) 270–289, https://doi.org/10.1002/net.21736.

[32] F. González, C. Melo-Riquelme, L. de Grange, A combined destination and route choice model for a bicycle sharing system, Transportation 43 (2016) 407–423, https://doi.org/10.1007/s11116-015-9581-6.

[33] F.E. Pedroso, F. Angriman, A.L. Bellows, K. Taylor, Bicycle use and cyclist safety following boston's bicycle infrastructure expansion, 2009–2012, American Journal of Public Health 106 (2016) 2171–2177, https://doi.org/10.2105/AJPH.2016.303454.

[34] C. Rissel, S. Greaves, L.M. Wen, M. Crane, C. Standen, Use of and short-term impacts of new cycling infrastructure in inner-Sydney, Australia: a quasi-experimental design, International Journal of Behavioral Nutrition and Physical Activity 12 (2015) 129, https://doi.org/10.1186/s12966-015-0294-1.

[35] M. Yuan, Q. Zhang, B. Wang, Y. Liang, H. Zhang, A mixed integer linear programming model for optimal planning of bicycle sharing systems: a case study in Beijing, Sustainable Cities and Society 47 (2019) 101515, https://doi.org/10.1016/j.scs.2019.101515.

CHAPTER TWO

Improvement of an online ride-hailing system based on empirical GPS data

Jinyu Chen[1], Wenjing Li[1], Qing Yu[2,3], Ryosuke Shibasaki[1], Haoran Zhang[4]

[1]Center for Spatial Information Science, The University of Tokyo, Kashiwa-shi, Chiba, Japan
[2]Department of Computer Science and Engineering, Southern University of Science and Technology, Shenzhen, China
[3]The Key Laboratory of Road and Traffic Engineering, Ministry of Education, Tongji University, College of Transportation Engineering, Shanghai, People's Republic of China
[4]School of Urban Planning and Design, Peking University, Shenzhen, China

1. Introduction

As a great source of emission and energy consumption, transportation attracts the attention of many studies on emission reduction and energy-saving [1]. In recent years, sustainable transport in the city has arisen all over the world [2]. Among all kinds of sustainable transport, ride-hailing is a popular trend in big cities [3,4]. Ride-hailing refers to the services that dynamically match drivers' supply and customers' demand and allow customers to hire drivers to send them to destinations through online ride-hailing platforms, such as Uber (an American multinational transportation network company) and Didi Chuxing (the biggest ride-hailing service provider in China, in the following part of this chapter, we will use Didi as the reference for it). Ride-hailing system does bring many benefits to citizens and urban development. The average waiting time for adopting ride-hailing is dramatically shorter than the original taxi dispatch [5,6]. Also, people who live in the remote and rural areas where public transport can hardly reach can go to urban areas easily by the ride-hailing system, which indirectly promotes urbanization to go faster. Meanwhile, ride-hailing can provide more jobs for drivers [7] and improve driving efficiency [8]. As we all know, the emission from transportation can affect citizens' health and the amenity of the city [9].

Spreading ride-hailing is a popular trend [10]. Currently, there are many places where there is no mature ride-hailing service. There are still many vacancies in the local ride-hailing market. When one ride-hailing service company tries to develop a local market, there must be a phase of increasing user scale, which refers to the number of users. The emission behavior of the ride-hailing system during this phase is remained to be a puzzle. With the rise of user scale, the number of emissions of the system can constantly be increasing. The thing that is essential is how to observe and control the change that user scale brings to the efficiency of emission. Currently, most studies focus their attention on the emission behavior of developed ride-hailing systems. Few pieces of evidence discussed the emission behavior of developing one. As a crowdsourcing service, the participation scale is one key factor that affects the emission performance of the whole system. Thus, to promote cleaner shared transportation, the clear pattern of the relationship between emission performance and user scale should be studied further.

In addition, there are some scholars exploring the efficiency of novel technologies in the mature ride-hailing system. Korolko et al. [11] indicated that bipartite matching with time window batching and dynamic pricing can lower waiting time for both riders and drivers as well as capacity utilization, trip throughput, and total welfare. However, they only considered the dispatching in a real-time time window and didn't consider the travel demand in the future. What's more, Afeche et al. [12] pointed out that the interference from the service platform to avoid dispatching a driver to the area with low travel demand can be optimal. These two conclusions inspire us with the idea that if we can predict the distribution of travel demands in the future, it can help us optimize the dispatching of ride-hailing system, especially improving the utility of energy. Among current studies, there are no existing literature that quantifies and discovers this improvement. This gap also needs to be fulfilled and furtherly instructs the development of a ride-hailing system.

Operating such kind of research isn't an easy task. Solid and real travel demand data are required as the base of simulation and assessment. Next, the reliable prediction model is in a dominant position in the whole simulation as imprecise prediction can bring misjudge to dispatching decisions. In addition, suitable dispatching should be designed carefully, and the performance and applicability should be ensured.

The development of the method for urban data mining [13], as well as more and more occurrence of works on GPS data mining, enable us to analyze the emission performance from urban transportation GPS information [1]. In this chapter, we adopted massive Didi GPS records and designed a simulation method to mainly achieve two tasks: (1) Mining the relationship between the emission performance of the ride-hailing system and user scale and providing corresponding advice for promoting ride-hailing services. (2) Proposing a prediction-based dispatching method for the ride-hailing system to improve the efficiency of the system. We chose Chengdu City, a typical big city in China as the study case.

2. Related works

In recent years, ride-hailing is becoming a popular topic among researchers. They are concerned about the problem from various aspects. The mainstream research fields can be presented as the impact ride-hailing has brought to urban areas, regulation and policy on ride-hailing, future development expectations, and efficiency and benefit of ride-hailing.

For the impact of ride-hailing, scholars separated and discussed their options from various perspectives. Rayle et al. [5] indicated that in San Francisco, at least half of ride-hailing trips replaced traditional urban transportation modes like taxis and public transportation based on the comparison of survey data and trip data from ride-hailing and taxis. Henao et al. [14] discussed that 13% of survey respondents owned fewer cars because of ride-hailing after analyzing survey and socio-demographic data from 311 passengers. Different from the conclusion by Li, Erhardt et al. [15] found that in San Francisco, 2016, 22% of traffic delays may be reduced without the operation of ride-hailing based on a simulation employing a travel demand model.

For regulation and policy, Flores et al. [16] observed the process of the appearance of ride-hailing on San Francisco street, the conflict between the ride-hailing companies and regulatory agencies, and the resolution of the conflict through a new and better registration framework. On a higher level, Beer et al. [17] revealed that the regulations and their strictness vary in 15 different USA cities. What's more, the ride-hailing service providers tend to operate in areas with light, and nonfingerprint information registered regulations. Both studies revealed the current status of regulation and provided a guideline for future decision-making.

In future development expectations, autonomous vehicle is always an eternal topic. Bosch et al. [18] showed that autonomous service can reduce the cost of ride-hailing by 85% in Zurich. Wadud et al. [19] argued that there is a potential in the benefit brought by vehicle automation, while this potential depends on many factors like vehicle automation level and vehicle connection. Some scholars also focused on the development brought by electric vehicle technology. Tu et al. [20] battery electric vehicles with 200 km could satisfy the travel demand of ride-hailing drivers up to 47% or 78%, and 20% or 55% of total ride-hailing travel distance can be traveled by driven electric vehicle. Level-2 charging available at home, work, and public parking can boost the acceptance of up to 91% of drivers and 80% of the distance.

Regarding the efficiency and benefit of ride-hailing, most scholars discussed the environmental and energy-saving behavior of ride-hailing. Reducing the vehicle distance traveled became an important ruler in evaluating the energy behavior of ride-hailing. Some conclusions told that, however, the introduction of ride-hailing brought an increase in vehicle distance traveled. Schaller [21] found that in 2017, ride-hailing brought additional vehicle distance traveled summed up to 9.1 billion kilometers in nine US cities. Furtherly, some scholars put forward the point that the actual impact of ride-hailing depends. Tirachini et al. [22] did a Monto Carlo Simulation on the ride-hailing scenarios in Chile. They declared that if the mean occupancy rate is 2.9 pax/veh or higher, there is a higher possibility that the ride-hailing can cause less traveling distance. Rodier [23] summarized that the factors that can decide whether the traveling distance can be reduced are auto ownership, trip generation, physical and legal limits to driving, mode choices, and void vehicle relocation travel. The report emphasized that the void cruising distance can account for up to 20% of total traveling distance in high-density urban areas and 60% in lower-density suburban areas because of lower travel demand density. Therefore, an urgent effort is to decrease void cruising distance.

Dispatch and matching are the key issues to overcome this issue. The strategy of dispatch directly impacts the global void cruising distance. Recently, there exists a lot of literature considering optimizing the dispatch strategy. Xu et al. [24] proposed an optimization dispatch approach considering maximizing the future gain of drivers, which refers to the matchable pairs of driver-order, based on mining the empirical order demand pattern. Their simulation and real-world application result show that the approach can maximize the Gross Merchandise Volume of total drivers. Feng et al. [25] improved the matching issue of ride-hailing from the perspective of the waiting time of passengers. They developed a heuristic method and proved that the algorithm could give a near-optimal solution. However, they didn't directly consider the optimal void cruising distance. Also, their strategy only considers the matching based on the current existing demand. With the emerging works concerning the problem of predicting the ride-hailing demand [26], we have some solid methods to forecast the travel demand in future scenarios. By merging the future knowledge of the distribution of travel demand, we can improve the matching issue to minimize the void cruising distance, thus, minimizing the invalid energy consumption. However, there is scarce literature quantifying this improvement and give an analysis on the performance.

Especially, these studies mainly focused on analyses from historical evidence in places with the nearly saturated ride-hailing system. They only operated simulations on the complete dataset in places where the ride-hailing services have been operated for a long time. The number of users that participate in ride-hailing every day is relatively stable. Thus, most of them consider improving the emission performance from the perspective of technologies. As a crowdsourcing system, the emission performance of ride-hailing is also deeply affected by the number of users. They failed to discover the relationship between the number of users and emission performance. The meaning of such a study is to solve the problem that during the growth of riders in the system, how many registered drivers should be kept to reach a balance in both efficiency and emission performance Such a gap also needs to be further studied.

Simulation is a common method of studying ride-hailing systems. Maciejewski et al. [27] use the simulation setup of MATSim to simulate the proposed dispatching algorithm to prove the efficiency of their algorithm. Grau et al. [28] simulated an agent-based ride-hailing dispatch model for better improvement in driver earnings, user cost, and vacant versus occupied time. Mourad et al. [29] summarize various ride-hailing models for the simulation. In this study, we propose a Gibbs sampling-based simulation framework to further discover the emission behavior of the ride-hailing system during its development. We believe our work can fill this gap and provide advice for ride-hailing service providers.

Therefore, there are some gaps in current studies:

(1) There is a lack of solid and visible evidence of the changing pattern of emission behavior when the number of users in the ride-hailing system changes.

(2) Considering the real-time matching of driver and passenger with the combination of optimization method and prediction model to minimize the void cruising distance as well as maximize the energy utility.

(3) The simulation of the method on real-world data to improve the performance and applicability, as well as an analysis of the spatial-temporal pattern of emission behavior of two different dispatch strategies.

In this chapter, we will try to answer these questions by operating two simulations separately:

(1) Simulation on how user scale impacts the emission performance and efficiency of the ride-hailing system.

(2) Simulation on dispatch algorithm based on optimization method and prediction model and operating novel analysis.

3. Problem description

3.1 Emission performance and the user scale

3.1.1 Concept of emission performance

Before we give more details of the problem description, we need to give the concept of emission performance. It can be referred to directly by invalid emission proportion or indirectly void cruising distance proportion. As shown in Fig. 2.1, for each ride-hailing order request, the expected driver to finish the request must travel two trips, which refers to a pick-up trip and a delivery trip, respectively [30]. The distance of the pick-up trip, which is referred to by the dotted line in the figure, is defined as the void cruising distance as it won't serve the transportation and create income for the driver; the distance of the delivery trip, which is referred by the solid line is defined as the delivery distance. So, the exhaust emitted during the pick-up trip by the car is defined as invalid emission, and the one during the delivery distance is defined as valid emission. Thus, the proportion of void cruising distance to the total distance is the void cruising distance proportion, and similarly, the proportion of invalid emission can be thought of as the proportion of invalid emission to the total emission. Apparently, there is a relationship between the void cruising distance proportion and the invalid emission proportion. If we can get the void cruising distance proportion, the invalid

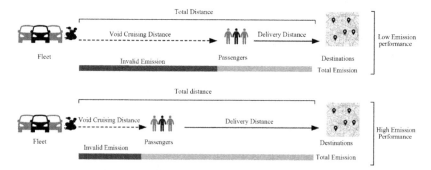

Figure 2.1 Illustration of emission performance.

emission proportion can also be computed, symbolizing the emission performance of the car-hailing system.

The main problem that this work tries to figure out is the difference in emission performance, which is directly influenced by drivers' trajectories under different scales of users available in the system. To the extent of the local market of ride-hailing systems, the ride-hailing service provider would try many methods to attract users to the system [31]. With the growth of regular users, the emission performance is also deeply affected. In this study, we will adopt a simulation framework to evaluate this impact and analyze the invalid emission proportion as the symbol for the emission performance. From the result of the analysis, we can have a clear observation of how user scale affects the emission performance of ride-hailing, thus, giving further advice on controlling the number of users in the system and keeping the emission performance of the system at a high level.

3.1.2 Emission performance and the user scale

Here, we will illustrate how the change of user scale in the ride-hailing system affects the emission performance that inspires our method. We will choose three cases as the illustration sample, as shown in Fig. 2.2. In the figure, d_j is the driver j, p_i is the passenger i. Suppose a scenario during the development of a ride-hailing system (a) The situation that may happen under the supplement of passenger scale (b) The situation that may happen under the supplement of driver scale (c) The situation that may happen under the supplement of driver and passenger scales simultaneously. The solid line refers to the original routine before the reduction; the dotted line refers to the routine drivers probably take after the supplement. The yellow triangle refers to the origin of the order; the blue circle refers to the destination; the red rectangle refers to the origin of the driver.

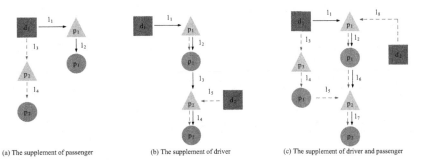

(a) The supplement of passenger   (b) The supplement of driver   (c) The supplement of driver and passenger

Figure 2.2 Illustration of the relationship between emission performance and user scale.

Fig. 2.2A shows the situation of the supplement of passenger scale. Formerly, driver d_1 is assigned to pick up the passenger P_1. If there exists a new passenger P_2 simultaneously and P_2 is assigned to d_1 to pick up, the driver d_1 will turn to pick up P_2 and give up P_1. This kind of change causes driver d_1's travel distance changes from $l_1 + l_2$ to $l_3 + l_4$ and the void cruising distance proportion in this situation changes from $\frac{l_1}{l_1+l_2}$ to $\frac{l_3}{l_3+l_4}$. Thus, the emission performance of d_1 changes. But it's hard to tell whether it increases or decreases.

Fig. 2.2B shows the situation of the supplement of the driver scale. Formerly, the order of passengers P_1, P_2 will be finished by driver d_1. With the appearance of d_2, P_2 may be picked up by another driver d_2. So the average void cruising distance proportion, in this case, changes from $\frac{1}{3}\left(\frac{l_1}{l_1+l_2} + \frac{l_3}{l_3+l_4}\right)$ to $\frac{1}{3}\left(\frac{l_1}{l_1+l_2} + \frac{l_5}{l_5+l_4}\right)$, which leads to the change of invalid emission proportion.

Fig. 2.2C shows the situation of the supplement of both driver and passenger scales. When driver d_2 and passenger P_3 are added to the scenario, the passenger P_1 may instead call for another driver d_2 to pick him or her up. By doing this, driver d_2 probably firstly turns to pick up passenger P_3 and then picks up his original passenger P_2. The average void distance proportion, in this case, changes from $\frac{1}{2}\left(\frac{l_1}{l_1+l_2} + \frac{l_6}{l_6+l_7}\right)$ to $\frac{1}{3}\left(\frac{l_8}{l_8+l_2} + \frac{l_3}{l_3+l_4} + \frac{l_5}{l_5+l_7}\right)$. And of course, like the former two situations, the emission performance shifts.

Besides the elaborations above, it should be pointed out that the scale of available drivers will also affect the emission performance from other perspectives. It can be illustrated in Fig. 2.3. (a) the original situation (b) The scale of drivers decreases. (c) The scale of drivers decreases more. With the reduction of the scale of drivers, the waiting time for a driver to take

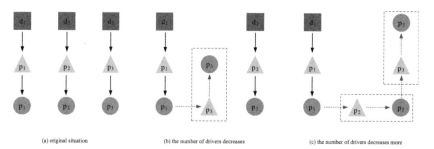

(a) original situation   (b) the number of drivers decreases   (c) the number of drivers decreases more

Figure 2.3 Illustration of affection of driver scale on the emission performance.

the order varies (maybe increases, maybe not). If one passenger waits for too long, he or she will be considered to give up the ride-hailing and take other transportation modes. Thus, affecting the emission performance of the ride-hailing system. For the same reason, the driver may also quit serving if he or she waits too long to take orders.

Fig. 2.3A gives the description of the original situation. The three passengers, p_1, p_2, and p_3, will be assigned to the three separate drivers, d_1, d_2, and d_3. However, in Fig. 2.3B, when d_3 is removed from the scene. Suppose p_1 and p_3 will be assigned to the same driver d_1 and p_2 to d_2. In this situation, p_3 has to keep waiting until d_1 drops p_1 and comes to pick him or her up. If the waiting time is beyond the tolerance of p_3, p_3 will cancel the order. Fig. 2.3C is a deeper case: d_2 is also removed from the scenario. The three passengers p_1, p_2, and p_3 must be assigned to the only d_1. At this point, p_2 and p_3 may both cancel their orders if the waiting time is beyond their tolerance, respectively.

In summary, whatever kind of change in user scale will both directly or indirectly influence the emission performance of the ride-hailing system. It is important to study different scales of drivers and passengers and find out how the scale of drivers and the scale of passengers impact the emission performance to promote future work. Due to the complex changes and multiple possibilities, a comprehensive simulation method is necessarily adopted to evaluate this relationship.

3.1.3 Research framework

Fig. 2.4 illustrates the process of the whole simulation method. The solid line refers to the process direction. The Didi Apps in users' (both passenger and driver) phones collect users' GPS data. The data source is from Chengdu, China, where the ride-hailing service has been operated for over 6 years.

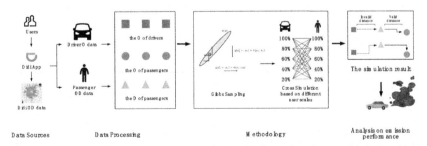

Figure 2.4 Flowchart of data processing, the method used in this study, and result to be achieved.

According to the report made by Didi Media Research Institute [32], the times of ride-hailing services are beyond the local taxi services, and the ride-hailing system serves over 1.4 million times 1 day. Thus, the dataset is suitable for study. The full dataset is suitable to be considered saturated. After receiving these data, we distract the origin of the driver (referring to Driver O in the figure) as well as the origin and destination of the passenger (referring to Passenger OD in the figure). These data also include the time stamps. In this chapter, our method wants to find the relationship between the scale of users and the emission performance. Our simulation method tries to study the situation under different user scales. We choose to sample from the dataset by a certain percentage to stimulate the scenarios of different scales of regular users in the ride-hailing system. Therefore, the result varies based on the partial dataset that is sampled in the simulation. So, instead of showing a single result, the mean of some times of simulation and their 95% confidence intervals will be illustrated. We use Gibbs sampling to sample these data by different percentages. The detail will be elaborated on in the methodology part. For a full simulation, the percentage is determined by 100%, 80%, 60%, 40%, 20%. A crosssimulation model is adopted to obtain the result we want under different combinations of the scale of drivers and passengers to make the model more universal. It also needs to be noted that since we focus on analyzing the minimal potential invalid emission proportion, so the situation of 100% scale of drivers and 100% scale of passengers will also be put in simulation instead of purely calculating from the dataset. The detailed methodology will be elaborated on in the rest of the method section.

The assumptions made in this part are shown as follows,

(1) In the sampling, the probability of each user adopting the ride-hailing and sampling of data is in independent distribution. This can be referred to by the principle of Gibbs sampling [33].

(2) Abnormal orders are not considered. Those trips with the same origin and destination or very short distances will be removed from the simulation set [34].

(3) The cost of each passenger and driver to adopt the ride-hailing will be considered. If a passenger waits for a driver to take the order longer than 15 min [34], the order will be canceled.

(4) The rejection of orders out of the driver's personal issue is not allowed [35].

(5) The participation of the driver is in the long term, which means that no driver will quit the system until the simulation is over. During the idle time, the driver will park their cars nearby the drop-off location [36].

3.2 Ride-hailing dispatch based on prediction and optimization

3.2.1 Metric of evaluation

In this section, we will introduce the metric to evaluate the performance of the proposed algorithm. As elaborated in the previous section, void cruising distance proportion is a good metric as it can clearly show and quantify the percentage efficiency of time, distance as well as energy. The equation of void cruising distance proportion can be implemented as:

$$P_{VD} = \frac{D_V}{D_V + D_D} \qquad (2.1)$$

where, P_{VD} is the void cruising distance proportion; D_V is void cruising distance; D_D is delivery distance.

This metric is also adopted in work by Ref. [14], where it is defined as efficiency. However, only a comparison of void cruising distance proportion seems not enough. In the work by Korolko [11], they also took the waiting time of passengers into consideration. This metric means to make sure the service quality because usually, passengers won't wait for someone to pick them up for too long in the real application. In this study, we also consider the cancellation of orders when someone waits for too long. The low cancellation rate Thus, in this study, we mainly consider three metrics listed void cruising distance proportion, waiting time of a passenger to wait for a driver to pick him up, and cancel rate of the order.

3.2.2 Research framework

The research framework used in this part is shown in Fig. 2.5. The data pre-processing part is similar to the one in part evaluating the relationship between user scale and emission performance. But we added one more step, which is to preprocess the OD data of orders into the desired format of the prediction model. The detailed steps will be elaborated on in the Methodology part. The proposed methodology can be divided into two parts: the prediction part and the dispatching part. The prediction part is mainly responsible for predicting the distribution of travel demand in the future based on a deep learning method. The input of this deep learning model requires historical observation corresponding metadata, and the output is the predicted spatial distribution of riding demand. The dispatching part focuses on optimizing the dispatch under the consideration of minimizing void cruising distance proportion based on the predicted distribution result in the future. To better combine the two parts. We adopt the time window

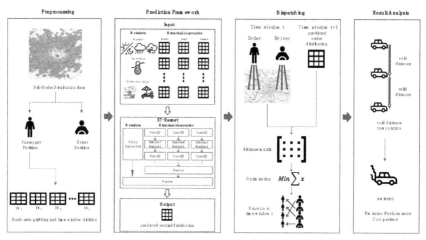

Figure 2.5 The framework used in this study.

method. The order and driver will be divided by serial time window as input [37]. For each time window, the prediction and optimization method will be separately operated once to decide the assignment of the driver to order. To better show the utility of the proposed algorithm. We will use a greedy algorithm operated in a time window as a baseline and compare the performance of two algorithms in result analysis. The assumptions made in this part are similar to the ones in part on Emission performance and user scale.

4. Study case

The GPS Dataset used in this study is provided by Didi. It includes the detailed information (Order ID, the time of the start and end of order, the longitude and latitude of origin and determination) except privacy information within 1 month in Chengdu City ranging from November 2, 2016 to November 30, 2016, except for some vacancies on 10 and 8. There are more than 6.6 million order records in the dataset. We exclude the orders with travel distances that are shorter than 500m, with the same origins and destinations as well as the same start time and end time, and very few ones that travel among cities [38]. After the preprocessing, 75.4% of orders remains. They will be used for the simulation and analysis. The visualization of the dataset in 1 day can be shown in Fig. 2.6. Most of the origins and destinations are located in the city center. The rest are distributed in the surrounding area. The distribution of ODs covered almost all the urban areas of Chengdu. The dataset can describe the case study well.

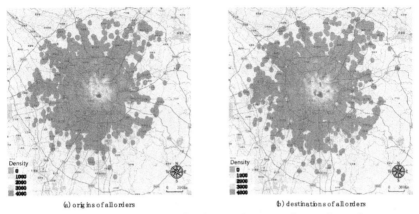

(a) origins of all orders   (b) destinations of all orders

Figure 2.6 Thermal map of order OD data on 1 day in Chengdu.

5. Methodology

5.1 Emission performance and the user scale

5.1.1 Reassignment system

The definition of availability of a driver. If driver i is taking another passenger to the destination or on the way to pick up in the time interval that passenger j can wait for a driver to pick him up, the driver i is considered unavailable to passenger j, else he is available.

When we sample a part of the dataset by a certain percentage to simulate the situation of the different number of users in the system, it is necessary to reassign the drivers to pick up orders and simulate a process of operation. Then, the emission performance can be computed. Under different scales of drivers and passengers in the simulation, an order from a passenger may be reassigned to another available driver based on their original GPS information to maximize the efficiency of the whole operating system. The reassignment algorithm is based on the shortest void distance principle, which means when an order is given in the system, it will be assigned to the driver that is available and nearest to the position of the passenger. This reassignment method will ensure the least distance for a driver to pick a passenger up. If all drivers are not available in the time period passenger wants to be picked up, the order will be canceled.

The code form of the reassignment algorithm is shown as algorithm 1. Notice that the whole simulation code is similar to the form of Python code. The meaning of mathematical symbols can be found in Nomenclature.

Algorithm 1. Reassignment
  Input: a single piece of order i and D_s
  Function: Find the available and most suitable driver for order i.

Output: the record of reassignment.

 1: for each driver $j \in D_s$:

 2: if $t_a \leq t_o + \theta_{max}$ (driver j is available to order i):

 3: driver $i \longrightarrow A_i$

 4: else:

 5: go to the next driver j +1

 6: if $A_i = \emptyset$:

 7: go to the next order i +1

 8: else:

 9: find the $md_i \in A_i$

 10: calculate t_p

 11: assign the order i to md_i

 12: update the original position and available time of md_i in D_s

 13: return the record of md_i & order i

After an order is reassigned to the driver, the driver will be considered not available to other passengers until he or she finishes the job. Then the GPS position and time stamp of the driver's OD will be updated according to the order. The reassignment will come to an end until all the orders are assigned to the drivers or canceled.

5.1.2 Gibbs Sampling for the generation of simulation samples

The sampling method plays an important role in the whole simulation process. In this study, Purely randomly selecting one part of data and putting them into simulation is not suitable because the simulation result deeply depends on the selection of data. The multiple possibilities should be considered. Additionally, the spatial-temporal pattern of demand and server varies due to regions, so blind sampling can't assure the full characterization of simulation results. As a result, a Gibbs Sampling is adopted in this study. Gibbs sampling can generate different simulation samples and consider the issue of full sampling. Ride-hailing is a high-dimensional system. The behavior of each user, either passenger or driver, can cause a chain effect on the operation of the whole system. Thus, we can imagine the relationship between the emission behavior and users as a function: emission behavior $= f$ (user$_1$, user$_2$, … …, user$_n$). Each parameter of the function is a single user. Thus, it is obvious that the function is high-dimensional. The sampling of the emission behavior is difficult. Gibbs sampling is used to solve such sampling problems with high dimensions. The principle of Gibbs sampling is to simulate the function step by step and slowly cover the main value of the function. The sampling method randomly selects a set of parameters for the first time in simulation (Suppose the number of parameters is n). Then, it will randomly change one parameter and remain the rest n-1 ones, then operate another time of the simulation. This process will be iterated repeatedly. In each iteration, the simulation result will be recorded. If the variance of the simulation result in the last several times of simulation is lesser than a threshold, the sampling process can be thought to be completed and come to an end. In this study, the dimension of the problem is very high, which can be up to 250, 000 and down to 50,000. Therefore, replacing one user at one time of sampling is unreasonable. It can hardly affect the final result. Instead, we choose to replace thousands of users after each time of the simulation. The detailed quantity depends on the percentage of users used in the simulation. In this study, firstly, we randomly pick a certain percentage of data in the whole dataset as the simulation samples. The rest of the dataset will be used as a backup set. After one time of simulation, a part of the simulation samples will be randomly replaced by the data in the backup set for another time of the simulation. To ensure the full consideration, the whole simulation process will be finished until it is considered to satisfy the convergence condition. In this study, e refers to the variance of the mean of all the void cruising distances in the last five times of simulation. When e is smaller than the convergence condition, the whole sampling process can be considered to be completed. Algorithm 2 gives the code form of Gibbs sampling.

Algorithm 2. Gibbs sampling.

Input: O, D, P_d and P_o

Function: find the distribution of the result of the simulation.

Output: the results of all times of iterations.

1: O_s ⟵ randomly selected P_o of data $\in O$

2: D_s ⟵ randomly selected P_d of data $\in D$

3: O_b ⟵ the rest (1 - P_o) of data in O

4: D_b ⟵ the rest (1 - P_d) of data in D

5: while($e > e_{max}$):

6:    for each order $i \in O_s$:

7:       record of reassignment ⟵ **Reassignment**(order i, D_s)

8:    calculate the results obtained

9:    calculate the e

10:   randomly selected a part of data $\in O_s$ ⟷ randomly selected a part of data $\in O_b$

11:   randomly selected a part of data $\in D_s$ ⟷ randomly selected a part of data $\in D_b$

12: return the results in all times of iterations

5.1.3 Crosssimulation module generation

Since the goal of this method is to find the difference in emission performance under the different scales of users, a full simulation is needed to get the complete result. Thus, a crosssimulation of different scales of samples is adapted. The original Data sets of drivers and passengers are randomly sampled by the percentage of 20%, 40%, 60%, 80%, and 100% separately. Then, the crosssimulation will be applied. It means all five kinds of the percentage of drivers and passengers will group with each other as the input of the simulation model. Then, the crosssimulation will give the output under different scenarios we need for analysis.

The flowchart form of the whole simulation process is shown in Fig. 2.7. Certainly, the whole simulation process will also include the step of dealing with data processing. *k* in the figure refers to the percentage of the scale of drivers; *l* in the figure refers to the percentage of the scale of orders.

5.1.4 Equation for result computation

In the result of every time of simulation, except the OD of each assigned or canceled order and driver, the results obtained from the crosssimulation include the distance, time interval that the driver travels to pick up the passenger and complete the order; the time length that drivers wait for an order to come; the time that passengers give the orders. The orders that originally existed in the real world were canceled in the simulation. Thus, we can compute the void distance proportion, the total distance that might be traveled or not be traveled.

After obtaining these results, we can compute the invalid emission proportion, the quantity of invalid emission, the quantity of total emission, and other results. The equations we use to link these two parts are from the COPERT (COmputer Program to calculate Emission from

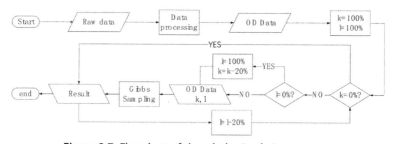

Figure 2.7 Flowchart of the whole simulation process.

Road Transportation), a manual written by European Environmental Agency. Since the measured standard, which COPERT complies with, is similar to the one adopted in China, the model is suitable for evaluating vehicle emissions in Chinese cities [39,40]. This manual provides the methodology and equations to calculate the emission of cars, and they are suitable for all countries. This manual contains methods to compute various kinds of emissions. The common equation of emission computation can be written as:

$$Q_{i,k} = \sum_j q_{i,j,k} l_j \tag{2.2}$$

where the $Q_{i,k}$ refers to the quantity of emission k of vehicle i; $q_{i,j,k}$ refers to the hot emission factor of emission k vehicle i during trip j; l_j refers to the length of trip j. $q_{i,j,k}$ can be calculated by:

$$q_{i,j,k} = \frac{\alpha_k v_{i,j}^2 + \beta_k v_{i,j} + \gamma_k}{\varepsilon_k v_{i,j}^2 + \zeta_k v_{i,j} + \eta_k} \tag{2.3}$$

The detailed information to calculate the emission factor $q_{i,j,k}$ can be found in the work by Ref. [38]. Since the quantity of emission mainly depends on the driving distance, the pattern among each kind of emission is the same. Thus, in this study, we will broadly elaborate on the emission pattern. Then, the total invalid emission quantity and invalid emission proportion can be calculated by the equation set (4)

$$\begin{cases} P_{void} = \dfrac{d_{void}}{d_{total}} \\ P_{e_{invalid}} = f(P_{void}) \\ E_{invalid} = E P_{e_{invalid}} \end{cases} \tag{2.4}$$

where, P_{void} is the proportion of void distance; d_{void} means the void distance that one driver travels to pick up one passenger and d_{total} is the total distance a driver travels to finish an order from a passenger. It includes $d_{invalid}$ and the distance that the driver travels from the origin of the passenger to the destination. $P_{e_{invalid}}$ is the proportion of vehicle invalid emissions; $E_{invalid}$ is the total quantity of vehicle invalid emissions. $f(x)$ is the function that turns the proportion of void distance to the proportion of invalid emission. E is total vehicle emission.

5.2 Ride-hailing dispatch based on prediction and optimization

5.2.1 Time window division

Time window division is a classic method used in many real-time dispatch problems [41]. One characteristic of this method is that it is easy to understand and implement. The illustration of time window division is shown in Fig. 2.8.

The process of time window division can be treated as a group of the timeline. The end of each time window is also the beginning of the last one. Suppose the length of the time window is l, the number of the time window is N, and the start time of simulation is 0. During the period of time window n, $n \in [1, 2, \ldots\ldots, N]$, the orders and available drivers given between time $(n-1)L$ and nl will be collected in the matching pool. Then, at the end of time window nl, the simulation algorithm will be operated to give the matching result. In this study, we choose the length of the time window to be 5 min, which makes 8352-time windows.

5.2.2 Baseline: greedy algorithm

The baseline algorithm we choose is the greedy algorithm. The greedy algorithm is a classical algorithm used in many real-time dispatch studies of pick-up and delivery problems [35,42]. In principle, the algorithm will iterate over every travel demand and find the closest driver who can pick up the order or follow the rule of first-come-first-serve [43]. When an order is given into the system, the algorithm will search the current candidate drivers and assign the nearest one to order. Generally speaking, the algorithm only considers the optimized solution for every single object. Although this method is easy to implement and manage, it is naturally uncoordinated and tends to prioritize immediate passenger satisfaction over global supply utilization. In the Result and analysis part, we will illustrate the performance of the greedy algorithm.

5.2.3 Prediction model

Travel demand prediction is currently a hot research topic in the field of Computer Science [26,44]. The mainstream of current methods is deep

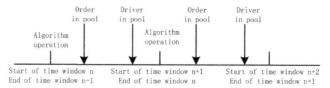

Figure 2.8 Time window division.

learning. The deep learning model tries to stimulate the thinking process of humans. People can feed the training materials to the deep learning model and make the model learn how to generate the desired output. The general structure of deep learning is shown in Fig. 2.9.

The input layer is used to input the features. The hidden layers contain the parameters for computation. The output layer will give the desired output. During the training process, the model will try to find the optimal parameters in the hidden layers and minimize the difference between the ground truth and computed output.

Many researchers developed various deep learning neural networks that concern this problem. In recent years, there exists a lot of achievements, like the convolutional LSTM neural network [45]. The prediction model we use in this study is the ST-Resnet [46]. This is a deep learning neural network based on the residual unit. The structure of ST-Resnet is shown in Fig. 2.10.

The input of this prediction model is divided into two parts, which are separately historical observation and metadata. The output is the spatial distribution in the future. The desired input format of historical observation is the matrix in essence. Preprocessing is needed to convert spatial data to the matrix. Firstly, we extract the order data in each time window. Next, we apply the regional grid method [47]. The concept is to convert the spatial distribution data to image-like data, which is in the form of a matrix. We divided the study area with a square grid with a size of 3690 m × 3690 m. This makes the whole study area gridded with the size of 40 × 40. Then,

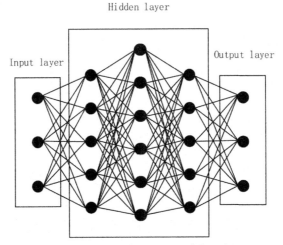

Figure 2.9 The general structure of deep learning.

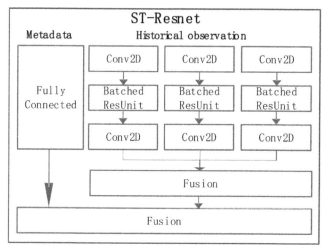

Figure 2.10 The graphical structure of ST-Resnet

we count the number of orders in the area of each cell in each time window. The quantity of orders is the element of each matrix. Finally, we can get a sequence of matrixes abstracted from Spatio-temporal data. Since the length of the time window is 5 min, from preprocessing of the data in 1 month, we can get a total of 8352 matrixes. In the prediction model, the input of observation is divided into three sequences, separately recent, near, and distant. Recent: a sequence of continuous matrixes of historical observation closely before the time window we want to predict; near a sequence of continuous matrixes of historical observation that is 1 day before near; distant: a sequence of continuous matrixes of historical observation that is 1 week before recent. We choose the length of the sequence to be 6. Thus, if we use x_n, $n \in [2022, 8351]$ to represent the output, the input can be represented as

$$
X \begin{cases}
\{x_i | i \in [n-6, n-5, n-4, n-3, n-2, n-1]\} \\
\left\{ x_j \middle| j \in \begin{bmatrix} n-288-6, n-288-5, n-288-4, n-288-3, n-288-2, \\ n-288-1 \end{bmatrix} \right\} \\
\left\{ x_z \middle| z \in \begin{bmatrix} n-2016-6, n-2016-5, n-2016-4, n-2016-3, \\ n-2016-2, n-2016-1 \end{bmatrix} \right\}
\end{cases}
$$

$$(2.5)$$

The input dimension of historical observation is 40 × 40 x 6 × batch size.

Another part of the input is the metadata. Generally speaking, metadata includes all the information that can have an impact on the spatial distribution of order. In the original paper, the author used weather data and date information. Thus, in this study, we marked the hour that the time window is located in 1 day, the day in 1 week, the week in 1 year of each time window, and the mark of whether the day is a holiday or not (holiday is marked as 1; workday is marked as 0) as the date information. Meanwhile, we also use the weather and temperature data as the weather data. The table of detailed weather data is shown as follows:

Table 2.1 Weather data is used in the prediction model.

Weather	The highest temperature of the day	The lowest temperature of the day
[Partly cloudy, cloudy, sunny, little rainy]	[9,22]	[4,13]

The temperature data will be rescaled to [-1, 1] by the equation:

$$\frac{tem - tem_{min}}{tem_{max} - tem_{min}} \times (t_{max} - t_{min}) + t_{min} \qquad (2.6)$$

where tem is the temperature we want to rescale; tem_{min} is the minimal observed temperature; tem_{max} is the maximal observed temperature; t_{max} is the upper bound of the rescaled interval; t_{max} is the lower bound of the rescaled interval.

We have introduced all the input data needed in this prediction model. In the following part, we will elaborate on how the model deals with input and get trained for prediction.

For the metadata part:

The date information and weather information will be separately turned into numerical data by the one-hot encoding method [48]. Then, two one-hot encoded data will be concatenated together as one matrix. The feature of metadata information will be extracted by a fully-connected layer implemented as:

$$Y = Relu(aX + b) \qquad (2.7)$$

Y is the output feature; X refers to the on-hot encoded input numerical data; a is the transform matrix; b is the bias matrix; $Relu$ is the activation function, which can be implemented as:

$$Relu(x) = \begin{cases} 0, & x < 0 \\ x, & x \geq 0 \end{cases} \tag{2.8}$$

The output feature will be then reshaped to the size of $40 \times 40 \times 6$, the same size as historical observation.

For the historical observation part:

As shown in Fig. 2.8, there are three individual input channels recent, near and distant. We will introduce the structure of one channel as all three channels are the same. The first layer is a 2D convolutional layer with the kernel size of 3×3 and 64 filters that extract the feature of the input sequence to the matrix of size $40 \times 40 \times 64$. Then, the following part is a sequence of residual units. The job of each residual unit is to deeper analyze the features. Suppose we adopt l residual units in the sequence. The universal equation can be implemented as:

$$X_{l+1} = X_l + F(X_l; \theta_l) \tag{2.9}$$

where, X_{l+1} is the output of the residual unit; X_l is the input; $F(x)$ is the function of the residual function; θ_l Refers to all the trainable parameters in the residual function.

The residual function contains two groups of the combination of $Relu$ and convolution. Thus, this makes the equation of residual function:

$$Y = F(X_l; \theta_l) = Relu(W * X + b) \tag{2.10}$$

where Y is the output of residual function; W is the transform matrix; $*$ is the convolution operation; b is the bias matrix.

Notice that between the two groups, there is a batch normalization layer [49].

After an iteration in the sequence, the result will go through the final 2D convolutional layer and be fused together. The method of fusion is to add the matrixes from three channels together into one. Then, this one matrix will be added with the reshaped output feature of metadata. Finally, the summed-up feature will be handled by a Tanh function and turned to be the output of the prediction result.

During the training process, we use the former 20% of the dataset as the test set and the latter 80% as the training set. The optimizer for the gradient descent is Adam [50], which has shown a better performance among all the optimizers. Adam tries to solve the problem of gradient descent with the idea of the moment. The first and second moments can be computed as:

$$m_t = \beta_1 m_{t-1} + (1 - \beta_1)g_t \tag{2.11}$$

$$v_t = \beta_2 v_{t-1} + (1 - \beta_2)g_t^2 \tag{2.12}$$

where m_t and v_t are moving averages, g_t is gradient on the current mini-batch, and β is a newly introduced hyper-parameter of the algorithm. They have really good default values of 0.9 and 0.999, respectively. The vectors of moving averages are initialized with zeros at the first iteration. Thus, $m_0 = 0, v_0 = 0$.

In principle, the first and second order will be corrected by:

$$\widehat{m_t} = \frac{m_t}{1 - \beta_1^t} \tag{2.13}$$

$$\widehat{v_t} = \frac{v_t}{1 - \beta_2^t} \tag{2.14}$$

Finally, the parameter of the model can be updated by:

$$w_t = w_{t-1} - \alpha \frac{\widehat{m_t}}{\sqrt{\widehat{v_t}} + \varepsilon} \tag{2.15}$$

w is the parameter of the model; α is the learning rate, and ε is the hyper-parameter that is 0.0001 in default.

By far, we have completed the introduction of the prediction model. In the result analysis, we will illustrate the accuracy of the prediction model.

5.2.4 Optimization

Optimization is a classical mathematical method used in many research fields, including ride-hailing [51]. Generally speaking, the concept of optimization is to optimize the objective function and find the globally optimal solution. The performance of the optimization algorithm deeply depends on the knowledge of conditions, which, in this case, is the information of drivers and orders. More information can help us get a more optimal solution.

The core of the dispatch strategy used in this study is that when we consider the dispatch problem in time window n, besides the existing knowledge of drivers and orders in time window n, the predicted distribution of orders in time window $n+1$ will also be taken into account. Thus, the objective function is to minimize the global pick-up distance in both time windows:

$$\min\left(f = \sum_i \sum_j S_{i,j} D_{i,j}\right) \tag{2.16}$$

subject to:

$$\sum_j S_{i,j} \leq 1 \tag{16.1}$$

$$\sum_i S_{i,j} \leq 1 \tag{16.2}$$

where, $S_{i,j}$ is the decision variable that decides whether driver i to pick up passenger j or not; $D_{i,j}$ is the distance of driver i to pick up passenger j.

Constraint 10.1 aims to ensure that one driver can be maximally assigned with one order; constraint 10.2 aims to assure that one order can be maximally assigned with one driver. Here, we can choose to impose one more constraint:

$$\sum_i \sum_j S_{i,j} = \max(I, J) \tag{16.3}$$

This constraint can serve the purpose of trying its best to satisfy orders with currently available drivers. The difference is that without the constraint, a part of the drivers will not be dispatched to the order in the optimized solution because there may be an order that is much closer to him, while with the constraint if there is no other candidate driver for the order, the driver will be dispatched in the current time window. In this study, we will also compare the performance of the algorithm with and without the constraint.

From the target function, the problem is an ILP (integer linear programming) problem. The basic method to solve ILP is the Simplex algorithm [52]. Its basic concept is to first construct an initial solution, which is a feasible and finite solution. If the initial solution isn't the globally optimal one, then the algorithm will introduce nonbase variables to replace a base variable for a better solution. The iteration is repeated until the globally optimal one is found. The process of the optimization algorithm is shown in Fig. 2.11.

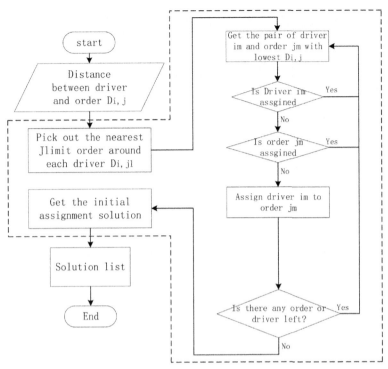

Figure 2.11 Flow chart of the optimization algorithm.

In the first step, we construct the distance matrix of each pair of drivers and order. The driver list only contains the available drivers in the current time window n; the order list contains orders both in the current time window n and future time window $n+1$. The column of the matrix refers to the list of drivers, and the row refers to the list of orders. The element $D_{i,j}$ means the distance between the position of driver i and the origin of order j. Because we can only predict the number of orders in each cell, we lack information on the exact spatial distribution of orders in each cell. Therefore, it's hard to compute the exact distance between predicted orders and existing drivers. To solve this problem, we furtherly divide each cell of a 40 × 40 grid into a 10 × 10 grid (See Fig. 2.12).

Each cell of a larger grid can be furtherly divided by a 10 × 10 grid. Then, we do statistics on the historical spatial distribution of orders in each 10 × 10 grid. Each cell of a smaller grid will be marked by a probability that order may exist in this cell. Based on the statistical result, we can estimate where the orders may be located in if there are orders predicted in the larger cell. The predicted orders will be allocated in the cell with a higher

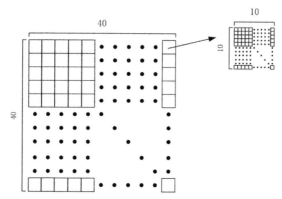

Figure 2.12 Cell division.

probability. We assume the location of predicted orders at the spatial center of the cell of a 10×10 grid. After that, we can compute the distance between the driver and predicted orders. Then, the following part is more like a greedy algorithm, where we pick out the pair of order and driver in the ascending order of distance to construct an initial solution of matching. In the next step, we try to improve this solution by iteration until we get the optimal solution. Since the result is the decision variable $S_{i,j}$, all variables are nonnegative, which satisfies the standard form of the simplex algorithm. The flow chart of the simplex algorithm is shown in Fig. 2.13.

The algorithm will first check whether the initial solution is the optimal one. If not, the algorithm will introduce basic variables into the constraints and turn the constraints and target function into a set of equations. Then, the algorithm will randomly choose a variable with a positive coefficient, for example, x_i to increase. Next, the algorithm will choose the strictest equation with x_i and rewrite the equation to one with only x_i on the left-hand of the equation. This is used to replace all x_i. This is called the pivot. Finally, if all the coefficients are nonpositive, the solution reaches the optimal one, else the above process will be repeated.

6. Result analysis

6.1 Emission performance and the user scale

6.1.1 Void distance proportion analysis

The plots of simulation results are shown in Fig. 2.14. The solid red curve refers to the mean of void cruising distance proportion. The area with the same color is the 95% confidence interval. The five subfigures show the

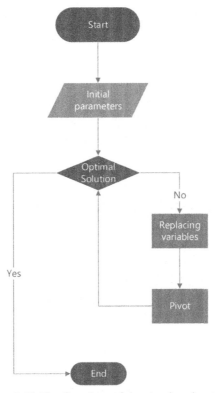

Figure 2.13 The flowchart of the simplex algorithm.

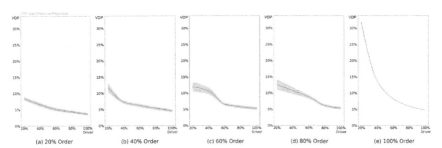

Figure 2.14 The plot of void cruising distance proportion.

difference in void cruising distance proportion when the scale of orders is set to a certain percentage. (a) Orders $= 20\%$ (b) Orders $= 40\%$ (c) Orders $= 60\%$ (d) Orders $= 80\%$ (e) Orders $= 100\%$. If we remain on the scale of orders, with the increase in the scale of drivers, the average void cruising distance proportion decreases in the five subfigures. It infers that when the mobility demand in the area is determined, the supplement of drivers to the shared transportation system will help decrease the mean void cruising distance proportion. By the comparison of these five figures, the linear relationship weakens with the increase in the percentage of orders. When the scale of travel demand is at the 100% level, the void distance proportion increases rapidly with the decrease of the scale of drivers; while it increases much more stably at the 20% level. This tells us that when the travel demand in the system is great in an area, the addition of demand satisfiers will effectively reduce the void cruising distance, thus, reducing the invalid emission. Here is the possible explanation. Consider the situation where the travel demand is huge while the servers are far not enough, the cars are busy trying to satisfy every travel demand in the system as soon as possible, so when an order is given into the system, there are few candidates drivers in the matching sequence. As common knowledge, it is hard to find a driver who can pick up the order within a short void cruising distance. From the analysis above, the effectiveness of supplements in improving the emission performance depends on the total travel demand. The greater the demand is, the more effective the supplement is. Besides, if we compare situations when the scale of drivers is set to 100%, even though the scale of orders varies, the void cruising distance proportion doesn't change much, and the confidence intervals are still obvious in the figures until the scale of orders mounts to 100%. This indicates that the scale of orders is the leading factor in determining the void distance proportion. It is mainly because that order is the served object in the system. The ODs of orders served in the system won't change under any circumstances—The passenger will only quit the system when his or her travel demand is not satisfied. In contrast, the ODs of drivers are deeply influenced by the different orders in the system. So, when the travel demands in the system are relatively stable in the system, the void distance proportion is relatively determined.

These findings tell us that in real cases, when a ride-hailing system is initially introduced in one area, an evaluation of the ride-hailing market not only serves the purpose of assessing the potential travel demand and commercial value [53], the policy-making of balancing the number of registered drivers in the system is also necessary. The operators can observe the void cruising distance proportion of historical service records to judge whether the current quantity of drivers is enough to serve the travel demand. Overall, the relationship between the void cruising distance proportion and the number of drivers is not a linear one. We can observe that the change of void cruising distance proportion is insensitive to the growth of driver numbers in the system when the proportion of drivers is equal to or larger than the one of orders. This indicates that the number of drivers has reached an equal or higher level than the number of passengers. The effort of making policies to attract more drivers is unnecessary. In this case, the critical ratio of the number of drivers to orders is 1:9. What's more, we also found a rapid interval before the critical ratio, where the increase of driver number can more effectively decrease the void cruising distance proportion. These two key features can be a clear sign of the suitable number of drivers in the system. In the future, deeper parameters that can affect the ratio and overall model can be explored to transfer the conclusion to other areas.

6.1.2 Emission performance analysis

After obtaining the simulation results, we can compute the invalid emission proportion of NO_x. The plots of calculation results are shown in Fig. 2.15.

The trend and shape of the invalid emission proportion curve are very similar to the one of void distance proportion, despite the variety of types of emission and quantity. So, we can say that the invalid emission proportion is closely related to the void distance proportion, a positive correlation. Thus, we can conclude that the emission performance is closely related to the user scale, and the larger the demand scale is, the more sensitive the emission performance is to the driver scale. By far, we can bridge the impact of user scale on emission performance. This impact is important for future decisions. With

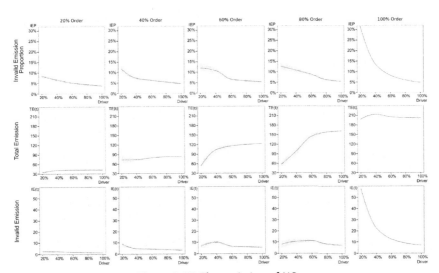

Figure 2.15 The emission of NOx.

this impact, if some metrics that ensure the high efficiency of the ride-hailing system want to be limited to a threshold, the scale of users that may satisfy this request can be computed. For example, if a car-hailing service provider wants to restrict the average void distance to a certain value, we can find this high-efficiency area of the scale of users for decision-makers as guidance.

6.1.3 High-efficiency area computation under metric constraints

This subsection aims at providing a sample to obtain the probable area of the user scale if we want some metrics to be considered to be limited into a range and does a little discussion. We choose three metrics for the discussion: maximal average invalid emission proportion, maximal average order cancel proportion, and maximal average waiting time for a driver to take an order. The first metric is meant to ensure the emission performance wouldn't be worse than a certain value; the second metric is meant to ensure the interest of the ride-hailing service platform and the travel satisfaction proportion of passengers who adopt ride-hailing; the third metric is meant to ensure the interest of the driver. Now we set two metric sets to simulate two scenarios for the purpose of showing the difference in the area. Reference metric set: Average invalid emission proportion $\leq 9.2\%$ Average order cancel proportion $\leq 35.8\%$ Average waiting for the time for a driver to take an order ≤ 1.75h; higher performance metric set: Average invalid emission proportion $\leq 7.6\%$; Average order cancel proportion $\leq 13.2\%$; Average waiting time for a driver to take an order ≤ 1.50h.

The area of the corresponding scale of drivers and orders can be shown in Fig. 2.16. The red one refers to the reference metric set, and the green one refers to the higher performance metric set. In the reference metric set, when the scale of orders and drivers are both greater than about 135,300 (near 80%) and 15,200 (near 60%) respectively, a square area, under any combination of quantity of driver and order, these three metrics can be satisfied anyway. When both are under this quantity, the area is restricted in a valley down straight to the situation where there are about 5100 drivers and 33,800 orders. It is near around 20% of drivers to 20% of orders case. In a higher performance metric set, we restrict the three metrics tighter. Then we get the area of the corresponding scale shown in Fig. 2.10. It can be seen that the square area shrinks to around 20,300 (80%) for the axis of the scale of the driver. The valley area extension is limited to the point where X-axis is approximately 101,400 (60%), and Y-axis is roughly 15,200 (60%). These two cases indicate that if some metrics want to be realized, we can mine the history data and find the approximate user scale in the ride-hailing system.

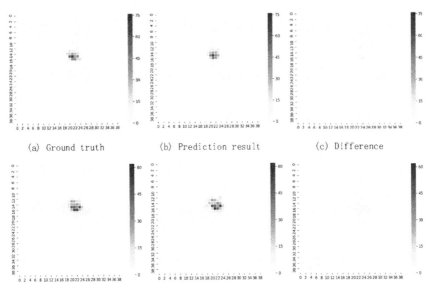

(a) Ground truth   (b) Prediction result   (c) Difference

Figure 2.16 The area of the scale of driver and order under two metric sets.

6.2 Ride-hailing dispatch based on prediction and optimization

6.2.1 Result of prediction

An important parameter of ST-Resnet is the number of residual units used in the model. In the original paper, the author indicated that the more residual units in the neural network, the deeper the neural network is, and the more accurate the prediction is. However, more residual units mean more memory usage during the training and slower training. To find a balance between the accuracy and computation resources, we choose the number of residual units to be 21. There are totally over 4.4 million trainable parameters in the model, which is quite a large quantity.

In the field of computer science, multiple forms of losses are used to evaluate the performance of prediction models like mse (mean squared error) and mae (mean absolute error). However, these losses are usually used to compare the performance among different prediction models and hardly give a direct impression of the accuracy. In this study, we adopt the mape (mean absolute percentage error) as the metric of accuracy, which can directly show the differences, and is computed by:

$$A_{diff} = |A_{GT} - A_{PR}| \qquad (2.17)$$

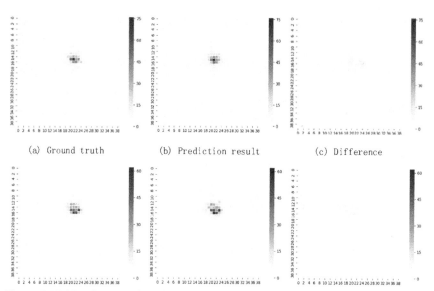

Figure 2.17 Visualization of prediction result (A) ground truth matrix (B) predicted matrix (C) the difference between ground truth and prediction.

where, A_{diff} is the difference matrix; A_{GT} is the ground truth; A_{PR} is the prediction result.

After completing the training, we compute the mape of the test set to be 0.01,169, which means that for each cell of the grid, the difference between the prediction result and ground truth is about 1.169%. In addition, we also visualize the prediction result, and the ground truth is shown in Fig. 2.17.

The figures on the left side are the ground truth matrixes of the spatial distribution of order distribution; the figure in the middle is the corresponding prediction result; the figure on the right is the heatmap of the difference between ground truth and prediction result. We can see from the figure that there is little difference between the ground truth and the prediction result. The prediction is relatively accurate and enough to put into the simulation.

6.2.2 Result of dispatch

Here, we will separately introduce the performance of the greedy algorithm, proposed optimization algorithm, and proposed optimization algorithm with an additional constraint. The performance of the three algorithms is shown in Table 2.2.

From the table, we can see that the greedy algorithm shows a poorer performance. The average waiting time for the passenger is over 10 min. At the same time, almost half of the orders will be canceled in the simulation. This

Table 2.2 Comparison of different algorithms by metric.

Algorithm Metric	Baseline: Greedy algorithm	Proposed method without optional constraint	The proposed method with optional constraint
Average waiting time of passenger	654.36 s	219.23 s	217.02 s
Average void cruising distance proportion	12.31%	3.83%	3.70%
The proportion of canceled orders	48.35%	0.00149%	0.00%

is mainly because, in the baseline algorithm, we don't provide priority to the orders that have been waiting long enough. In a real-world application, for commercial purposes, the ride-hailing dispatch platform may provide priority to the orders that have been waiting for a long time. Besides, when operating the dispatch, the Didi dispatch platform will provide each order to several candidate drivers to raise the chances that the order will be taken. Thus, the cancel rate will be much lower in the real application. In the simulation, the proportion of canceled orders of the optimization method is much lower than the one of the optimization method. Besides, the average waiting time of passengers in the optimization method is only 1/3 times of the greedy algorithm. This shows that the optimization algorithm can more easily and quickly answer the travel demand from customers. What's more, from the perspective of void cruising distance proportion, the optimization method shows a better performance, which is lesser than 1/3 times of the greedy algorithm. The overall result shows that the proposed algorithm surpasses the traditional greedy algorithm. The statistic of distribution of metrics is shown in Fig. 2.18.

From left to right, the figures show the result of the separately greedy algorithm, optimization method without optional constraint and with optional constraint. The upper figures show the waiting time of passengers, and the lower ones show the void cruising distance proportion. The x-axis is the value of the metric, and the y-axis can be treated as the "probability." The larger the y value is, the higher probability is. The integration of the result of the greedy algorithm is small mainly because of the high cancellation proportion. We can have a clear vision that the proposed algorithm can effectively suppress the waiting time and void the distance proportion of most cases into a low interval. The waiting time in all of the cases is under 1000 s, which is about 16 min; the highest void cruising distance proportion

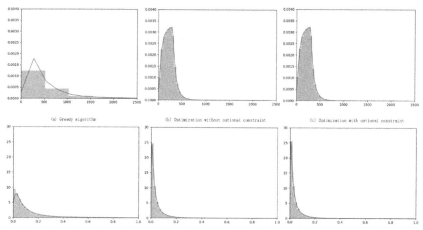

Figure 2.18 The statistical result of metrics.

is about 25%. While on the other hand, there are some extreme cases in the greedy algorithm. Some have been waiting for over 2500 s. In a small part of cases, the picking-up distance is near half of the delivery distance. This furtherly proves the stability of the performance of the proposed algorithm.

If we make a transverse comparison between the optimization method with and without the optional constraint, we can find that the optimization algorithm with the optional constraint performs better than without the constraint. A smaller proportion of canceled orders and shorter waiting time is natural. We also notice that it accidently brings lesser void cruising distance proportion. To better understand the mechanism behind this, we conduct an experiment under the perfect prediction, which means that there is no error in the prediction result. The result of the metrics is separate, the average waiting time of passengers: 219.31 s; average void cruising distance proportion: 3.83%; the proportion of canceled orders: 0.00%. We can see from the comparison that the only difference is that perfect prediction help eliminate the canceled orders in the simulation. This can furtherly prove the high accuracy of prediction. What may cause the difference between the result of the optimization algorithm with and without optional constraint is probably the uncertainty of distance in the prediction. In the process of solving the optimization problem, we compute the distance between each order and driver in both the current and predicted time window and construct a distance matrix. Because we lack the information on the exact spatial distribution of orders in each cell, this causes many uncertainties in the simulation and affects the performance of optimization. Since currently, most of the prediction of travel demand is mainly based on the area gridding method, we recommend more to pay main effort on optimizing the current dispatch problem. The prediction result aims to provide guidance on which group of drivers are better choices for dispatching at present.

7. Conclusion and future work

Under the background of energy-saving and emission reduction, many studies focus on traffic emissions [54]. It is pointed out that void cruising for the next passenger causes a lot of unnecessary exhaust emissions [55].

The main idea of this study is divided into two parts. The first is to propose a simulation method to evaluate the impact of the scale of users in the ride-hailing system on the emission performance and provide a guideline for controlling the number of users for ride-hailing service providers. To better adopt the method, massive Didi data from Chengdu in 1 day were used as the dataset. The method included the data process—extraction of OD of orders and drivers, Gibbs sampling, crosssimulation, and result computation. From the result obtained by the simulation, we found that under the circumstance of a certain scale of travel demands in the scenario, the void distance proportion decreased with the increase of the scale of drivers and when the scale of travel demands increased. But, the trend of rising the void cruising distance proportion varies by different scales of travel demands. The greater the travel demand is, the more rapidly the void distance proportion increases. It indicated that the greater the travel demand in an area is, the more efficient the supplement of the driver is to reduce the void distance proportion. Moreover, we find two key features of judging the suitable number of drivers in the system, where before is a rapid interval and after is a gentle one. Since there is a strong relationship between the void distance proportion and invalid emission proportion, we also plotted the relationship between the invalid emission proportion as well as quantity and the scale of drivers under a certain quantity of travel demand. Then, we found an extremely similar pattern. At this point, we can have a clearer vision of the impact of the emission performance and user scale. When Ride-hailing service providers try to introduce a ride-hailing system into a new area, they can use this relationship to estimate the suitable number of registered drivers in the system as a guideline to attract or control the number of drivers or passengers. Finally, we also proposed a sample for the high-efficiency area computation of the scale of users in the ride-hailing system under certain metric constraints. Two metric sets are determined to find the different areas of the scale of users under different metrics.

The second part is to propose a dispatch method based on both prediction and optimization methods to improve the efficiency of the ride-hailing system. We use the same dataset for simulation. We firstly preprocess the data into desired input format of historical observation needed by the prediction model and collect the metadata for additional input. Next, we adopt the ST-Resnet as the deep learning neural network for prediction and successfully train the prediction model. The rescaled MAPE is rather small and enough for the simulation of the dispatch algorithm. Then, we introduce the dispatch algorithm based on the optimization method. We state the target function to optimize and the constraint, including the optional one, which can impose a full satisfaction of orders. We use the greedy algorithm, which is used widely in the current real-time dispatch system, as the baseline and compare the performances. We find that the proposed method out performances the baseline and shows a good stability of performance on the evaluation metrics, which proves a great potential in real-time application. In addition, we also find that the algorithm shows better performance with the optional constraint. This is mainly because of the uncertainties in the location of predicted orders. Thus, we suggest imposing the constraint that maximizes the number of served orders in solving the current dispatch problem. By far, we have successfully answered and filled the research gaps mentioned in the literature review.

There are certainly some limitations in this work. For example, the simulation method in evaluating the impact of user scale is very dependent on regional historical data. Now, if we want to transfer this model to other cities, we may need other local historical ride-hailing data. In future work, we can improve this model with some critical city information, such as the landmark position to make this model more common. In the part of dispatch, we mainly use the statistical result to estimate the location of predicted orders in the future. Adopting smaller cells can help get a more accurate location. However, it will inevitably make the spatial distribution matrix sparser, thus, making the model hard to be trained. In the future, if better prediction methods like GCN (graphical convolutional network) can be developed better, we can improve this limitation by adopting them.

References

[1] H. Zhang, X. Song, T. Xia, M. Yuan, Z. Fan, R. Shibasaki, et al., Battery electric vehicles in Japan: human mobile behavior-based adoption potential analysis and policy target response, Applied Energy 220 (2018) 527–535.

[2] H. Zhang, X. Song, Y. Long, T. Xia, K. Fang, J. Zheng, et al., Mobile phone GPS data in urban bicycle-sharing: layout optimization and emissions reduction analysis, Applied Energy 242 (2019) 138–147.

[3] R.R. Clewlow, G.S. Mishra, Disruptive Transportation: The Adoption, Utilization, and Impacts of Ride-Hailing in the United States, University of California, Davis, 2017. Institute of Transportation Studies, Davis, CA, Research Report UCD-ITS-RR-17-07.

[4] R.R. Clewlow, G.S.J.U.C. Mishra, Davis, Institute of Transportation Studies, C.A. Davis, Research Report UCD-ITS-RR-17-07. Disruptive Transportation: The Adoption, Utilization, and Impacts of Ride-Hailing in the United States, 2017.

[5] L. Rayle, D. Dai, N. Chan, R. Cervero, S. Shaheen, Just a better taxi? A survey-based comparison of taxis, transit, and ridesourcing services in San Francisco, Transport Policy 45 (2016) 168−178.

[6] B. Li, D. Zhang, L. Sun, C. Chen, S. Li, G. Qi, et al., Hunting or waiting? Discovering passenger-finding strategies from a large-scale real-world taxi dataset, in: 2011 IEEE International Conference on Pervasive Computing and Communications Workshops (PERCOM Workshops), IEEE, 2011, pp. 63−68.

[7] Y. Guo, F. Xin, S.J. Barnes, X. Li, Opportunities or threats: the rise of online collaborative consumption (OCC) and its impact on new car sales, Electronic Commerce Research and Applications 29 (2018) 133−141.

[8] J. Cramer, A.B. Krueger, Disruptive change in the taxi business: the case of Uber, The American Economic Review 106 (2016) 177−182.

[9] Z. Wang, F. Chen, T. Fujiyama, Carbon emission from urban passenger transportation in Beijing, Transportation Research Part D: Transport and Environment 41 (2015) 217−227.

[10] R.R. Clewlow, G.S. Mishra, Disruptive Transportation: The Adoption, Utilization, and Impacts of Ride-Hailing in the United States, 2017.

[11] N. Korolko, D. Woodard, C. Yan, H. Zhu, Dynamic Pricing and Matching in Ride-Hailing Platforms, 2018. Available at: SSRN.

[12] P. Afeche, Z. Liu, C. Maglaras, Ride-hailing Networks with Strategic Drivers: The Impact of Platform Control Capabilities on Performance, Columbia Business School Research Paper, 2018, pp. 18−19.

[13] G.R. Calegari, I. Celino, D. Peroni, City data dating: emerging affinities between diverse urban datasets, Information Systems 57 (2016) 223−240.

[14] A. Henao, W.E. Marshall, The impact of ride-hailing on vehicle miles traveled, Transportation 46 (2019) 2173−2194.

[15] G.D. Erhardt, S. Roy, D. Cooper, B. Sana, M. Chen, J. Castiglione, Do transportation network companies decrease or increase congestion? Science Advances 5 (2019) eaau2670.

[16] O. Flores, L. Rayle, How cities use regulation for innovation: the case of uber, lyft and sidecar in san Francisco, Transportation Research Procedia 25 (2017) 3756−3768.

[17] R. Beer, C. Brakewood, S. Rahman, J. Viscardi, Qualitative analysis of ride-hailing regulations in major American cities, Transportation Research Record 2650 (2017) 84−91.

[18] P.M. Bösch, F. Becker, H. Becker, K.W. Axhausen, Cost-based analysis of autonomous mobility services, Transport Policy 64 (2018) 76−91.

[19] Z. Wadud, D. MacKenzie, P. Leiby, Help or hindrance? The travel, energy and carbon impacts of highly automated vehicles, Transportation Research Part A: Policy and Practice 86 (2016) 1−18.

[20] W. Tu, P. Santi, T. Zhao, X. He, Q. Li, L. Dong, et al., Acceptability, energy consumption, and costs of electric vehicle for ride-hailing drivers in Beijing, Applied Energy 250 (2019) 147−160.

[21] B. Schaller, The New Automobility: Lyft, Uber and the Future of American Cities, 2018.

[22] A. Tirachini, A. Gomez-Lobo, Does ride-hailing increase or decrease vehicle kilometers traveled (VKT)? A simulation approach for Santiago de Chile, International Journal of Sustainable Transportation 14 (2020) 187−204.

[23] C. Rodier, The Effects of Ride Hailing Services on Travel and Associated Greenhouse Gas Emissions, 2018.

[24] Z. Xu, Z. Li, Q. Guan, D. Zhang, Q. Li, J. Nan, et al., Large-scale order dispatch in on-demand ride-hailing platforms: a learning and planning approach, in: Proceedings of the 24th ACM SIGKDD International Conference on Knowledge Discovery & Data Mining, 2018, pp. 905−913.

[25] G. Feng, G. Kong, Z. Wang, We Are on the Way: Analysis of On-Demand Ride-Hailing Systems, 2017. Available at: SSRN 2960991.

[26] H. Yao, F. Wu, J. Ke, X. Tang, Y. Jia, S. Lu, et al., Deep multi-view spatial-temporal network for taxi demand prediction, in: Thirty-Second AAAI Conference on Artificial Intelligence, 2018.

[27] M. Maciejewski, J. Bischoff, Large-scale microscopic simulation of taxi services, Procedia Computer Science 52 (2015) 358−364.

[28] J.M.S. Grau, M.A.E. Romeu, E. Mitsakis, I. Stamos, Agent based modeling for simulation of taxi services, Journal of Traffic and Logistics Engineering 1 (2013) 159−163.

[29] A. Mourad, J. Puchinger, C. Chu, A survey of models and algorithms for optimizing shared mobility, Transportation Research Part B: Methodological 123 (2019) 323−346.

[30] R.J. O'Neil, K. Hoffman, Decision diagrams for solving traveling salesman problems with pickup and delivery in real time, Operations Research Letters 47 (2019) 197−201.

[31] X. Cheng, S. Fu, G. Yin, Does subsidy work? An investigation of post-adoption switching on car-hailing apps, Journal of Electronic Commerce Research, Forthcoming (2016). https://ssrn.com/abstract=2953448.

[32] Institute DMR, Report on Big Data of Intelligent Travel in Chengdu, 2016.

[33] D. Marcotte, D. Allard, Gibbs sampling on large lattice with GMRF, Computers & Geosciences 111 (2018) 190−199.

[34] M.M. Vazifeh, P. Santi, G. Resta, S. Strogatz, C. Ratti, Addressing the minimum fleet problem in on-demand urban mobility, Nature 557 (2018) 534.

[35] A.M. Arslan, N. Agatz, L. Kroon, R. Zuidwijk, Crowdsourced delivery—a dynamic pickup and delivery problem with ad hoc drivers, Transportation Science 53 (2018) 222−235.

[36] Transportation ICfEa, Online Ride-Hailing Network and Fuel Consumption: A Driver's Perspective, 2017.

[37] L. Zheng, L. Chen, J. Ye, Order dispatch in price-aware ridesharing, Proceedings of the VLDB Endowment 11 (2018) 853−865.

[38] Y. Sui, H. Zhang, X. Song, F. Shao, X. Yu, R. Shibasaki, et al., GPS data in urban online ride-hailing: a comparative analysis on fuel consumption and emissions, Journal of Cleaner Production 227 (2019) 495−505.

[39] H. Cai, S. Xie, Estimation of vehicular emission inventories in China from 1980 to 2005, Atmospheric Environment 41 (2007) 8963−8979.

[40] J. Lang, S. Cheng, Y. Zhou, Y. Zhang, G. Wang, Air pollutant emissions from on-road vehicles in China, 1999−2011, Science of the Total Environment 496 (2014) 1−10.

[41] C. Yan, H. Zhu, N. Korolko, D. Woodard, Dynamic Pricing and Matching in Ride-hailing Platforms, Naval Research Logistics (NRL), 2019.

[42] Y. Khazbak, J. Fan, S. Zhu, G. Cao, Preserving location privacy in ride-hailing service, in: 2018 IEEE Conference on Communications and Network Security (CNS), IEEE, 2018, pp. 1−9.

[43] R. Zhang, M. Pavone, Control of robotic mobility-on-demand systems: a queueing-theoretical perspective, The International Journal of Robotics Research 35 (2016) 186—203.

[44] D. Wang, Y. Yang, S. Ning, Deepstcl: a deep spatio-temporal convlstm for travel demand prediction, in: 2018 International Joint Conference on Neural Networks (IJCNN), IEEE, 2018, pp. 1—8.

[45] K.F. Chu, A.Y. Lam, V.O. Li, Travel demand prediction using deep multi-scale convolutional LSTM network, in: 2018 21st International Conference on Intelligent Transportation Systems (ITSC), IEEE, 2018, pp. 1402—1407.

[46] C. Jia, S. Wang, X. Zhang, S. Wang, S. Ma, Spatial-temporal residue network based in-loop filter for video coding, in: 2017 IEEE Visual Communications and Image Processing (VCIP), IEEE, 2017, pp. 1—4.

[47] X. Ma, Z. Dai, Z. He, J. Ma, Y. Wang, Y. Wang, Learning traffic as images: a deep convolutional neural network for large-scale transportation network speed prediction, Sensors 17 (2017) 818.

[48] M. Cassel, F. Lima, Evaluating one-hot encoding finite state machines for SEU reliability in SRAM-based FPGAs, in: 12th IEEE International On-Line Testing Symposium (IOLTS'06), IEEE, 2006, p. 6.

[49] S. Ioffe, C. Szegedy, Batch Normalization: Accelerating Deep Network Training by Reducing Internal Covariate Shift, 2015 arXiv preprint arXiv:150203167.

[50] D.P. Kingma, J. Ba, Adam: A Method for Stochastic Optimization, 2014 arXiv preprint arXiv:14126980.

[51] T. Sühr, A.J. Biega, M. Zehlike, K.P. Gummadi, A. Chakraborty, Two-sided fairness for repeated matchings in two-sided markets: a case study of a ride-hailing platform, in: Proceedings of the 25th ACM SIGKDD International Conference on Knowledge Discovery & Data Mining, 2019, pp. 3082—3092.

[52] V. Klee, G.J. Minty, How good is the simplex algorithm, Inequalities 3 (1972) 159—175.

[53] C. Frei, M. Hyland, H.S. Mahmassani, Flexing service schedules: assessing the potential for demand-adaptive hybrid transit via a stated preference approach, Transportation Research Part C: Emerging Technologies 76 (2017) 71—89.

[54] Z. Huang, F. Cao, C. Jin, Z. Yu, R. Huang, Carbon emission flow from self-driving tours and its spatial relationship with scenic spots—A traffic-related big data method, Journal of Cleaner Production 142 (2017) 946—955.

[55] X. Luo, L. Dong, Y. Dou, N. Zhang, J. Ren, Y. Li, et al., Analysis on spatial-temporal features of taxis' emissions from big data informed travel patterns: a case of Shanghai, China, Journal of Cleaner Production 142 (2017) 926—935.

CHAPTER THREE

Research on vehicle routing problem and application scenarios

Lu Wenyi
Center for Spatial Information Science, The University of Tokyo, Kashiwa-shi, Chiba, Japan

1. Introduction

Vehicle Routing Problem, or VRP, has been discussed since last century in the field of both civil used and industrial transportation. It helps identifying a route for a set of customers with fixed positions [1], and on this basis some further problems like the Vehicle Routing Problem with Time Windows (VRPTW) and The Dial-a-Ride-Problem (DARP) derive from the original VRP [2,3]. The Vehicle Routing Problem first started with the famous Traveling Salesman Problem, described as given a list of cities and their distance graph, find a shortest route to cross all the cities then returns to the place of departure with no other repetitive visit [4,5]. Tadei et al. and Huang et al. explored stochastic conditions of TSP and VRP respectively, showing the path selection leads to significant savings of costs [6,7]. Then with the rise of more customer requests and travel demands, new problems and solutions are generated in the fields of time constraints, travel economy, and order appointed multiple destinations, etc.

The development of applications in public transportations exploded with the prosperity of Internet, especially in 21st century. Rapid information exchange and collection methods with mobile phones and Internet offered new opportunities for modern public transportations. In 2010s, the sharing economy soon spawned the appearance of new public transportation methods like hitch rides and shared taxis [8,9]. These new commercial scenarios require operation models with higher precision, that is, digging out more optimal solutions compared with primitive rough predictive solutions. In industrial fields, VRP appears in merchandise distribution services or delivery services, allocation planning, etc. One classic scenario is delivery services, typically a truck carrying goods is supposed to deliver distribution

Handbook of Mobility Data Mining, Volume 3
ISBN: 978-0-323-95892-9
https://doi.org/10.1016/B978-0-323-95892-9.00006-1

quota to multiple corresponding stores. Demands of timeliness and travel distances are added to complicate the original VRP model, bringing challenges to algorithms and computing power.

2. Vehicle routing problem in MaaS shared-bus system

2.1 Introduction

Nowadays, Mobility as a Service (MaaS), a new idea of urban mobility framework, has been extensively discussed and studied, which provides convenience for users through fast response to instant travel requests and efficient transportation planning [10,11]. MaaS system performs well in mega cities with multiple transportation ways [12]. Among all sorts of transportation, subway takes on the most travel pressure [13]. Although subway system provides enormous convenience, commuters still face with difficulties about how to efficiently move between subway stations and destinations [14]. Unfortunately, transportation policy makers and private-sector transportation service providers seldom pay attention to these issues, which indicates that there are still lots of chances to further decrease traffic pollution and save public transportation resource [15,16].

With the development of technology, collecting personal GPS data becomes simpler and more convenient, which shows great potential [17−19]. By extracting travel demands from real human mobility data based on GPS records, in this paper, we propose a novel MaaS shared bus system framework. The system provides an efficient and environment-friendly solution for the short-distance movement around the subway station by arranging shared bus for different passengers.

To be more specific, optimal route of each shared bus is planned by establishing midway bus stations, which takes both operating costs and most of the customer demands into account. An ant colony optimization algorithm based method is developed to solve the route planning problem. The system is also capable to receive temporary requests raised by users through smartphone application.

More than this, we provide a real case experiment to test the efficiency of the shared bus system. We extract commuting demands between communities around subway stations and the stations. Based on the real travel demands, we analyze the environmental pollution that can be reduced to demonstrate the significance of our proposed system.

Our contribution includes but not limit to:

1. We develop a novel MaaS shared bus subsystem framework, which can optimize bus routes based on passengers' travel demands.
2. We extract real passengers' travel demands from big mobility dataset to test the efficiency of the shared bus system.
3. We analyze the reducible pollution in the real case to demonstrate the potential of shared bus system. We also explore how will different parameters affect the system performance.

2.2 Problem description

In this section, we intend to make a brief description to our problem. The overview of our problem can be summarized as Fig. 3.1.

Our goal is to provide shared-bus service for dense passenger flows to efficiently commute from subway stations to their destinations. Passengers getting off from trains in subway stations can take our service for the rest parts of their trips by providing their destinations and expected arrival time. We assume that each bus serves in a certain period.

(a) Bus operation pattern one

(b) Bus operation pattern two

Figure 3.1 Overview of the MaaS shared bus system.

To optimize the bus route, the first step is to decide midway bus stations, which should be considered thoroughly to reduce the walking distance of passengers and guarantee the restriction of expected arrival time. Since some of the passengers may alight in the same area or district, not all the destinations are chosen as midway stations. Then an optimal route should be planned based on the results derived from the first part, which is a one-origin multiple-destination vehicle routing problem. The vehicle starts from one starting station at a given time, each vehicle containing dozens of passengers heading to different destinations, and some of the passengers are supposed to alight at the same station at the same time. Each mid-way bus station will be passed only once, and every mid-way station will be attached to a certain alight time.

Assume that $U = u_1, u_2, \ldots, u_k$ denotes the group of k passengers that get off from trains and choose to take our service for the rest parts of their trips, their corresponding destinations $D = d_1, d_2, \ldots, d_k$ and expected arrival times $t_1, t_2, \ldots, t_k$ could be collected. A graph $G = (V, E)$ is utilized to represent distance relations between starting point of the bus and destinations, where $V = D \cup p_s$, p_s is the starting point of the bus and E is the shortest distance between two points on the road network. The bus route consists of n stations $S = s_1, s_2, \ldots, s_n, s_i \in V$. In particular, the first station and the last station are both the starting point, that is, $s_1 = p_s, s_n = p_s$. The standard speed of each bus can be represented as v. For a given departure time t_0, the arrival time of each station $t_1, t_2, \ldots, t_n$ could be computed iteratively by:

$$t_i = t_{i-1} + \frac{E(s_{i-1}, s_i)}{v}, \ \forall i \in [1, n] \tag{3.1}$$

In addition, it is not proper to let passengers arrive too early or too late. We set a tolerance time Δt to represent the maximum difference time between the arrival time that passengers could tolerate and their expected arrival time. Then for any passenger u_i who expect to get off at station s_j at t_{u_i}', we have:

$$t_{u_i}' - \Delta t \leq t_j \leq t_{u_i}' + \Delta t, \ \forall u_i \in U \tag{3.2}$$

Obviously, it is impossible to carry all passengers under the restrict limitations. So we set up an objective function to maximize the passengers to be delivered through the bus system, ultimately maximize the income of the service provider, which can also be achieved through decreasing the mileage of the buses. Thus, we utilize both passenger numbers and path length as the optimization parameters to establish the objective function.

2.3 Methodology

In this section, we tend to formulate an overview of the methodologies. We discuss the route planning procedure and the detailed algorithms used under the base of ant colony algorithms.

Ant colony optimization is a meta-heuristic algorithm, designed specifically for solving combinatorial optimization problems. This probabilistic technique was inspired by a nature phenomenon that some ants wandering on the ground randomly to search for food, and when the food is found, they will leave pheromone on the trail back to their nest. The successors then prefer to follow the trail rather than move randomly, while reinforcing the concentration of the pheromone. The pheromone evaporates overtime, reducing its attractive strength gradually if the ants who follow the trail failed to bring back food continuously.

The original ants may take two separate paths from the same start to the same destination. Assume that ants all move in the same speed, ants who take the longer path will cost longer time. The pheromone left in the longer path is supposed to evaporate more than other trails, leading the possibility of choosing the shorter path higher for the next ant. Through iteration, ants will eventually find the shortest path between destinations. In our problem, the ant system is described as following:

1. Ants are moving around on the road network as shared buses, and each ant has speed limitations in different roads according to local laws.
2. Each ant that successfully delivers passengers to their destinations is considered as s-ant, no matter how many passengers they delivered in total.
3. The pheromone left by each s-ant is computed according to multiple indexes, including the total distance the ant went through and the number of delivered passengers.

The pheromone will be updated after each iteration. The old pheromone will evaporate by a ratio set in advance, and then the newly generated pheromone will be added. In the first batch, an amount of N ants will be deployed to the original station, and since no former information is given, the possibilities of moving to station V_i are

$$P(0, i) = \frac{1}{m}, \ \forall i \in [1, m] \tag{3.3}$$

After the first batch, some routes are evaluated with higher pheromone for shorter path and more delivered passengers. In the next turn, these stations will be more easily chosen as the next station than other stations. After each iteration, pheromone is updated according to the ant that delivered the most passengers to their destinations within the shortest path. For iteration k among the total iteration times M, assume the best ant has a route:

$$R_k = \{W_1, W_2, W_3, .., W_n\}, k \in (1, 2, 3 ... M), W_n \in V \tag{3.4}$$

The total number of delivered passengers is

$$Pas_k = \sum_{i=1}^{n} D(W_i) \tag{3.5}$$

The total distance of path is

$$Dis_k = \sum_{i=1}^{n-1} d_{i,i+1} \tag{3.6}$$

Then the new pheromone graph is updated by:

$$Phe(V_i)_k = \begin{cases} Phe(V_i)_{k-1} \times \mu + \dfrac{Q \times D(V_i)}{Dis_k}, & \text{if } V_i \in R_k \\ Phe(V_i)_{k-1} \times \mu, & \text{if } V_i \notin R_k \end{cases} \tag{3.7}$$

The coefficient Q tends to balance the influence from the passenger number and the total distance of the path. Since after each iteration, existed pheromone will evaporate a certain percentage, the proportion of the surplus pheromone is denoted by μ. After adequate iterations, the ants will gradually find the most efficient path to deliver the most of the passengers within their time constraints, while taking the shortest route.

Algorithm 1.

Single Ant Route Search Algorithm $FindRoute(G(V, E), Phe[V_i], t_0)$

Require: The graph of distance between each pair of candidate positions $G(V, E)$; the expected arrival time of each candidate t_i; the pheromone graph $Phe[V_i]$; the start time of the ant t_0; the maximum time difference between actual arrival time and expected arrival time δt_{max}; the ant speed v.

Ensure: The delivered passenger number n and the path. $Path$

1: Set an array $table_i \leftarrow True$ for each candidate, $n \leftarrow 0$, $Path \leftarrow Empty$, temporary time $t \leftarrow t_0$
2: // Find a path to deliver passengers
3: **while** $table$ not all $False$ **do**
4:     Randomly pick i in open-table if $Phe[i] = True$
5:     $\delta t = \frac{E(V_i, V_{temp})}{v}$
6:     **if** $-t + \delta t - t_i| \leq \delta t_{max}$ **then**
7:         $n + = 1$
8:         $t + = \delta t$
9:         $Path.append(V_i)$
10:     **end if**
11:     $table_i = False$
12:     $V_{temp} = V_i$
13: **end while**
14: **return** $n, Path$;

Each ant follows the Algorithm 1 to move step by step until it no longer finds a feasible candidate position, under the strict time-window restrictions and the influence from the past pheromone to the surrounding environment. However, a single ant may not be able to discover the global optimal solution, thus adequate ants are necessary. The algorithm 2 describes the top-level conceptual model of ant dispense and pheromone update.

Algorithm 2. Best Route Search Algorithm

Require: The graph of distance between each pair of candidate positions $G(V, E)$; The number of ants s; The start time of the ants t_0; The pheromone graph $Phe[V_i]$; The iteration times M The evaporate ratio μ.

Ensure: The delivered passenger number n and the path. $Path$

```
 1: Initialize pheromone graph ∀Phi[Vᵢ] = 1, n ← 0, Path ← Empty
 2: // In iteration times, generate n ants, each ant finds its best route
 3: for k = 1 to M do
 4:     // Iteration times
 5:     for j = 1; j < s; j + + do
 6:         // Ant number
 7:         p, Path_tmp = FindRoute(G(V, E), Phe[Vᵢ], t₀)
 8:         if n ≤ p then
 9:             n = p
10:             Path = Path_temp
11:         end if
12:     end forDis_k = Σᵢ₌₁^len(Path) d_Path[i],Path[i+1]
13:     //Pheromone Update by temporary best route
14:     for ∀Vᵢ do
15:         if Vᵢ ∉ Path then
16:             Phe[Vᵢ]* = μ
17:         end if
18:         if Vᵢ ∈ Path then
19:             Phe[Vᵢ] = Phe[Vᵢ] * μ + (Q*D(Vᵢ))/Dis_k
20:         end if
21:     end for
22: end for
23: return n, Path;
```

2.4 Experiment of real world benchmark

In this section, we test the robustness of the proposed system under a real-world scenario. We also test the flexibility of our system by considering possible changes in real-world operations. Finally, we analyze the environmental pollution that can be reduced to highlight the importance of a well-designed shared bus system.

2.4.1 Experimental set up

A real world scenario is usually in a large or mega city with multiple transportation modes. To construct the benchmark, we extract passengers' travel demands from a big mobility dataset in Tokyo, Japan. The original dataset is a part of "Konzatsu-Tokei (R)" Data provided by Zenrin DataCom INC. "Konzatsu-Tokei (R)" Data refers to people flows data collected by individual location data sent from mobile phone under users' consent, through Applications provided by NTT DOCOMO, INC. Those data is processed collectively and statistically in order to conceal the private information. Original location data is GPS data (latitude, longitude) sent in about every a minimum period of 5 min and does not include the information to specify individual [20,21]. ※ Some applications such as "docomomap navi" service (map navilocal guide).

After several preprocessing including map matching, travel mode detection, and stay point clustering, we collect the crowd flow, in which people just get off the subway and tend to move to next destination. Considering the size of our raw dataset, we pick five major subway stations and their surrounding areas in Tokyo, Japan as target study sites: Ikebukuro, Shibuya, Shinagawa, Shinjuku, and Tokyo. The morning peak between 7:00 a.m. and 8:00 a.m. is selected as target period. Of each station, the crowd flow involves more than fifty-thousands' passengers in the target period.

Based on the mobility pattern of the crowd flow, we sample and generate passengers' requests for taking bus, in which their expected arrival time are set as their ground truth arrival time. We set the default request number of each bus as 20. If requests are too many for a single bus, one delivery turn will take more than 40 min, making some of passengers wait too long on the bus. On the other hand, less requests lead to less income for operators while the operating expense decrease inconspicuously.

The default tolerance time for passengers is set as 3 min. The tolerance time can be set longer if we intend to deliver more passengers, or shorter if we intend to provide the most precise service for passengers. More information about the practical operation can help to optimize the benefits of our service.

The default number of buses is set as 3, which means three buses can carry passengers at the same time. The target period is divided into six slices with 10 min. As shown in Fig. 3.2, three buses set out alternately and get back to the subway station after all passengers being delivered. Then the bus pick up another batch of passengers and set out at the beginning of next 10 minutes slice. For instance, a bus sets out at 7:00 a.m., at which time it carries passengers whose expected arrival time is in the 0—10 min slice, 10—20 min slice or 20—30 min slice. After delivering all passengers and getting back at 7:35 a.m., the bus sets out again at 7:40 a.m. to deliver new passengers whose expected arrival time is between 7:40 a.m. and 7:50 a.m.

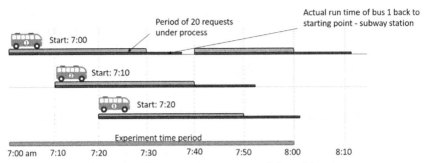

Figure 3.2 The operation patterns of shared buses.

The experiment is conducted on a PC with 8-core 4.0 GHz CPU and 16 GB of RAM, using Google Map as a demonstration board and all results are stored in a look-up table.

2.4.2 Experimental results and analysis

Fig. 3.3 visualize two simulated routes of a bus as an example. The red mark denotes the starting point of the bus, which is also the subway station. Each green and yellow mark represents a request from one person. The yellow marks are passengers that are successfully delivered, and the green marks represent people who cannot be sent in time and are not served. The purple line denotes the route of the bus. In Fig. 3.3A, we randomly generated 50 travel demands with different positions as destinations in Tokyo city, and also randomly set their expected arrival time within 1 hour to examine the validity of our route planning algorithms. Fig. 3.3B demonstrates the planned route of 20 real requests around Tokyo station.

Table 3.1 reveal two metrics to measure the performance of the system for different stations, including delivery ratio and time difference. Delivery ratio is defined as the number of delivered passengers dividing the total number of requests. Time difference denotes the absolute value of the difference between actual time of delivery and passengers' expected arrival time.

Under default conditions, the average delivery ratio varies from 0.159 in Shinagawa station to 0.329 in Shinjuku station, mainly caused by indeterminacy factors like the distribution distinction of the requests between different stations. The average time difference in different stations is relatively similar, which verifies the consistency of our algorithm.

When the maximum tolerance time gets longer, it is obvious that delivery ratio and time difference both increase. On the one hand, longer tolerance time gives the bus higher fault tolerance rate, which makes it possible to carry more passengers; on the other hand, more passengers inevitably make the average waiting time longer. Fig. 3.4 demonstrates the violin plot of the average time difference distribution with different maximum tolerance time. From the figure, we can see that the average time difference usually lies at around half of the maximum tolerance time, which proves that our algorithm can effectively ensure the delivery time.

We also visualize the change trend of average ridership (or delivered passengers) with different parameters in Fig. 3.5. In (a), the number of buses is different. As more buses are put into use, more passengers will be delivered,

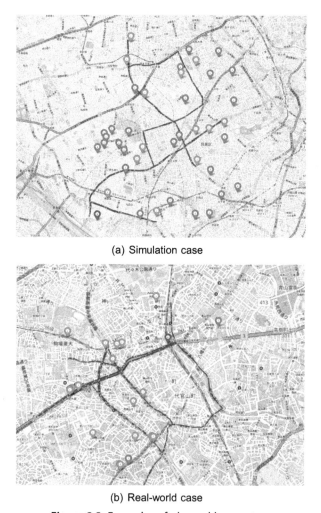

(a) Simulation case

(b) Real-world case

Figure 3.3 Examples of planned bus routes.

Table 3.1 Experimental results with different maximum tolerance time.

		Ikebukuro	Shibuya	Shinagawa	Shinjuku	Tokyo	Average	Variance
min tolerance time	Average delivery ratio	0.243	0.253	0.117	0.286	0.232	0.230	0.016
	Average time difference(min)	1.218	1.251	1.231	1.230	1.238	1.233	0.136
min tolerance time	Average delivery ratio	0.324	0.291	0.159	0.329	0.267	0.279	0.017
	Average time difference(min)	1.774	1.855	1.881	1.774	1.798	1.805	0.203
min tolerance time	Average delivery ratio	0.343	0.316	0.185	0.378	0.307	0.310	0.016
	Average time difference(min)	2.259	2.433	2.521	2.334	2.426	2.371	0.304
min tolerance time	Average delivery ratio	0.390	0.346	0.213	0.387	0.331	0.337	0.016
	Average time difference(min)	2.842	2.982	3.183	2.853	2.979	2.936	0.410
min tolerance time	Average delivery ratio	0.398	0.380	0.255	0.424	0.363	0.367	0.014
	Average time difference(min)	3.440	3.540	3.894	3.414	3.528	3.528	0.481

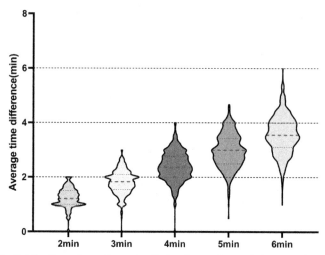

Figure 3.4 Distribution of results under 2–6 min maximum tolerance time. The thick red dotted line represents the mean value, and the thin red lines represent the quartiles.

which is observable when bus number is less than 4. However, when more than five buses are put into use, the final bus starts at 7:40 due to our preset bus operation patterns, so it will only receive passenger requests between 7:40 and 8:00, which is 10 min less than former buses, thus carrying less passengers. In (b), the maximum tolerance time is different. Similar with Table 3.1, the increase in maximum tolerance time makes the buses possible to carry more passengers, and the sufficient tolerance time leads to stable increase in final ridership.

Then we compute and compare the traffic pollution generated by shared bus and private car. The emission standard we use is from the regulation made by Ministry of the Environment [22]. We use the emission standard made before 2009 and the trajectory data is from 2011. Therefore, all of the vehicles meet the standard. The emission standard provides the general emission coefficient that can be utilized to compute the quantity of pollutants including CO, NMHC, NOX and PM based on the travel distance. In this study, we use 1.92 g/km (CO), 0.08 g/km (NMHC), 0.08 g/km (NOX) and 0.007 g/km (PM) as the emission coefficient for private cars and gasoline buses; 0.84 g/km (CO), 0.032 g/km (NMHC), 0.11 g/km (NOX) and 0.007 g/km (PM) for diesel buses.

As shown in Fig. 3.6, we separately compute the emissions of our shared bus using gasoline and diesel as energy source, and then compute the

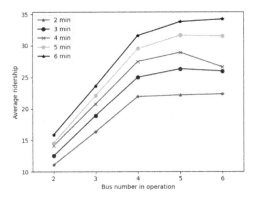

(a) Average ridership with different number of buses

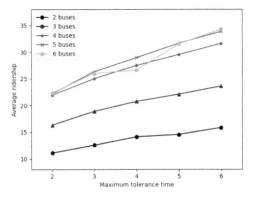

(b) Average ridership with different maximum tolerance time

Figure 3.5 Experimental results of average delivered passenger number in multiple circumstances.

emission of a scenario that if all potential passengers move to their destinations by private gasoline cars. The numeric results are the average of 300 times 3-bus operations with requests between 7:00 a.m. and 8:00 a.m. in grams. The emission of Shinagawa case tends to be higher due to longer average operation distance, but opposite in average private car usage. Buses using diesel have a higher emission load than using gasoline in NOX, but less in CO, NMHC and PM emission. However, no matter which kind of energy supply is used for buses, the pollution is much less compared to gasoline cars in all metrics.

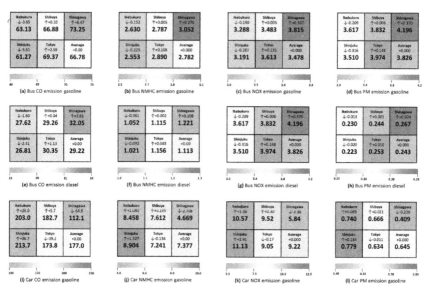

Figure 3.6 [Best viewed in color] (A) average MaaS bus CO emission in grams while using gasoline, (B) average MaaS bus NMHC emission in grams while using gasoline, (C) average MaaS bus NOX emission in grams while using gasoline (D) average MaaS bus PM emission in grams while using gasoline, (E) average MaaS bus CO emission in grams while using diesel, (F) average MaaS bus NMHC emission in grams while using diesel, (G) average MaaS bus NOX emission in grams while using diesel, (H) average MaaS bus PM emission in grams while using diesel, (I) average car CO emission in grams while using gasoline, (J) average car NMHC emission in grams while using gasoline, (K) average car NOX emission in grams while using gasoline, (L)average car PM emission in grams while using gasoline.

2.5 Conclusion

In this section, we propose a shared bus system for commuter delivery with meta-heuristic methods to solve the route planning problem. We take the punctuality of buses into consideration to explore the delivery quality under different maximum tolerance time. Our service is tested by extracted real-world travel demands in Tokyo to demonstrate the robustness and feasibility. Compared with normal travel by private cars, our bus service is environmental friendly, producing much less emission in CO, NMHC, NOX and PM.

Still, this work is the early stage of MaaS guided shared transportation services. It remains space for improving the algorithm in promoting the accuracy in station-path matching and decreasing the possibilities of detour. Another optimizing direction is to take both delivering and picking up services into consideration to advance the income of bus service operators and also provide more comfortable services for commuters.

3. Application Scenario of Vehicle Routing Problem in Logistics Transportation

3.1 Introduction

In logistics industry, customized strategies are designed for commercial customers, and to maximize the efficiency and minimize the required operation costs, basically the number of trucks put into use and the total mileage. In early ages, the delivery routes are planned by empiricism, without the assistance of calculation tools. With the help of maps and mileage counting methods, the logistics industry grew toward scientificity. Grid management is introduced to transportation and dispatching enterprises. Take China for instance, cities are divided into areas of administrative divisions; each area has a corresponding intermediate center. Merchandises are transported to transfer centers, and these centers are responsible for the next level of distribution, from intermediate terminals to smaller terminals, and to retailers at last. This architecture design is being used in most delivery companies in China, but maintaining such intermediate centers are costly as well, and it is only a simplification of transportation framework rather than improving efficiency in mode of distribution. Therefore, we tend to design a new method for merchandise delivery using VRP as base model, and the model is tested in a real-world scenario.

3.2 Problem description

We consider the scenario of logistics transportation for a food factory. The factory produces convenience foods every early morning, pack them up and deliver to retailer stores in its corresponding sales area. Normally, the operation plan is not fixed for each truck, since the convenience food demand vary from day to day. In weekdays, the demand for convenience food may be larger compared with weekends, and different stores also have their own different demand period. To analyze the best delivery plan for this specific scenario, we need detailed data of current delivery scheme. The trucks used by the factory for delivery were all equipped with GPS recorders for operation data logging. The logs collected by recorders mainly include the operation categories like start working, end working, and unloading. Each operation includes a current truck mileage, a time stamp, and its location information. The trucks start from the same location of freight center near the factory to load up the foods, then visit the shops successively, and return to the factory depot. With the logs of mileage, we can obtain the total mileage of the trucks in different tie scales. The dataset we use include the logs in December 2020, and we take Dec. 1, 2020 for concrete analysis. In Dec. 1st, 2020, a total of 69 trucks were deployed for transportation, and the total mileage was 11,434.35 km. Fig. 3.7 shows the location of shops visited in Dec. 1, 2020 and the location of the factory.

3.3 Methodologies

The log data includes the sequence of visited stores, but have no detailed record of routes, so we reconstructed the routes of each truck. Since the total load of each truck is definite, a re-scheduling of the sequence of visiting the stores will not change the allocations of the stores, that is, each truck still corresponds to the same store allocations. Therefore, for each truck, the problem can be simplified as the Traveling Salesman Problem, finding a shortest

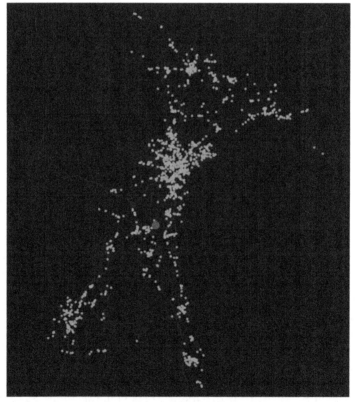

Figure 3.7 Distribution of the positions of the stores, each blue dot (light gray in print) represents an existing store, and the red dot (dark gray in print) represents the factory.

path to pass by all the mid-points and return to the location of departure with no repetitive visits. The same method described in Part.1, the ant colony algorithm is applied in this scenario for an optimized route. Fig. 3.8A shows the original routes that reconstructed according to the recorded transport sequence. Fig. 3.8B shows the optimized route generated by the optimization algorithm which has been precisely explained in the Section.2 bus sharing system design above. Obviously, the optimization leads to changes of the orders of visiting the corresponding stores for most of the trucks. The new routes and distances are calculated by the map routing and distance matrix services provided by ORS.

The new total mileage of the trucks is 9016.59 km, a significant decrease compared with the original 11,434.35 km records. It reveals the great potential of logistics optimization in our scenario that for one factory in 1 day a carefully designed route planning procedure can save around 2,500 km mileage.

The optimization, however, is only a simple change in the sequence of visiting. We wonder if we can provide an optimal solution to the real-world problem of logistics in all aspects, rather than optimize only the routing part of the delivery. From truck capacity, delivery transportation area division to route planning, we hope to see that a full-stack design can further help the reduction of the operation costs.

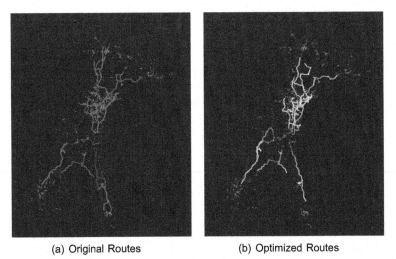

(a) Original Routes   (b) Optimized Routes

Figure 3.8 Captures of the original routes recorded and the optimized routes.

To realize our optimization, we need some vital information which was not included in our dataset logs. The truck capacities influence the truck usage, and the merchandise demand quantity influence the allocation of the trucks. Both of these information are not given, so we make assumptions based on the given data. In Dec. 1st, 2020, a total of 69 trucks were used for delivery. Some stores were visited by more than one trucks, meaning that these stores may have larger demand than the other stores. We define that every single visit to a store by a truck is delivering one unit of merchandise, so a total of 2128 visits were happened in Dec. 1, 2020. In 1 month scale, there were a total of 2016 trucks and 63,224 unit visits. The average delivery units for a truck in Dec. 1, 2020 is 30.84, and the number in December 2020 is 31.36. Based on the hypothesis that every unit visit transports the same quantity of the merchandise, we assume the truck capacity as 31 units. The quantity demanded of each store can be represented by the visit times of the trucks. Since we assume that every visit of the truck delivers the same quantity of the merchandise, the more trucks visit a store, the more demand it has.

3.3.1 DBSCAN

We first re-divide the corresponding stores of the trucks with a clustering method called Density-Based Spatial Clustering of Application with Noise(-DBSCAN). DBSCAN was proposed by Martin Ester, Hans-Peter Kriegel, Jörg Sander and Xiaowei Xu in 1996 [23]. It is a nonparametric algorithm basing on the density that groups together the points that are closely packed. In DBSCAN, two parameters are required as inputs: ε epsilon and *minPts*, the minimum number of points to form a dense region. The algorithm starts with an arbitrary point that has not been visit. This point's ε-neighborhood is retrieved, and if it contains sufficient points, a cluster is formed. Otherwise, this point will be labeled as a noise point for the moment. If this point is found in another point's ε-neighborhood, it will hence be part of a cluster again. Points in a cluster will add all the points in its ε-neighborhood to its former cluster, and this process continues until the density-connected cluster is completely found. After that, a new arbitrary point is again retrieved and processed.

One precondition in DBSCAN is how we define the distance between the shops. We use the Euclidean Distance to represent, because we have the latitude and longitude records of each store in our logs, making the calculation easier. Fig. 3.9 below shows that when different epsilon distance is given, the clustering results we have.

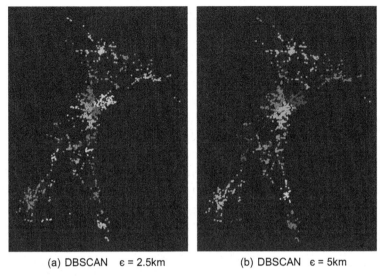

(a) DBSCAN є = 2.5km   (b) DBSCAN є = 5km

Figure 3.9 Clustering results with different epsilon value in DBSCAN.

In DBSCAN, we set the number of minimum points in a cluster as one, because all the points are valid and should not be classified as noise points. Keeping all the points valid leads to a new problem that the pool of clusters contains clusters with very few stores, some even only contain one store. We gather these clusters together to form a larger cluster, to avoid the condition that the total demand value in a cluster does not match the truck capacity. When the demand value is small compared with a much higher truck capacity, the loading rate of the truck will be low.

The cluster merging combines small clusters together to form a larger cluster. In our case, a discrete small cluster will find its closest neighborhood cluster by comparing the distance between the centers of mass of each cluster. The clusters merge until at least 15 stores are contained. The next procedure is to allocate the trucks for each cluster. We take the classic Knapsack Problem [24] as reference, to load the demands in a cluster with the least number of trucks. Then each truck will have its new corresponding stores to deliver. The final procedure is the same as described before, the ACO algorithm to sort out a shortest path for the truck to deliver the demand merchandise to the stores.

3.3.2 Fast Unfolding

In social networks, each user is a node and the connections between the nodes, like following each other, form the basic structure of social networks. Some of the users have closer relationships, while some other appear to be sparse. We call the tight connected parts of the network as communities. In community detection, many methodologies were proposed, such as the Girvan-Newman algorithm named after Michelle Girvan and Mark Newman [25] and the Label Propagation Algorithm [26]. The Fast Unfolding algorithm, also called Louvain Method, was created in 2008 by Blondel et al. [27]. In community detection, Newman et al. proposed the concept of modularity [28]. This concept is used for the measurement of the quality of partition (Q). We use equation below to describe the computation of modularity Q in community C:

$$Q = \frac{1}{2m} \sum_{i,j} \left[A_{i,j} - \frac{k_i k_j}{2m} \right] \delta\left(c_i c_j\right) \tag{3.8}$$

In which,

$$m = \frac{1}{2} \sum_{i,j} A_{i,j} \tag{3.9}$$

representing the sum of all the weights of the links in C, and $A_{i,j}$ is the weight between node i and node j.

$$k_i = \sum_j A_{i,j} \tag{3.10}$$

k_i is the weights of all the links to node i, and c_i is the belonging community of node i. $\delta(i, j)$ is used for the confirmation of whether node i and node j are in the same community, and if they are, returns 1 and if not, returns 0.

The Fast Unfolding algorithm contains two steps basically.

1. Modularity Optimization, to remove node i from its community to its neighboring communities, and if the gain of the value of modularity is positive, the node is placed in the new community.
2. Community Aggregation, to merge the nodes in the same community into one new node, thus reconstruct the whole social network.

The upon process repeat until the community structure does not change any more, and we obtain the final division of the communities. In our scenario, we still use the Euclidean Distance to substitute the weight between the nodes. However, we prune the links longer than certain distances to study how keeping different length of weights influence the results of division. Fig. 3.10A shows the network when we only keep the links shorter than 2.5 km, and Fig. 3.10B shows the network with links shorter than 5 km. Similar to the DBSCAN, when shorter constraints are given, the number of communities or clusters increase largely. We use ε to represent the pruning distance as well to match it in DBSCAN.

The rest parts of allocating trucks to each cluster and planning the routes for each truck is the same as upon.

3.3.3 Experiment and result analysis

The experiment is conducted under a stable 2.2 GHz 8-core CPU environment. The ACO computation part in each calculation has the same 50 ants and 500 iteration times to guarantee the convergence. The results are listed in Table 3.2 below.

We tested the mileage needed under 31 units capacity with both DBSCAN and Fast Unfolding algorithms. In the previous part, we discussed that an assumption must be made before because we do not have the relevant information about the truck capacity. We take 31 units as an attempt but 31 is the average capacity. If we use it as the maximum capacity of the trucks, the truck usage will never be less than that recorded in the original logs. Therefore, we set another capacity, 35, as a new option. Fig. 3.11A shows the trend of the truck usage and total mileage under 31 capacity using

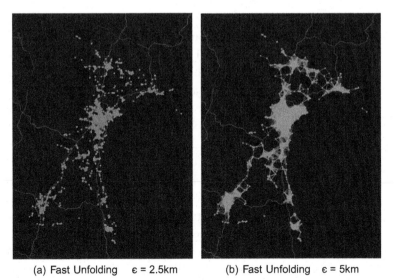

(a) Fast Unfolding   ε = 2.5km   (b) Fast Unfolding   ε = 5km

Figure 3.10 Community detection results with different pruning distance in fast unfolding.

Table 3.2 Experimental results with different ε and clustering method under 31 and 35 units truck capacity.

	Truck capacity	ε(km)	Cluster number	Truck usage	Total Mileage (km)
DBSCAN	31	5	15	70	11,286.47
		2.5	14	76	8549.35
		2	22	79	8410.00
		1.5	23	80	8440.22
		1	30	86	8597.47
	35	5	15	62	10,006.96
		2.5	14	70	8041.11
		2	22	73	7947.37
		1.5	23	69	7541.47
		1	30	74	7607.23
Fast unfolding	31	5	10	75	8614.13
		2.5	21	78	8194.38
		2	25	79	8036.04
		1.5	32	81	8127.22
		1	36	85	8141.14
	35	5	10	75	7460.49
		2.5	21	72	7628.96
		2	25	74	7620.40
		1.5	32	75	7469.69
		1	36	76	7722.3

DBSCAN and Fast Unfolding, and Fig. 3.11B shows the trend of the truck usage and total mileage under 35 capacity.

We can see that when capacity is 31, when ε decrease from 5 to 1 km, the truck usage increase in both scenarios, but the mileage decrease at first and then stable at around 8,500 km. Despite $\varepsilon = 5km$ using DBSCAN, all other mileages are lower than both original mileage and the optimal mileage. The trend of truck usages in accord with our assumption, all larger than the original 69 trucks, from at least 70 trucks to maximum 86 trucks. When capacity increase to 35, things change in some aspects. The truck usages in DBSCAN still get higher than the original usage, but in Fast Unfolding, when $\varepsilon = 5km$, the truck usage is only 62. Typically, the mileage in Fast Unfolding is shorter than DBSCAN, but under 35 capacity and $\varepsilon = 1km$, the mileage of DBSCAN is slightly shorter than the mileage of Fast Unfolding. To get a best performance in optimization, when capacity is 35, using Fast Unfolding with an epsilon value of 5 km can get both the shortest mileage and the least truck usage. When capacity is 31, using Fast Unfolding with 2.5 km or 2 km as epsilon both make similar fine results.

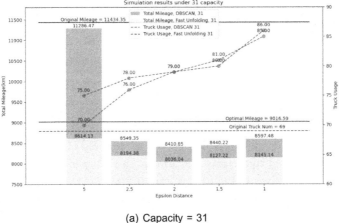

(a) Capacity = 31

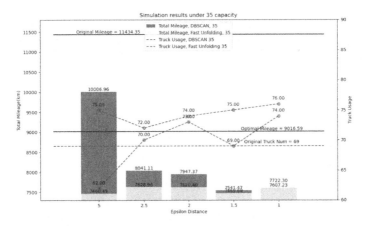

(b) Capacity = 35

Figure 3.11 Truck usage and total mileage under 31 capacity using DBSCAN and fast unfolding.

3.4 Conclusion

In the section of Application Scenario of Vehicle Routing Problem in Logistics Transportation, we discussed a typical scenario of delivering merchandise to retailer stores from factories. We get an optimistic solution just by re-scheduling the sequence of visiting the stores and find a new shortest path for the trucks. The optimized route decrease from 11434.35 to 9016.59 km using the same amount of trucks. We also discussed that if assumptions are made to clarify some key parameters like truck capacity and shop demands, we can further optimize the whole transportation procedure using different clustering algorithms to re-allocate the trucks. We hope to obtain more detailed dataset and make the optimization with higher reliability.

4. Summary and prospect

In this part, we summarize our work in the field of the applications of VRP. We illustrated two classic scenarios in our daily life, one is the stylish bus sharing system for subway nearby commuting and the other is the logistic transportation in city scale. For the bus sharing part, we proposed a feasible system to maximum the served passenger number with limited buses, and we studied how the changes of user experience influence the final load capacity. For the logistic part, we optimize the scheme basing on the original records, and we further optimize the full-stack procedure with some reasonable assumptions. Our proposed scheme can save more than 3,000 km mileage for a factory every day, bringing much economic benefits.

References

[1] P. Toth, D. Vigo, The Vehicle Routing Problem, SIAM, 2002.

[2] L.M. Gambardella, É. Taillard, G. Agazzi, Macs-vrptw: a multiple colony system for vehicle routing problems with time windows, in: New Ideas in Optimization, McGraw-Hill, 1999, pp. 63–76.

[3] J.-F. Cordeau, G. Laporte, The dial-a-ride problem (darp): variants, modeling issues and algorithms, Quarterly Journal of the Belgian French and Italian Operations Research Societies 1 (2) (2003) 89–101.

[4] J. Beardwood, J.H. Halton, J. Michael Hammersley, The shortest path through many points, in: Mathematical Proceedings of the Cambridge Philosophical Society, vol. 55, Cambridge University Press, 1959, pp. 299–327.

[5] R. Bellman, Dynamic programming treatment of the travelling salesman problem, Journal of the ACM 9 (1) (1962) 61–63.

[6] F. Maggioni, P. Guido, R. Tadei, The multi-path traveling salesman problem with stochastic travel costs: building realistic instances for city logistics applications, Transportation Research Procedia 3 (2014) 528–536.

[7] Y. Huang, L. Zhao, T. Van Woensel, J.-P. Gross, Time-dependent vehicle routing problem with path flexibility, Transportation Research Part B: Methodological 95 (2017) 169–195.

[8] M.C. Gonzalez, C.A. Hidalgo, A.-L. Barabasi, Understanding individual human mobility patterns, Nature 453 (7196) (2008) 779–782.

[9] H. Hosni, J. Naoum-Sawaya, A. Hassan, The shared-taxi problem: formulation and solution methods, Transportation Research Part B: Methodological 70 (2014) 303–318.

[10] M. Kamargianni, W. Li, M. Matyas, A. Schäfer, A critical review of new mobility services for urban transport, Transportation Research Procedia 14 (2016) 3294—3303. Transport Research Arena TRA2016.

[11] H. Zhang, J. Chen, Q. Chen, T. Xia, X. Wang, W. Li, X. Song, R. Shibasaki, A Universal Mobility-Based Indicator for Regional Health Level. Cities, 2021, p. 103452.

[12] C. Mulley, J.D. Nelson, S. Wright, Community transport meets mobility as a service: on the road to a new a flexible future, Research in Transportation Economics 69 (2018) 583—591. Competition and Ownership in Land Passenger Transport (selected papers from the Thredbo 15 conference).

[13] S. Ribeiro, M. Figueroa, F. Creutzig, C. Dubeux, J. Hupe, S. Kobayashi, Global Energy Assessment—toward a Sustainable Future. Chapter 9—Energy End-Use: Transport, vol. 06, 2012.

[14] Y. Sui, H. Zhang, X. Song, F. Shao, Y. Xiang, R. Shibasaki, R. Sun, Y. Meng, C. Wang, S. Li, et al., Gps data in urban online ride-hailing: a comparative analysis on fuel consumption and emissions, Journal of Cleaner Production 227 (2019) 495—505.

[15] T. Tamaki, H. Nakamura, H. Fujii, S. Managi, Efficiency and emissions from urban transport: application to world city-level public transportation, Economic Analysis and Policy 61 (2019) 55—63 (Special issue on: Future of transport).

[16] Q. Yu, H. Zhang, W. Li, X. Song, D. Yang, R. Shibasaki, Mobile phone gps data in urban customized bus: dynamic line design and emission reduction potentials analysis, Journal of Cleaner Production 272 (2020) 122471.

[17] Q. Yu, H. Zhang, W. Li, Y. Sui, X. Song, D. Yang, R. Shibasaki, W. Jiang, Mobile phone data in urban bicycle-sharing: market-oriented sub-area division and spatial analysis on emission reduction potentials, Journal of Cleaner Production 254 (2020) 119974.

[18] H. Zhang, P. Li, Z. Zhang, W. Li, J. Chen, X. Song, R. Shibasaki, J. Yan, Epidemic versus economic performances of the covid-19 lockdown in Japan: a mobility data analysis, Cities (2021) 103502.

[19] Y. Sui, H. Zhang, W. Shang, R. Sun, C. Wang, J. Ji, X. Song, F. Shao, Mining urban sustainable performance: spatio-temporal emission potential changes of urban transit buses in post-covid-19 future, Applied Energy 280 (2020) 115966.

[20] Q. Yu, W. Li, H. Zhang, D. Yang, Mobile phone data in urban customized bus: a network-based hierarchical location selection method with an application to system layout design in the urban agglomeration, Sustainability 12 (15) (2020) 6203.

[21] Q. Yu, W. Li, D. Yang, H. Zhang, Mobile phone data in urban commuting: a network community detection-based framework to unveil the spatial structure of commuting demand, Journal of Advanced Transportation 2020 (2020), 8835981, https://doi.org/10.1155/2020/8835981.

[22] Ministry of the environment from japanese government. motor vehicle exhaust emission standards. https://www.env.go.jp/en/air/aq/mv/table_290628.pdf.

[23] M. Ester, H.-P. Kriegel, J. Sander, X. Xu, et al., A density-based algorithm for discovering clusters in large spatial databases with noise, in: Kdd, vol. 96, 1996, pp. 226—231.

[24] P.C. Chu, J.E. Beasley, A genetic algorithm for the multidimensional knapsack problem, Journal of Heuristics 4 (1) (1998) 63—86.

[25] M. Girvan, M.E.J. Newman, Community structure in social and biological networks, Proceedings of the National Academy of Sciences 99 (12) (2002) 7821—7826.

[26] X. Zhu, Z. Ghahramani, Learning from Labeled and Unlabeled Data with Label Propagation, 2002.

[27]   D.B. Vincent, J.-L. Guillaume, R. Lambiotte, E. Lefebvre, Fast unfolding of communities in large networks, Journal of Statistical Mechanics: Theory and Experiment 2008 (10) (2008) P10008.
[28]   M.E.J. Newman, Modularity and community structure in networks, Proceedings of the National Academy of Sciences 103 (23) (2006) 8577—8582.

CHAPTER FOUR

Travel demand prediction model and applications

Wenxiao Jiang
Center for Spatial Information Science, The University of Tokyo, Kashiwa-shi, Chiba, Japan

1. Introduction

With the development of deep learning techniques, deep learning approaches are also applied in the transportation domain. Travel demand prediction, as an important task of transportation, has attracted more and more attention. It can be applied in many fields, such as road construction, public transport introduction, transportation planning, and some new areas like online ride-sharing and online ride-hailing. A deep spatio-temporal convolutional long short-term memory (LSTM)-based deep learning traffic demand forecasting framework is proposed by Wang et al. [1]. Another deep learning model, called multiscale convolutional LSTM, is proposed by Chu et al. [2]. Inspired by deep learning techniques for image and video processing, this model considers travel demand as image pixel values. Moreover, a deep architecture called residual spatio-temporal network for travel demand prediction is proposed by Guo and Zhang [3]. It comprises fully convolutional neural networks and a hybrid module consisting of an extended convolutional LSTM, convolutional neural network (CNN), and traditional LSTM.

In this chapter, a convolutional LSTM-based travel demand prediction model is built, and technical potential analysis is proposed to evaluate the travel demand prediction model in a ride-hailing dispatching system simulation. The travel demand is defined as the location where passengers appear in the ride-hailing dispatching system simulation. An index called empty distance is employed to show the performance of the travel demand prediction model. In this simulation, traditional dispatching always sends the closest driver to passengers. However, from the global perspective, this is not an optimal solution since it causes massive unnecessary travel distance. For example, as Fig. 4.1 (A) shows, there are two drivers, D1 and D2, waiting for passengers' orders, and passengers P1 and P2 appear in chronological order. In the traditional dispatching system, when the passenger P1 appears,

89

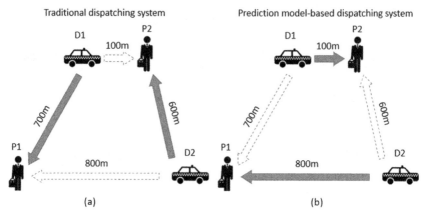

Figure 4.1 The problem of the traditional dispatching system.

the closest driver D1 is dispatched to take P1's order, and then when the passenger P2 emerges, the dispatching system could only send driver D2 to pick the passenger up because driver D1 is unavailable now. However, it is clear to see that (B) the prediction model-based dispatching is a better dispatching strategy than (A) in Fig. 4.1. The traditional dispatching system cannot achieve this way as it cannot predict the appearance of passenger P2 near the driver D1 in a short time, but the travel demand prediction model could circumvent the deficiencies of the traditional dispatching system. Forecasting the travel demands in the future allows the dispatching system to reduce unnecessary travel distance, and how much the unnecessary travel distance is reduced is adopted to evaluate the performance of the travel demand prediction model.

2. Deep learning

2.1 Convolutional neural networks

CNN is one of the most common deep network architectures. According to Aloysius and Geetha [4], this method was inspired by the visual cortex of animals [5]. The recognition, a neural network model for a mechanism of visual pattern recognition, which is proposed by Fukushima [6]; is regarded as the predecessor of CNN. Then, the article written by LeCun et al. [7] presents a back-propagation network for handwritten digit recognition, and it is considered the pioneering work in CNN. CNN is a promising tool for solving image recognition problems because of its structure [8].

In the past decade Krizhevsky et al. [9] trained a large, deep CNN named AlexNet to classify images in the ImageNet LSVRC contest and achieved a winning top-5 test error rate. Their CNN model has become one of the most influential CNN models in image recognition, and many variations of CNN models are based on this model Simonyan and Zisserman [10]. presented work to investigate how the convolutional network depth affects its accuracy in image recognition. The models they built are called VGGNets. The result shows that the depth of 16−19 weight layers makes a significant improvement compared with others. Szegedy et al. [11] proposed a deep CNN model named GoogLeNet. They increased the depth and width of the network while keeping the computational budget constant. To optimize the quality of the model, the model decisions were based on the Hebbian principle and the intuition of multi-scale processing. He et al. [12] presented a residual learning framework based on CNN layers to ease the training of networks. Their comprehensive empirical evidence shows that the residual networks are easier to optimize and have better accuracy. However, apart from image recognition, the CNN models can also be applied to transportation. A paper [13] proposes a CNN-based method that learns traffic as images and predicts traffic speed with high accuracy on a large scale. A novel three-dimensional CNN model [14] is proposed for traffic data prediction. The 3D convolution layers are introduced to automatically capture the correlations of traffic data in both spatial and temporal dimensions.

The convolutional layers are the core of the CNN model. They are used to extract features from input data, and thus they can learn the feature representations. There are three components that are important for the convolutional layers: kernel, padding, and stride. The two-dimensional CNN is used as an example to explain the procedure. Thus, the input data is a big matrix.

The kernel is a small matrix that can be adapted to extract features from the input matrix by doing a convolution. As shown in Fig. 4.2, there are two different sizes of the kernel with the input matrix. The orange matrix is the input matrix. The yellow rectangle is the kernel. It slides all over the orange matrix to do convolutions and build the green matrix, which is the part of the output matrix. A comparison of Fig. 4.2 (A) and (B) can find that the results in the green matrix are different because of different kernel sizes. It means that the kernel size can affect the results directly. Also, there is a study [15] discussing the kernel size impact on the CNN model. Four different sizes of the kernel are evaluated using sensitivity, specificity, and accuracy parameters.

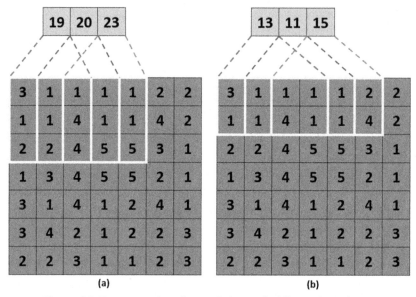

Figure 4.2 Two examples of convolution with different kernel size.

Padding is used to set all elements outside of the input matrix to zero, as shown in Fig. 4.3. Since the size of the results from the convolution layer is different compared to the input matrix, padding can guarantee that the output matrix size is the same as the input matrix size or the custom size.

Stride is the distance that the kernel moves over the input matrix each time. As shown in Fig. 4.4, (A) is the kernel with a stride that is equal to 1, and (B) is the kernel with a stride that is equal to 2. The size and number of the output matrix can be totally different.

2.2 Recurrent neural networks

A recurrent neural network (RNN) is widely used in research that is concerned with sequential data. The typical feature of the RNN model is a cyclic connection, which enables the RNN to possess the capacity to update the current state based on past data and current input data [16]. The foundational research on RNN models was proposed in the 1980s [17]. One of the early RNN models that can produce a content-addressable memory is introduced by Hopfield [18]. An RNN model for supervised learning on sequential data is proposed by Jordan [19]. Based on this idea, Elman [20] presents an approach in which the hidden unit patterns of the RNN model are feedbacked to themselves. However, the traditional RNN model cannot

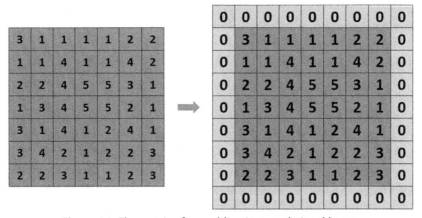

Figure 4.3 The matrix after padding in convolutional layers.

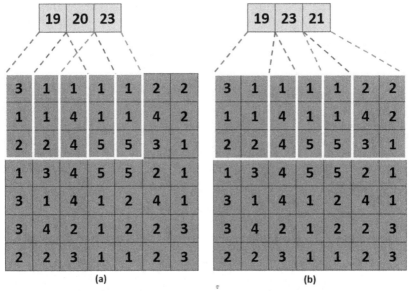

Figure 4.4 The convolutional layers with different stride.

handle the case where the distance of the relevant data is too far in the sequential input data.

In order to deal with the long-term dependencies Hochreiter and Schmidhuber [21] proposed the LSTM model. According to their study, the LSTM model can solve complex, artificial long-time lag tasks that cannot be solved by traditional RNN models. It is a popular model and is

still in use today. A hierarchical system [22] is presented for labeling unseg-
mented sequential data at multiple scales with an LSTM network. An LSTM
network-based model [23] is designed for an English and a large French-
language modeling task. He and Droppo [24] proposed a generalized formulation of the LSTM network for speech recognition. In their experiments, it
is shown that their model has good performance and achieves an 8.2% relative word error rate reduction on the 2000-hour Switchboard data set. Also,
in transportation, Zhao et al. [25] presented a novel traffic prediction model
by introducing the LSTM network. Different from conventional prediction
models, the temporal–spatial correlation in traffic systems are considered in
their model. Altche and de La Fortelle [26] proposed a trajectory prediction
model based on the LSTM network. It can accurately predict future longitudinal and lateral trajectories for vehicles on the highway.

The most commonly used LSTM network is called the LSTM with a
forget gate, which was proposed by Gers et al. [27]. They introduced a
forget gate to the original LSTM, and the architecture of the LSTM with
a forget gate is shown in Fig. 4.5. Based on the architecture, the LSTM layer
can be mathematically described in Eq. (4.1) [16].

$$f_t = \sigma\left(W_{fh}h_{t-1} + W_{fx}x_t + b_f\right) \qquad (4.1)$$

$$i_t = \sigma\left(W_{ih}h_{t-1} + W_{ix}x_t + b_i\right)$$

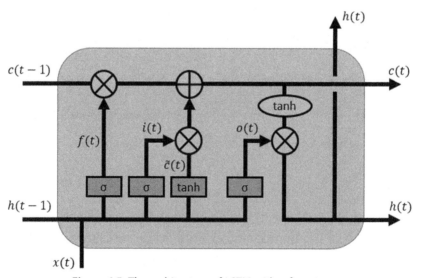

Figure 4.5 The architecture of LSTM with a forget gate.

$$\widetilde{c_t} = tanh(W_{\widetilde{c}h}h_{t-1} + W_{\widetilde{c}x}x_t + b_{\widetilde{c}})$$

$$c_t = f_t \odot c_{t-1} + i_t \odot \widetilde{c_t}$$

$$o_t = \sigma(W_{oh}h_{t-1} + W_{ox}x_t + b_o)$$

$$h_t = o_t \odot tanh(c_t)$$

where W denotes the weight matrices. h_{t-1} is the hidden state of the layer at time $t-1$. b is the bias. f, i, c, and o are the forget gate, input gate, cell gate, and output gate, respectively. The value of forgets gate f ranges from 0 to 1. When the value is 1, it means that the LSTM layer keeps all the information. Conversely, when the value is 0, it means that the layer throws away all the information. σ is the sigmoid function. $\odot$ is the Hadamard product.

3. Travel demand prediction model

Although the LSTM is adopted in many fields and works well on a large variety of prediction problems based on time series data [28,29], it still has not a good performance for travel demand prediction problems. The reason is that spatial features are as important as temporal features in the travel demand prediction problems, and the LSTM is difficult to extract spatial features.

Convolutional LSTM is a novel LSTM architecture that is proposed to overcome the major drawback of LSTM, which does not take spatial correlation into consideration. In the studies that have data structures similar to spatio-temporal prediction [30,31], convolutional LSTM architecture shows a better performance than LSTM architecture. The travel demand prediction problem is one of the spatio-temporal prediction problems. Therefore, it is very suitable for using convolutional LSTM architecture.

The structure of the travel demand prediction model, which is based on the convolutional LSTM architecture, is shown in Fig. 4.6. The convolutional LSTM layer, which contains 32 hidden states and 3×3 kernels, is employed to learn features of the travel demand data, and the convolutional 2D layer with one hidden state and 3×3 kernels are implemented for prediction. The input of each step is a sequence of demand data represented by 256×256 grids. The output is the prediction result that indicates the travel demand for a certain time period in the future.

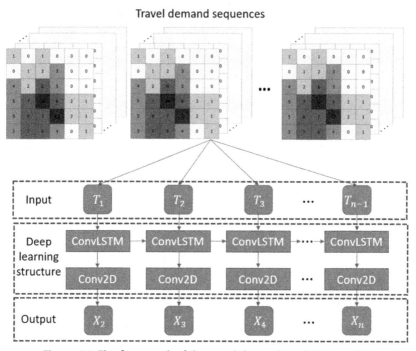

Figure 4.6 The framework of the travel demand prediction model.

4. Study case

The dataset used for the travel demand prediction model is the order data of the Didi Express service provided by the Didi Chuxing GAIA Initiative in Chengdu, a subprovincial city serving as the capital of southwest China's Sichuan province. The time span of the datasets is approximately 1 month, from November 2, 2016, to November 30, 2016. The order data of November 10th is missing due to the incompleteness of the data pool. The order data include Order ID, Start billing timestamp, End billing timestamp, Pick-up longitude/latitude, and drop-off longitude/latitude. Because the order data of November 10th is missing, the order data is naturally divided into two parts to maintain data continuity in time: the first part, which is from November 11, 2016, to November 30, 2016, is used for training the prediction model; the second part, including from November 2, 2016, to November 9, 2016, is used for testing the prediction model. Fig. 4.7 shows the spatial distribution of passengers' pick-up locations in 1 day, which is used as travel demand data. For training the travel demand

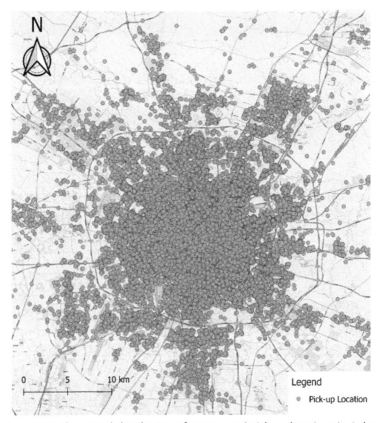

Figure 4.7 The spatial distribution of passengers' pick-up locations in 1 day.

prediction model, the study area is divided into 256×256 grids. The dataset is chunked into small parcels, which only contains the data every 5 min, and the parcels are classified into their cell of grids, as shown in Fig. 4.8. Every eight parcels (40 min) are leveraged to predict the results for the next 5 min.

5. Result and discussion

The error metrics Root Mean Squared Error (RMSE) and Mean Absolute Error (MAE) are used to measure the accuracy of the travel demand prediction model. The prediction model based on the LSTM structure is introduced for comparison. In the LSTM prediction model, an LSTM layer is implemented for capturing the characteristics of variables, and a fully connected layer is used for prediction. Table 4.1 shows that the travel demand

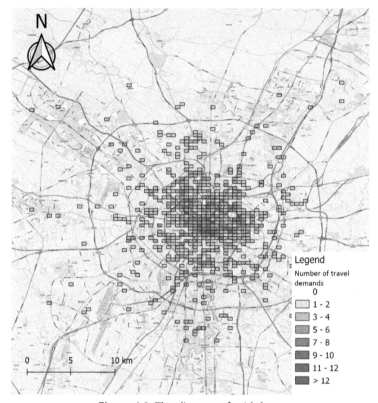

Figure 4.8 The diagram of grid data.

Table 4.1 The error metrics between convolutional LSTM and LSTM structure.

	RMSE	MAE
LSTM	0.11561	0.01238
Convolutional LSTM	0.10819	0.01004

prediction model based on the convolutional LSTM structure performs better than its counterpart. The RMSE and MAE dropped 6.42% and 18.90%, respectively, compared to the LSTM structure.

To further demonstrate the performance of the travel demand prediction model, the predicted result of the model is compared with real travel demand data extracted from Didi's dataset. Taking November 3rd, 2016, as an example, Fig. 4.9 (A) shows the spatial distributions of the quantity of travel demand in the typical time periods, which is generated by the convolutional LSTM-based travel demand prediction model. Fig. 4.9 (B) illustrates

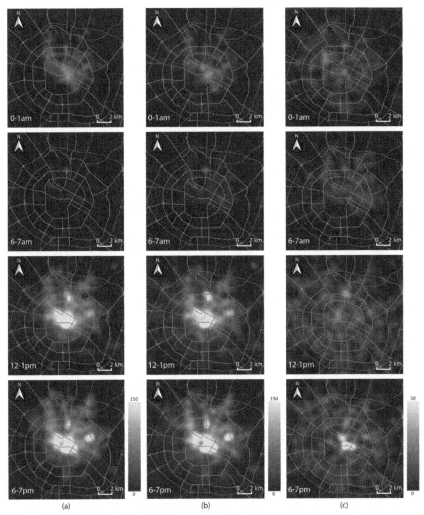

Figure 4.9 The spatial distribution difference of quantity of travel demand between prediction results and real data in the typical time periods.

the spatial distributions of the quantity of travel demand based on Didi's real data. The shapes of the two results are similar at the macroscopic level. In other words, the travel demand prediction model has adequately learned the features of travel demand variation. The spatial distributions of difference between the predicted results and the real data are shown in Fig. 4.9 (C). There are just a few prediction errors at midnight and in the morning, but at noon and especially during the rush hour at night, the errors increase significantly in the center of Chengdu city.

6. Technical potential analysis of travel demand prediction model

Since the emergence of online ride-hailing has attracted a lot of attention, the research attention on travel demand-supply has rapidly risen to a new high level. The modeling of travel demand and driver supply prediction has become one of the important research topics for online ride-hailing. Ke et al. [32] proposed a deep learning approach, named the fusion convolutional LSTM network, to forecast short-term passenger demand under an on-demand ride service platform in Hangzhou, China. Also, a unified linear regression model with more than 200 million dimensions of features is built in a study [33] to predict the taxi demand. Furthermore, there is literature [34] that analyzed the uber demand prediction performance of one temporal model and two spatio-temporal models for different scenarios. To improve the efficiency of driver supply, Lee and Sohn [35] developed a parametric duration model using some new operational characteristics and variables such as weather, land use, demographics, socioeconomic, and accessibility of public transportation.

However, among these prediction models, most of them focus on using traditional error metrics to show the performance of their models but rarely simulate a ride-hailing dispatching system to show their impact on saving unnecessary travel distance. Therefore, a new ride-hailing dispatching system simulation is required to provide a more comprehensive result by recording all the possible situations between drivers and passengers. To accomplish this goal, a multi-scenario-based method is proposed to evaluate the technical potentials of the travel demand prediction model in ride-hailing dispatching system simulation.

6.1 Scenarios

The dispatching system simulation is divided into two parts: the travel demand prediction model and the ride-hailing dispatching system model. The travel demand prediction model is responsible for providing prediction results. With the outcome, the dispatching system simulates the matching between drivers and passengers. In this study, there are three scenarios proposed for evaluating the travel demand prediction model: the traditional dispatching system, the prediction model-based dispatching system, and the perfect prediction model-based dispatching system. The difference between these three scenarios is in the travel demand prediction result. In the prediction model-based dispatching system, the prediction results are supplied from the proposed travel demand prediction model. There are no prediction results used in the traditional dispatching system. The perfect prediction model-based dispatching system employs real travel demand data as the prediction results to generate the performance upper bound of the prediction model.

6.2 Indexes
6.2.1 Empty distance
To evaluate the efficiency of the travel demand prediction model, an index called empty distance is proposed. The empty distance is used to indicate the travel distance from the drivers to the location of picked-up passengers. In this study, the location data are represented by longitude and latitude. The empty distance is therefore calculated by the Haversine formula. Each empty distance result is recorded under the dispatching simulation for evaluation.

6.2.2 Relative performance
Relative performance is introduced to demonstrate the difference between the results of the travel demand prediction model and perfect prediction results that have 0 error prediction under the dispatching simulation. It is inversely proportional to the negative impact of the prediction error from the prediction model. Relative performance is calculated by Eq. (4.2).

$$R_p = \left| \frac{V_m - V_t}{V_p - V_t} \right| \tag{4.2}$$

where R_p is the relative performance. V_m, V_t, and V_p are the same type of value provided by dispatching system simulation based on three scenarios: the prediction model-based dispatching system, the traditional dispatching system, and the perfect prediction model-based dispatching system, respectively. For instance, the relative performance of average empty distance is calculated by the values of average empty distance resulting from the prediction model-based dispatching system, the traditional dispatching system, and the perfect prediction model-based dispatching system.

6.3 Input and output

There are three types of input data required for the simulation: driver location, passenger location, and prediction result. All types of input data are derived from driver data and order data of the Didi Express service provided by the Didi Chuxing GAIA Initiative. The order data is the same as mentioned in Section 3.4. The driver data covers about 26,000 Didi vehicles in Chengdu, and the data of November 8th is missing due to the incompleteness of the data pool. The driver data include Driver ID and its corresponding Order ID. Considering the real driving conditions, some invalid data points are filtered out, such as the ones with excessive short travel distances (shorter than 500 m), zero idle or delivery time, average travel speed beyond urban speed limits, and a sudden distance deviation over 100 m. Since there is no initial location data of drivers before drivers pick up passengers, the initial position for each driver is assumed to be the drop-off location of the first order. Therefore, the first order of each driver is not included in the simulation. Since the initial driver locations are identical in all these scenarios, this assumption has a negligible impact on the performance evaluation of the prediction model. Also, there is an assumption that the driver will wait for the next order in the location when the passenger gets off. The passenger location is the pick-up location of each order. Although this assumption would have an impact on the driver locations, the spatial distribution of driver locations would not change much from a macro perspective. In addition, this assumption has the same impact on all three scenarios. Therefore, it only causes a slight bias in the technical potential analysis.

As shown in Fig. 4.10, the driver location data are derived from the Didi driver data. The passenger location data are extracted from the order data directly, but the prediction result data is provided by the travel demand prediction model, which is trained on the order data. The passenger location data include passenger IDs, passenger departure locations, passenger destinations, order start time, and order end time. Passenger departure locations and passenger destinations are represented by longitude and latitude. The driver location data contain the driver IDs, driver initial locations, and the driver working schedules. Similarly, the driver's initial location is represented by longitude and latitude. In the ride-hailing dispatching system simulation, the prediction result data is optional input data. Depending on the different scenarios, it could be the blank results, the grid results of the travel demand prediction model, or the grid results provided by real data.

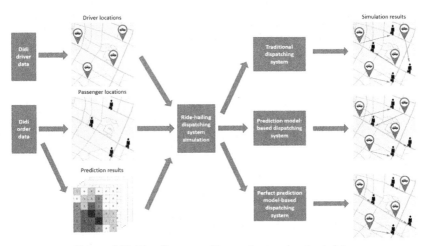

Figure 4.10 The diagram of input data and output data.

The output data is the matching results between drivers and passengers provided by the ride-hailing dispatching system simulation from these three scenarios. It consists of the driver ID, the passenger ID, the empty distance, the total distance, the order start time, and the order end time. The time span of the output data is the same as the test data of the travel demand prediction model, but November 2nd and November 8th are excluded due to the lack of driver data. In this study, the order time and the empty distance are primarily analyzed for prediction model evaluation.

6.4 Ride-hailing dispatching system simulation

The ride-hailing dispatching system simulation is employed to evaluate the matching between drivers and passengers using the driver location data, passenger location data, and prediction result data. There is a flowchart in Fig. 4.11 that explains how the dispatching system simulation works. Firstly, the passenger location data is sorted in chronological order and streams as the input data to the ride-hailing dispatching system. Secondly, the driver location data is read to find the closest driver for each passenger. This driver must be within the working hours and not dispatched for another passenger. Thirdly, it is needed to judge if there are prediction results data provided by the travel demand model. If no prediction results data is available, which is in the scenario of a traditional dispatching system, the system sends this driver to pick up passengers directly. Otherwise, the prediction results data is loaded as input data. Fourthly, the driver information is saved if it

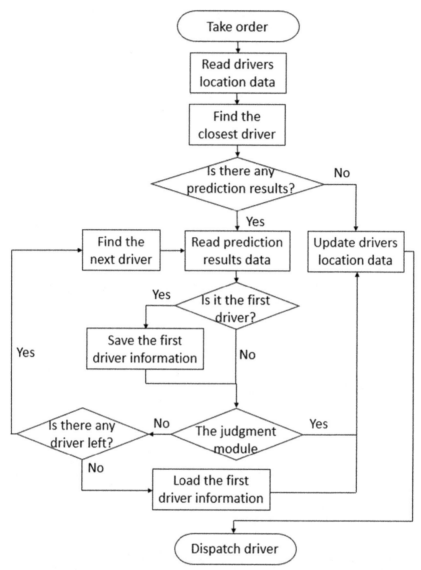

Figure 4.11 The flowchart of ride-hailing dispatching system simulation.

is the first driver. Fifthly, there is a module to judge whether to dispatch the current driver based on the driver location data and the prediction results data. If the module decides that the driver is not dispatched, for example, a new passenger will appear near this driver, which could save a lot of distance. This driver won't be dispatched to pick up the passenger. Instead, the driver will wait for the new passenger. Then, the next closest driver is found to repeat the process until the module decides to dispatch the current driver. If all drivers are not allowed to be dispatched by the module, the saved first driver is dispatched to pick up a passenger, which is the same as the scenario of a traditional dispatching system. Finally, the current driver location data is updated for the next order. The destination of the passenger is the new driver's location, and the newly available time of the driver is calculated by Eq. (4.3).

$$T_{new} = T_{old} + (T_{end} - T_{start}) + (D_{empty} / V_{average}) \qquad (4.3)$$

where T_{new} is the newly available time of the current driver. T_{old} is the old available time. T_{start} and T_{end}, which are obtained from the order data, represent the time when passengers are picked up and dropped off by drivers, respectively. D_{empty} is the empty distance, and $V_{average}$ is the average speed of the day. If the available time exceeds the time when the current driver ends work, the driver is deleted from the driver location data.

The judgment module is adapted to determine whether to dispatch the current driver depending on the determination conditions as shown in the following: (1) The driver and passenger are in the different cells, and the distance between them is greater than the diagonal distance of 1 cell. (2) In the cell where this driver is, the number of orders should be less than the number of drivers. (3) If the first driver does not meet the conditions mentioned above, there is another condition needed to be considered the empty distance difference between the current driver and the first driver to the passenger is less than the distance the first driver could save. Besides, if the current driver does not meet this condition, the drivers after this cannot satisfy this condition, so the first driver will be dispatched. When the three conditions are satisfied, the current driver will be sent for the passenger because the module thinks that dispatching this driver could save unnecessary travel distance.

6.5 Result of ride-hailing dispatching system simulation

Fig. 4.12 compares the average empty distance of each day among the traditional dispatching system, the prediction model-based dispatching system, and the perfect prediction model-based dispatching system. The result from the perfect prediction model-based dispatching system shows the upper bound of the travel demand prediction model. It illustrates how much the impact of the prediction error is. Compared with the traditional

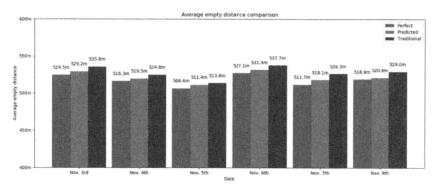

Figure 4.12 The average empty distance comparison among traditional dispatching systems, prediction model-based systems, and perfect prediction systems.

dispatching system, the convolutional LSTM-based prediction model has different degrees of decrease in the average empty distance every day. The prediction model reduces the average empty distance by 8.2 m on Nov. 7th and decreases by 2.4 m on Nov. 5th. The reason for such differences is that the locations of the passengers and drivers are not identical every day. The performance of the prediction model thus floats up and down. The average saved empty distance of the whole time period simulated by the prediction model is 6.1 m. According to the statistics, the prediction model saves 1164 km per day compared to the traditional dispatching system. Therefore, it is concluded that the prediction model has positive effects on reducing unnecessary travel distance between drivers and passengers. However, compared to perfect prediction results, it is found that the relative performances of average empty distance are 57.7%, 62.2%, 32.2%, 58.9%, 56.3%, and 79.9% from November 3 to November 9, respectively, excluding November 8. The average relative performance is 58.9%, which means the performance of the travel demand prediction model still has 41.1% upside potential.

In the dispatching system simulation, not every ride-hailing dispatch uses the demand prediction model because the large cell size causes many ride-hailing dispatches to fail to meet condition (1) of the judgment module. Therefore, the daily saved average empty distance does not seem to be significant. To further demonstrate the performance of the prediction model, the usage count of the prediction model and the perfect prediction model per day is recorded. It is noticed that the usage count of the prediction model is only 84% of the perfect prediction model. In addition, Fig. 4.13 shows in a histogram the average empty distance saved by using the prediction model

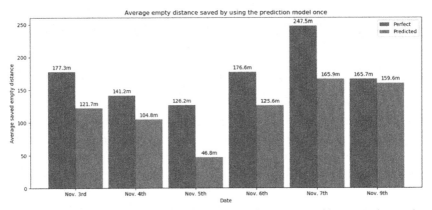

Figure 4.13 The histogram of the average empty distance saved by using the prediction models once.

and the perfect prediction model once, compared to the traditional dispatching system. On average, the prediction model saves 120.7 m every time it is used, but the upper bound of the demand prediction model is about 172.4 m. The relative performance is approximately 70%.

The distribution of the average empty distance difference between the prediction model/the perfect prediction model and the traditional dispatching system on an average day is shown in Fig. 4.14. The number of ride-hailing dispatches in which the empty distance is less than 500 m increases by approximately 1800 per day. In the range from 500 to 4000 m, it has different degrees of decrease because the prediction model provides better ride-hailing dispatches for drivers. However, due to the negative impact of the prediction model, some passengers cannot be picked up by the closest

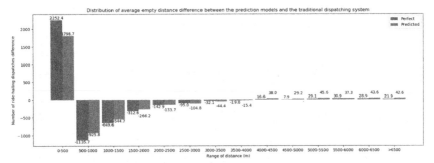

Figure 4.14 The distribution of average empty distance difference between the prediction models and the traditional dispatching system.

drivers, which causes the number of ride-hailing dispatches to increase slightly in the range of greater than 4000 m. Although the trends are similar between the demand prediction model and the perfect prediction, the perfect prediction model transfers more ride-hailing dispatches from the range 500−4000 to the range 0−500, and the negative impact is slighter.

Fig. 4.15 demonstrates the temporal distribution of the total empty distance difference between the prediction models and the traditional dispatching system on an average day. The results of the perfect prediction model indicate that from 7:00 to 17:59 and 21:00 to 00:59, the prediction model should have a good performance, but only in the time period from 8:00 to 10:59, 12:00 to 14:59, 16:00 to 16:59, and 22:00 to 0:59, the relative performance is greater than 50%. During evening rush hours from 18:00 to 20:59, the performance of the prediction model is not promising. However, this result does not occur during morning rush hours from 08:00 to 10:59. The reason is that people conduct sparse-to-dense movement in the morning and do the opposite in the evening. Fig. 4.16 shows the temporal distribution of the average empty distance. During morning rush hours, the average empty distance is 771.45 m compared to 242.51 m during evening rush hours. Thus, it is difficult to find room to save travel distance when the empty distance is short. In the time period from 1:00 to 6:59, the performance is also bad because the number of passengers and drivers is sparse. The prediction model is unable to provide many options. Besides, an innovative finding is that the prediction error is significant from 18:00 to 18:59, as shown in Fig. 4.9 (c), but it does not cause much negative impact. The incorrect dispatches only have little effect. On the other hand, from 6:00 to 6:59, although the prediction error is small, the model cannot find the

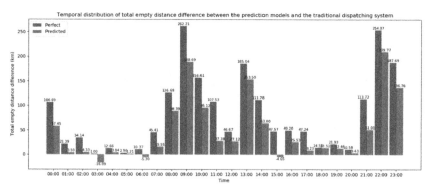

Figure 4.15 The temporal distribution of total empty distance difference between the prediction models and the traditional dispatching system.

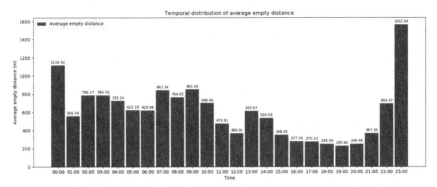

Figure 4.16 The temporal distribution of average empty distance.

opportunities to save empty distance and even causes an extra negative value. It is concluded that at different time periods of the day, the impact of the prediction errors on the performance of the prediction model is different.

Based on the findings in this study, there are some suggestions for future travel demand prediction models and ride-hailing dispatching systems: (1) The travel demand prediction model has sound effects on reducing unnecessary travel distance, but the accuracy of the demand prediction model is still necessary to be further improved. Although the error metrics show that the results of the prediction model are close to the real results, in the ride-hailing dispatching system simulation, the empty distance saved by the model is still far from the saved empty distance based on real data. At some time periods and locations, the prediction error is still significant. (2) The cell size of grid prediction results is crucial for ride-hailing dispatching. The larger the cell size, the harder it is to find the opportunity to save empty distance in the ride-hailing dispatching system simulation. (3) Because of the deficiency of the travel demand prediction model, the number of driver dispatches that the empty distance in the range of greater than 4000 m rises slightly. Some rules are supposed to be made by the dispatching system to optimize the problem of drivers and passengers being too far apart. (4) Even if the error metrics are the same at different time periods of the day, the impact of the prediction errors on the performance of the travel demand prediction model is different. In some time periods, a traditional dispatching system or other algorithm-based model should be adopted to dispatch drivers, rather than the system based on a prediction model.

7. Conclusion

LSTM network is a deep learning architecture that is well suited to process time-series data and extract temporal features. However, the travel demand data is in spatio-temporal data. The LSTM network can only extract the temporal features but ignores spatial features in the travel demand data. The convolutional LSTM is a novel LSTM architecture that is proposed to overcome the major drawback of LSTM, which does not take spatial correlation into consideration. In this study, a convolutional LSTM-based travel demand prediction model is trained by using data provided by Didi Chuxing. The results show that the RMSE and MAE decreased by 6.42% and 18.90%, respectively, compared to the LSTM structure.

For evaluating the performance of the travel demand prediction model from a different aspect, a ride-hailing dispatching system simulation is proposed. How much the unnecessary travel distance is reduced is adopted to evaluate the performance of the travel demand prediction model. The ride-hailing dispatching is simulated in three scenarios: traditional dispatching system, prediction model-based dispatching system, and perfect prediction model-based dispatching system. The simulation results reveal that the total empty distance was reduced by 1164 km per day by using the prediction model, and it has 41.1% upside potential. Also, some suggestions are provided for ride-hailing demand prediction models and ride-hailing dispatching systems.

References

[1] D. Wang, Y. Yang, S. Ning, Deepstcl: a deep spatio-temporal convlstm for travel demand prediction, in: 2018 International Joint Conference on Neural Networks, IEEE, 2018, pp. 1—8.

[2] K.F. Chu, A.Y.S. Lam, V.O.K. Li, Travel demand prediction using deep multi-scale convolutional LSTM network, in: Proceedings of the 21st International Conference Intelligent Transportation Systems (ITSC), November 2018, 2018, pp. 1402—1407.

[3] G. Guo, T. Zhang, A residual spatio-temporal architecture for travel demand forecasting, Transportation Research Part C: Emerging Technologies 115102639 (2020).

[4] N. Aloysius, M. Geetha, A review on deep convolutional neural networks, 2017 International Conference on Communication and Signal Processing (ICCSP) (2017) 0588—0592.

[5] D.H. Hubel, T.N. Wiesel, Receptive fields and functional architecture of monkey striate cortex, The Journal of physiology (1968).

[6] K. Fukushima, Neocognitron: a self-organizing neural network model for a mechanism of pattern recognition unaffected by shift in position, Biological Cybernetics (1980), 1980.

[7]   Y. LeCun, B. Boser, J.S. Denker, D. Henderson, R.E. Howard, W. Hubbard, L.D. Jackel, Handwritten Digit Recognition with a Backpropagation Network, in: NIPS. Citeseer, 1990, 1990.

[8]   M.V. Valueva, N.N. Nagornov, P.A. Lyakhov, G.V. Valuev, N.I. Chervyakov, Application of the residue number system to reduce hardware costs of the convolutional neural network implementation, Mathematics and Computers in Simulation 177 (2020) 232−243, 2020.

[9]   A. Krizhevsky, I. Sutskever, G.E. Hinton, ImageNet classification with deep convolutional neural networks, in: NIPS, 2012, 2012.

[10] K. Simonyan, A. Zisserman, Very Deep Convolutional Networks for Large-Scale Image Recognition, 2014 arXiv preprint arXiv:1409.1556, 2014.

[11] C. Szegedy, W. Liu, Y. Jia, P. Sermanet, S. Reed, D. Anguelov, D. Erhan, V. Vanhoucke, A. Rabinovich, Going Deeper with Convolutions, CVPR, 2015, 2015.

[12] K. He, X. Zhang, S. Ren, J. Sun, Deep residual learning for image recognition, in: IEEE Conference on Computer Vision and Pattern Recognition (CVPR), IEEE, 2016, pp. 770−778.

[13] X. Ma, Z. Dai, Z. He, J. Ma, Y. Wang, Y. Wang, Learning traffic as images: a deep convolutional neural network for large-scale transportation network speed prediction, Sensors 17 (4) (2017) 818.

[14] S. Guo, Y. Lin, S. Li, Z. Chen, H. Wan, Deep spatial-temporal 3D convolutional neural networks for traffic data forecasting, IEEE Transactions on Intelligent Transportation Systems (2019), 2019.

[15] S. Öztürk, U. Özkaya, B. Akdemir, L. Seyfi, Convolution kernel size effect on convolutional neural network in histopathological image processing applications, in: International Symposium on Fundamentals of Electrical Engineering (ISFEE), IEEE, 2018.

[16] Y. Yu, X. Si, C. Hu, J. Zhang, A review of recurrent neural networks: LSTM cells and network architectures, Neural Computation 31 (7) (2019) 1235−1270.

[17] Z.C. Lipton, J. Berkowitz, C. Elkan, A Critical Review of Recurrent Neural Networks for Sequence Learning, arXiv:1506.00019, 2015.

[18] J.J. Hopfield, Neural networks and physical systems with emergent collective computational abilities, Proceedings of the National Academy of Sciences 79 (8) (1982) 2554−2558.

[19] M.I. Jordan, Serial Order: A Parallel Distributed Processing Approach. Technical Report 8604, Institute for Cognitive Science, University of California, San Diego, 1986.

[20] J.L. Elman, Finding structure in time, Cognitive Science 14 (2) (1990) 179−211.

[21] S. Hochreiter, J. Schmidhuber, Long short-term memory, Neural Computation 9 (8) (1997) 1735−1780.

[22] S. Fernández, A. Graves, J. Schmidhuber, Sequence labelling in structured domains with hierarchical recurrent neural networks, in: Proceedings of the 20th International Joint Conference on Artificial Intelligence, Morgan Kaufmann, San Mateo, CA, 2007.

[23] M. Sundermeyer, R. Schluter, H. Ney, LSTM neural networks for language modeling, in: Interspeech, 2012, pp. 194−197.

[24] T. He, J. Droppo, Exploiting LSTM structure in deep neural networks for speech recognition, in: Proceedings of the IEEE International Conference on Acoustics, Speech and Signal Processing, IEEE, Piscataway, NJ, 2016, pp. 5445−5449.

[25] Z. Zhao, W. Chen, X. Wu, P.C.Y. Chen, J. Liu, LSTM network: a deep learning approach for short-term traffic forecast, IET Intelligent Transport Systems 11 (2017) 68−75.

[26] F. Altche, A. de La Fortelle, An LSTM network for highway trajectory prediction, in: Proceedings of the IEEE International Conference on Intelligent Transportations Systems (ITSC), IEEE, 2017, pp. 353–359.

[27] F.A. Gers, J. Schmidhuber, F. Cummins, Learning to forget: continual prediction with LSTM, Neural Computation 12 (10) (2000) 2451–2471.

[28] A. Alahi, K. Goel, V. Ramanathan, A. Robicquet, F.F. Li, S. Savarese, Social lstm: human trajectory prediction in crowded spaces, in: CVPR, 2016.

[29] A. Graves, N. Jaitly, A.-R. Mohamed, Hybrid speech recognition with deep bidirectional LSTM, in: Automatic Speech Recognition and Understanding (ASRU), IEEE Workshop on, 2013, pp. 273–278.

[30] X. Shi, Z. Chen, H. Wang, D.Y. Yeung, W.K. Wong, W. Woo, Convolutional Lstm Network: A Machine Learning Approach for Precipitation Nowcasting, 2015 arXiv preprint arXiv:1506.04214.

[31] L. Zhang, G. Zhu, P. Shen, J. Song, Learning spatiotemporal features using 3DCNN and convolutional LSTM for gesture recognition, in: 2017 IEEE International Conference on Computer Vision Workshops, 2017.

[32] J. Ke, H. Zheng, H. Yang, X. Chen, Michael), Short-term forecasting of passenger demand under on-demand ride services: a spatio-temporal deep learning approach, Transportation Research Part C: Emerging Technologies 85 (2017) 591–608.

[33] Y. Tong, Y. Chen, Z. Zhou, L. Chen, J. Wang, Q. Yang, J. Ye, The simpler the better: a unified approach to predicting original taxi demands on large-scale online platforms, in: Proceedings of the 23rd ACM SIGKDD International Conference on Knowledge Discovery and Data Mining, ACM, 2017.

[34] S.S. Faghih, A. Safikhani, B. Moghimi, C. Kamga, Predicting Short-Term Uber Demand Using Spatiotemporal Modeling: A new york City Case Study, 2017 arXiv preprint arXiv:1712.02001.

[35] W.K. Lee, S.Y. Sohn, Taxi vacancy duration: a regression analysis, Transportation Planning and Technology 40 (2017) 771–795.

CHAPTER FIVE

Railway usage behavior analysis based on mobile phone big data

Yanxiu Jin
Center for Spatial Information Science, The University of Tokyo, Kashiwa-shi, Chiba, Japan

1. Introduction

Cities have always been central to human development and technological progress, and they often evolve in response to the changing needs and aspirations of their inhabitants [1]. There are three core urban development concepts: urban form, urban interactions, and urban spatial structure. Urban spatial structure is defined as the geographic location and integration of different urban elements and the inherent mechanism of urban form and interaction [2]. Experience shows that urban structure reflects the distribution of infrastructure and functions and influences people's behavior, the overall economic performance of cities, and environmental sustainability [3,4]. With rapid global urbanization, economic development, and growth in city size, uncontrolled urban growth has caused urban problems, primarily arising from the imbalance between supply and demand [5]. Phenomena such as congestion and pollution caused by the lack of adequate public transportation systems, degradation of the vitality of urban centers, the concentration of resources such as education jobs in some areas, and long commutes all reflect urban imbalances.

It is essential to build compact, balanced, and sustainable urban structures to cope with the rapid growth of cities. Various studies have shown that primary urban elements are factors that shape and influence the urban structure, such as transportation [6,7], road networks [8], building distribution [9], land-use patterns [10], and human behavior [11,12]. However, the city is large and complex, and it is not easy to combine the above elements for a comprehensive analysis. A railway station is a small area that can combine most urban elements. Starting the analysis from the station can provide some inspiration for the study of urban spatial structure.

Rail transit has become a pioneer in effectively alleviating urban traffic with its unique advantages of being economical, environmentally friendly,

Handbook of Mobility Data Mining, Volume 3
ISBN: 978-0-323-95892-9
https://doi.org/10.1016/B978-0-323-95892-9.00005-X

113

and efficient. Rail transit dramatically facilitates people's travel and plays a crucial role in optimizing the urban spatial structure and boosting regional economic development [13,14]. In the early 1990s, a New Urbanism gradually emerged in the United States. The concept of Transit Oriented Development (TOD) advocates the use of stations as development centers, combining multiple building functions to form a network of mixed land uses and high-density development nodes connected by transportation corridors. It emphasizes the development of public transportation systems as an urban spatial structure and transit station areas as a core function of urban development and diversity of land use. Land use is influenced by the rail station areas, thus increasing the services of the public transport station areas and the use of the public transport system [15,16].

However, even in TOD-based concept planning and construction, uneven development can still occur (Fig. 5.1). Similarly, the impact on rail transit ridership varies depending on the urban context and regional economic characteristics [17]. Policymakers, urban planners, or subway managers must understand station usage and the major factors affecting its use to provide effective strategies to increase or optimize travel demand.

With the emergence of data sources related to information and communication technologies (ICT) and the popularity of cell phones, a large

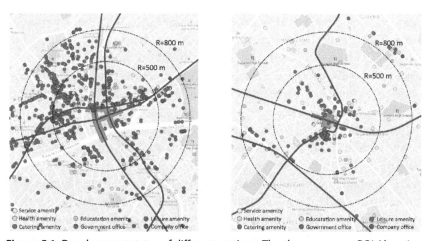

Figure 5.1 Development status of different stations. The dots represent POIs' location, and the color represents the category of the POI. Both Shibuya station and Otsuka station are on the JR Yamanote line. However, there is a big difference in the size of the stations and the number of interchanges between them. In addition, the density, diversity, and number of POIs near Shibuya station are much higher than those at Otsuka station.

amount of personal data with spatial-temporal information is available for urban studies in various fields. Moreover, human mobility big data supports a better understanding of travel behavior [18]. The emergence of these big spatial data allows us to quantify the usage and development of railroads. More and more scholars are studying TOD through big spatial data and exploring the impact of the built environment on the travel behavior of crowds [19]. However, few such studies have been based on GPS records, and those based on GPS records have focused more on movement behavior between origins and destinations [20]. Cervero showed that entry and exit behavior is closely related to passengers' travel choices [21]. Therefore, it is more appropriate to use GPS data and focus our perspective on inbound and outbound trips by GPS data to clarify rail usage behavior.

This study explores the change in passengers' ride behavior and station usage at different distances and classifies and summarizes stations' characteristics based on 10 million GPS trajectory data. We believe that our work can help urban planners and transportation managers better understand the usage of various stations and the factors that influence railway usage behavior. It will also provide some help for future optimization of station facilities, service improvement, and policy development related to cities and transportation.

2. Literature review

Since the development of stations in different regions is uneven, many researchers have attempted to classify TODs based on various characteristics of stations and neighborhoods. The TOD typology, which explores different classifications' differences and common features, has also emerged [22]. Node-place is the most widely known TOD typology classification model that explores the characteristics of stations in two dimensions, the "node-index" (describing the variety and frequency of transit supply) and the "place-index" (describing the functional mix of the station area) [23]. Subsequently, many authors then modified the original model to further explore the possibility of a third dimension. Cao et al. used an optimized node-place model, which added the dimension of passenger flow to cluster 169 stations in Tokyo by TOD type and analyzed and compared the characteristics of different operators' stations [24]. New sources of information and communication technology-related data continue to emerge, and the methods for classifying stations and TOD studies have been enriched [25]. extracted five main factors from the selected station features to cluster the stations using the smart card data [25]. They classified the metro stations of Shanghai Metro lines 3,5,9 into several station types with different congestion grades using the K-means clustering method. Kong et al. explored how to delineate TOD areas, identify potential TOD areas, and characterize the functions of TOD in megacities through public transit data, POIs, and taxi trajectories data [19]. Zhou et al. exploit big and open data to quantitatively examine the relationships between TOD attributes and TOD outcomes [26]. The above studies show that big data, such as trajectory data, can complement or even replace traditional data for further study of TOD and railway stations.

In some studies based on questionnaires of the residential population, passenger travel behavior is defined as how far passengers are willing to walk to the station [21]. provides a detailed analysis of the effects of TOD on passenger behavior using data from the 1-day travel diary of residents in California. Residents who live within 800 m of the station are 20% more likely to use public transportation than those between 800 m and 4.8 km from the station [11]. Jiang et al. add that people's walking distance increases when the built environment of station neighborhoods has specific characteristics [27]. However, the stations are not utilized by residents exclusively, and other non-residents' travel behaviors are ignored in these studies. On the other hand, some studies adopt ridership from smart card data to define passenger travel behavior [28,29]. Compared to the questionnaire, the smart card data is more inclusive of all passengers, but lacks the information about passengers's intention on their way to station. In summary, railway travel behavior defined by questionnaires or smart card data suffers from a lack of passenger comprehensiveness. However, GPS trajectory data, which reflect the passenger's location, can compensate for the distance attribute neglected in existing studies due to data limitations or cost constraints. This study focuses on the railway usage behavior with different station buffers, classifies stations by railway usage behavior pattens, and discusses the characteristics of the different types to identify the factors that influence station usage.

3. Methodology

3.1 Framework

As shown in Fig. 5.2, an elaborate framework is formulated, which mainly contains the following four parts:

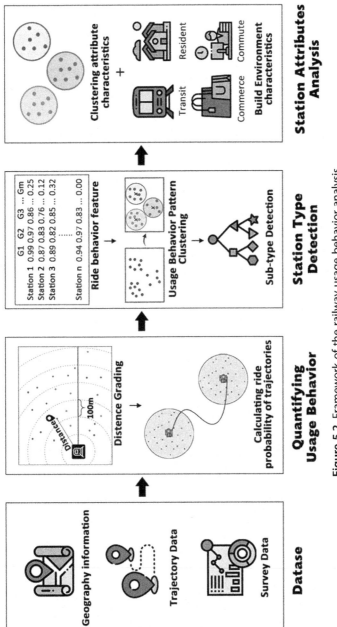

Figure 5.2 Framework of the railway usage behavior analysis.

3.1.1 Dataset preparation

This study's dataset includes geography information, trajectory data, and survey data. Geography information shows the coordinates of the station. Trajectory data, which records the locations of moving objects at certain moments, has long been an important means of studying human behavior and solving traffic problems. Survey data describes the population, land use, and development status of the station's area. Data processing prior to analysis is focused on Trajectory data and survey data.

- Survey data

  Aggregation and statistics according to the scope of selected indicators

- Trajectory data

  We have performed the following processing for the trajectory records:

  Step 1 travel mode detection:

  To determine the trip mode of the raw GPS recordings, this study used Travel Mode Detection Model constructed by Zhang et al. [30]. Firstly, divide each user's raw GPS recordings into stay and move segments based on the distance and time interval between positioning points. Then the move segments are divided into trips based on speed and velocity change rate. Finally, categorize the trips into travel modes (including walk, bike, car, and train) by random forest.

  Step 2 Map matching:

  Then, we need to match the trajectories to traffic networks. Consequently, we chose sparse map matching improved by [31]. The enhanced sparse map matching method involves searching the network for the nearest link of GPS positioning points to estimate a realistic route based on observation locations. For the train mode trajectories, the nearest station to each positioning point along the railroad is located is considered the target station. For the nontrain mode trajectories, we set the search area as a circle with a radius of 2 km centered on the station coordinates. The positioning point that appears in the station search area is considered the target station, but passengers did not take a train here. When two or more stations search for a positioning point simultaneously, the closest station is considered the target station.

  Step 3 Data cleaning:

  After the above two steps, the attributes of the data are anonymous ID, trajectory number, positioning point number, travel mode, timestamp, longitude, latitude, and target station ID. We select trajectories where both the origin and destination points are within the study area. In addition, we also need to refer to the running schedule of the railway station to screen out trajectories that deviated significantly from the time interval.

3.1.2 Quantifying usage behavior

The railway travel behavior is a limited definition in the current study, which could not reflect passenger travel behavior fully. We think of railway travel behavior not as the share of residents who use public transportation or how many passengers ride the railway at a station. Instead, it is how many people would prefer to ride the railway over other travel modes at different distances from the station. Hence, we propose the concept of distance grading and calculate the probability of railway usage corresponding to the distance grade. The distance grades and their corresponding probabilities are collectively referred to as **railway usage behavior**. Based on the above-processed dataset, we quantify the railway travel behavior by calculating the probability of railway usage for each station.

3.1.3 Cluster analysis

The railway usage behavior of stations varies due to different environmental characteristics and uneven development of the economic features. Besides the factors influencing railway usage behavior, this study also aims to conduct an attribution analysis of different railway usage behaviors. Cluster analysis could help us understand the differences between the categories and compare the characteristics of the categories, which might find the causes of the differences. Therefore, we used cluster analysis to group stations by railway usage behavior.

3.1.4 Station attribution analysis

Based on the clustering results, we analyze the features of the Usage Behavior Pattern of each station type. Beyond clustering features, we also analyze the built environment of stations in four aspects: transit, residential, commercial, and commuting. Finally, we summarize the attributes of each station type.

3.2 Deriving usage behavior probability

We propose the distance grading to calculate the railway usage behavior probability (Fig. 5.3). It could make discrete the continuous variables, reduce the noise contained in the features, improve the features' expressiveness, and facilitate the quantification of the probability of use at different distances.

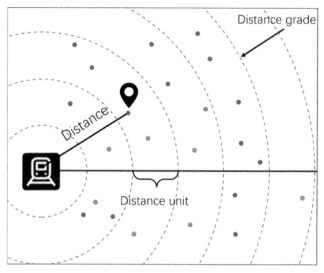

Figure 5.3 Definition of distance grade.

For each trajectory, the sum of the distance from the origin point to the target station and the distance from the destination point to the target station divided by the distance unit is considered as the distance grade (L_i) of it,

$$L_i = \frac{Do_i + Dd_i}{DU} \tag{5.1}$$

where Do_i is the distance from the origin point to its target station, Dd_i is the distance from the destination point to its target station, DU is the distance unit which should be set as an integer.

Therefore, there are different numbers of trajectories scattered between each distance grade. Trajectories can only be compared between different stations on a magnitude-to-magnitude basis. Thus, to quantify the railway usage at each station, it is necessary to calculate the probability of railway usage behavior. The probability of taking the railway at a certain distance grade of a station (P_{lk})) is the sum of the number of trajectories whose travel modes are Train divided by the total number of the trajectories for that grade,

$$P_{lk} = \frac{NT_{lk}}{NT_{lk} + NN_{lk}} \tag{5.2}$$

where NT_{lk} is the number of l-th distance grade trajectory segments which travel mode are Train at the k-th station, NN_{lk} is the number of l-th distance grade trajectory segments whose travel modes are not Train at the k-th station.

3.3 Station type detection

3.3.1 Usage behavior pattern clustering

To clarify the similarities and differences of railway usage among different stations, we perform clustering on 36 stations using the probabilities of railway usage behavior at the different distance grades of each station as their features.

In this section, we will introduce three algorithms for clustering.

Algorithm 1 - K-Means: It is one of the simplest algorithms that solve the clustering problem. When dealing with scattered point clouds, the K-means algorithm can be used to classify point cloud data and obtain compact and independent clusters quickly [32].

It is calculated as follows:

- First take any k sample points as the initial centers of the k clusters.
- For each sample point, calculate their distances from the k centers and group them into the cluster where the center with the smallest distance is located.
- Wait until all sample points have been grouped and recalculate the centers of the k clusters.
- Repeat the above process until the clusters into which the sample points are grouped no longer change.

K-means is relatively simple to implement, and its clustering effect is good, so it is widely used in clustering problems. However, K-means has some shortcomings: First, the number of clusters must be specified before the performance, but sometimes the value of k is difficult to estimate and give in advance at the beginning. Second, the centroids are chosen randomly at the beginning and recalculated in the later iterations until convergence. The result generated depends on the positions of the centroids at the beginning. Therefore, the results have large randomness. Third, the algorithm must constantly adjust the classification of objects and constantly calculate new clustering centroids after the adjustment, so when the amount of data is enormous, the time cost is high.

Algorithm 2—Hierarchical Clustering: Hierarchical clustering is one of the popular and easy to understand clustering techniques. This clustering technique is divided into two types:

Agglomerative ("bottom-up" approach): each observation starts in its own cluster, and pairs of clusters are merged as one moves up the hierarchy.

Divisive ("top-down" approach): all observations start in one cluster, and splits are performed recursively as one moves down the hierarchy.

Agglomerative is calculated as follows:

- Each observation starts in its own cluster. The distance between clusters is the distance between the observations
- Find the two closest clusters and merge them into one cluster.
- Recalculate the distance between the new cluster and all the old clusters.
- Repeat steps 2 and 3 until the clusters are finally merged into a given cluster number.

Hierarchical clustering is suitable for use when the amount of data is large, but it does not work well for clustering high-dimensional data. Moreover, although the number of clusters is not a necessary parameter for hierarchical clustering, we still need to determine the number of clusters as the termination condition of the algorithm.

Algorithm 3—Gaussian Mixture Model: Gaussian Mixture Model (GMM) is similar to k-means, except that the measure of similarity is changed from a distance to a probability distribution.

GMM assumes that there are a certain number of Gaussian distributions, each of which represents a cluster, then finds the best mean, variance, and weight of each Gaussian distribution by Expectation-Maximization (EM). Thus, the GMM tends to combine data points belonging to an individual distribution together.

It is calculated as follows:

- Specify the value of K and initially choose the value of each parameter at random.
- E step. Based on the assumed values of the parameters, give the expected estimates of the unknown variables.
- M-step. Based on the estimated values generated in the E-step, the complete data are used to update the parameters
- Repeat steps 2 and 3 until convergence.

Instead of getting a definite clustering label, the result of GMM is to get the probability of each cluster. Thus, GMM can be used not only for clustering but also for probability density estimation. However, it also requires specifying k-values and has a much higher computational cost than K-means. Estimating covariance becomes difficult when there are not enough points per mixture model and does not apply to small sample data.

The advantages and disadvantages of the three clustering methods have been summarized in Table 5.1.

The clustering algorithm and the optimal number of clusters for this work need to be determined based on stations' situations and the setting

Table 5.1 Cluster algorithms comparison.

Algorithm	Advantage	Disadvantage
K-means	Simple to implement; Good clustering effect	Results are randomization; High time cost when data is enormous
Hierarchical clustering	Suitable for big data	Bad effect on high-dimensional data
GMM	Calculate the probability of each cluster; Wide range of applications	High time cost; Not suitable for small sample data

of the distance unit. In Section 4, the clustering algorithm and parameters will be set according to the properties of the study area.

3.3.2 Subtype detection

Beyond the clustering result, we performed further subtype detection. Taking the probabilities of railway usage behavior as the indicators for clustering overlooks the passenger scale; thus, we took the passenger amount as the additional indicator for subtype detection based on the clustering result. We take the average count of entry and exit passengers at each station as the ridership and perform descriptive statistical analysis to explore the concentration trends and dispersion of the data. According to the results of the descriptive analysis, the optimal threshold amount of ridership can be set. The ridership of each station is compared with the threshold value, and then classify the stations into appropriate subtypes based on the comparison results.

3.4 Identification of build environment indicators

Indicator selection is also an indispensable part of exploring the impact factors for railway travel behavior. Although [13] proposed a well-known model called 3Ds—density, diversity, and design—as a framework for selecting built environment indicators, the measurement of 3Ds is not standardized. Thus, the built environment indicators vary from study to study. In addition to the 3Ds, recent literature has considered other area elements, such as the intensity of economic activity in the catchment and residential population attributes [33–35]. However, insufficient research focuses on the various indicators of functional attributes that make up the land use mix. Although indicators of functional attributes such as commercial and residential land use are the most widely introduced indicators, other functional land-use types such as educational and administrative are still in the minority.

Table 5.5

	Indicator	Scope	Data Source
Transit attributes	The number of transfer lines	In the station	Homepage of JR station
	The number of bus stops	500m	OSM
Residential attributes	Resident population	2km	National Land Information Division
	House price	2km	National Land Information Division
Commerce attributes	The number of shopping malls	2km	OSM
	The number of restaurants	2km	OSM
Commute attributes	Commuting population	2km	National Land Information Division
	The number of companies	2km	National Land Information Division

Since the indicator selection in this paper is based on urban functions, we refer to key land-use variables derived by X. Li et al. and the functional characteristics of Tokyo [36]. Finally, we classify the functional attributes of the built environment into four categories: Transit attributes, residential attributes, commerce attributes, and commute attributes. Based on our insights and factors identified by previous studies, two indicators highly correlated with travel behavior were selected for each category. Table 5.5 shows the indicators of the station build environment and their data sources.

4. Case study

4.1 Study area

As one of the largest urban areas in the world, Tokyo's complex and well-developed public transportation system plays an important role in the city and is the backbone of shaping the urban fabric. A large number of people rely on the railway system every day to commute and to use various facilities in Tokyo, and it accounts for 50% of the transportation market share. One of the busiest and most important lines in Tokyo is the JR Yamanote Line, which runs in a loop linking the city center (Tokyo Station) with most major transportation hubs and business districts. Since the government does not allow private railway operators to extend their lines within the JR

	Stations along the lines
	Private railway
	Tokyo metro subway
	JR Yamonote Line & JR Chuo Line (part)

0   2.5   5 km

Figure 5.4 Study area.

Yamanote Line, private railway operators have to build their terminals along the JR Yamanote Line. Millions of commuters who need to go to the city center have to transfer at JR Yamanote Line. Therefore, the JR Yamanote Line has become an important transportation corridor and forms Tokyo's two major metropolitan commuter railways with the JR Chuo-Sobu Line, which runs through the city's heart. This study examined 29 stations on the JR Yamanote Line and seven stations on the JR Chuo-Sobu Line, which connects to the JR Yamanote Line (Fig. 5.4). The data within Tokyo 23 wards are used in this study, and 2019/10/01-2019/10/31 is selected as the target timeperiod.

4.2 Station type detection results

4.2.1 Parameter settings

To calculate the probability of railway usage behavior and cluster the stations using the probabilities of railway usage behavior as features, we need to determine three parameters: the distance unit, the method of clustering, and the number of clusters.

First, we select 50, 100, and 200 m as alternative parameters for distance units and integers from two to eight for clusters' number k. Then we cluster the stations by K-means, hierarchical clustering, and GMM, respectively. Finally, the effect of clustering is observed and compared to select the best parameters.

The silhouette coefficient is a way to evaluate the effectiveness of clustering. The silhouette coefficient is used to describe the similarity between the target's cluster and other clusters. A more significant value indicates a higher degree of matching relationship between the target and its cluster and a lower degree of matching relationship with other clusters. Thus, the higher the value, the better the clustering result. If the value is small or negative, the number of clusters is not selected properly. It could be used to evaluate the effect of different algorithms or the effect of different parameters of running the specific algorithm based on the same original data.

Tables 5.2–5.4 show the silhouette coefficients for various parameters. When k is 3, the distance unit is 100m, the clustering algorithm is K-means, the silhouette coefficient is the largest, and the best clustering result. Therefore, this work will continue the analysis based on the above parameters.

Table 5.2 Silhouette coefficients of K-means.

	k = 2	k = 3	k = 4	k = 5	k = 6	k = 7	k = 8
50	0.282	0.345	0.132	0.125	0.049	0.063	0.083
100	0.452	0.474	0.352	0.068	0.271	0.199	0.195
200	0.377	0.222	0.225	0.182	0.182	0.134	0.150

Table 5.3 Silhouette coefficients of hierarchical clustering.

	k = 2	k = 3	k = 4	k = 5	k = 6	k = 7	k = 8
50	0.332	0.149	0.134	0.128	0.110	0.108	0.10
100	0.452	**0.466**	0.379	0.345	0.240	0.237	0.241
200	0.426	0.330	0.228	0.228	0.229	0.175	0.172

Table 5.4 Silhouette coefficients of GMM.

	k = 2	k = 3	k = 4	k = 5	k = 6	k = 7	k = 8
50	0.282	0.130	0.116	0.091	−0.025	0.060	0.057
100	0.452	0.292	0.282	0.346	0.227	0.146	0.155
200	0.219	0.230	0.201	0.217	0.106	0.138	0.166

4.2.2 Sensitivity Analysis

Although we have found the values of the optimal parameters in the previous section, we would like to explore further the effect of the setting of the distance unit on the clustering results. Thus, we do the sensitivity analysis using the control variables method. Set the optimal number of clusters as three and the clustering method as K-means, then change the distance unit and reperform the clustering to observe the changes in the results. We set the distance units to 50, 100, and 200m and plotted the following usage behavior patterns. As shown in Fig. 5.5, the trend of usage behavior patterns is almost unchanged under the three distance units. Under the distance unit of 50m, the pattern fluctuation is most apparent, while when the distance unit is 200m, the pattern fluctuation tends to be flat. As the distance unit is set smaller, the number of outliers increases, and the statistical significance becomes weak. Therefore, the probability of ride behavior is not sensitive to the effect of the distance unit.

4.2.3 Usage behavior pattern clustering

After k-means clustering, the characteristics of three clusters are depicted in Fig. 5.6, which shows the usage behavior pattern at each cluster of stations. The left figures for each cluster show the box plot of the usage behavior probabilities at the stations belonging to the cluster and the cluster average usage behavior probabilities with distance grades. The right figures show the location of stations belonging to each cluster on the railways.

Cluster A—Transit-led station. There are six stations in Cluster A. When the passengers are at the 20th distance grade, the passenger has more than 80% probability of choosing to ride at this station. The probability of railway usage behavior at the station with the distance grades from 20 to 25 decreases sharply and then flattens out. Even if the total distance of the origin and destination points from their target stations is 3.4 km, there is a 50% probability of railway usage behavior.

Cluster B—Balanced station. Cluster B contains 15 stations, and the trend of the probability of railway usage behavior with distance grades is similar to that of Cluster A. There is a high probability of railway usage behavior in the area nearby the station. In contrast, when the distance grade is greater than 5, the overall railway usage behavior probabilities are lower than Cluster A. We believe that a certain service radius characterizes these stations, and the probability of railway usage behavior within the service radius is relatively high. Once larger than the service radius, the probability of railway usage behavior decreases rapidly with increasing distance.

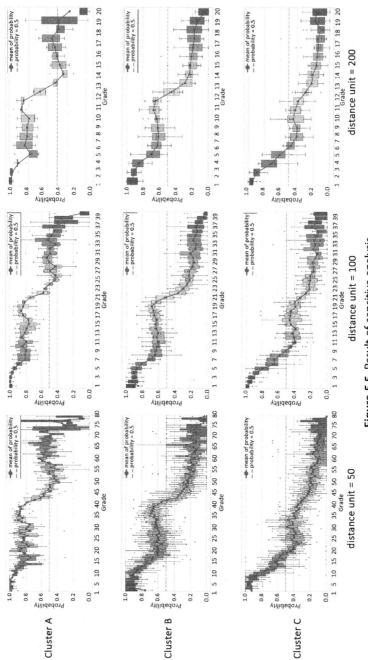

Figure 5.5 Result of sensitive analysis.

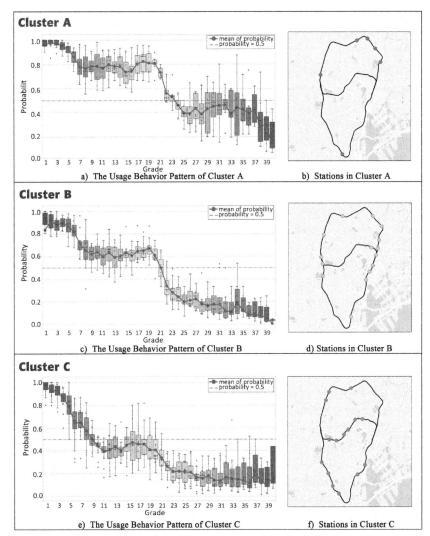

Figure 5.6 The probability of railway usage behavior and distribution in different clusters.

Cluster C—Non-transit-led station. Cluster C contains 15 stations, typified by an almost gentle decrease in the probability of railway usage behavior with increasing distance. At the distance grade of 9, the probability of railway usage behavior is already less than 50%. Therefore, the function of transportation at such stations is probably not the main factor in attracting passengers, and their transportation functions mainly service people near the station.

4.2.4 Subtype detection

To select additional indicators for classifying station subtypes, we adopted the average hourly count of trajectories as the station's ridership. Then the scatter plot of the count of trajectories at each station and the violin plot of probability density were plotted. As shown in Fig. 5.7A, the upper quartile is a clear dividing line, with stations densely below the upper quartile and dispersed above the upper quartile. Therefore, the upper quartile of the trajectory count, that is, 5860, was chosen as the threshold value. In each cluster, if the average hourly count of trajectories is more significant than 5860, it is assigned to a new group and vice versa. Thus, all stations were divided into five groups for station subtypes detection. Fig. 5.7B shows the average hourly count of trajectories at each station and the new grouping result. Finally, Group 1 corresponds to the stations in cluster A. Cluster B was divided into two groups, with nine stations in group 2 and 6 stations in group 3. Similarly, cluster C is divided into two groups, with 12 stations in cluster 4 and 3 stations in cluster 5. In the next part, the characteristics of the built environment of the five groups are discussed.

4.3 Built environment analysis

Now that we have defined the types of each station, we would like to summarize the characteristics of the built environment of each group in terms of four dimensions: transit attributes, residential attributes, commute attributes, and commerce attributes. Box plots of the indicators for each group and their averages are shown in Fig. 5.8A. To visually compare the differences between the groups, we do the data Standardization and draw the radar plot as shown in Fig. 5.8B.

Group 1—Commuting rigid demand stations. Compared with the other groups, the common characteristics of the stations in Group1 are lower housing prices, fewer companies, and less commercial development, which could only be sufficient to meet the basic needs of the neighborhood. Therefore, more people prefer to live here than to work here, which leads to less working and more residence populations in the areas near these stations. Meanwhile, the transit attributes of these stations are not vital, and passengers do not have much choice of transit routes. Thus, these stations are necessary for commuters who live in the surrounding area of the station. The radar plot of Group1 shows that the residential attributes are much stronger than the other attributes, which also shows an imbalance between the attributes.

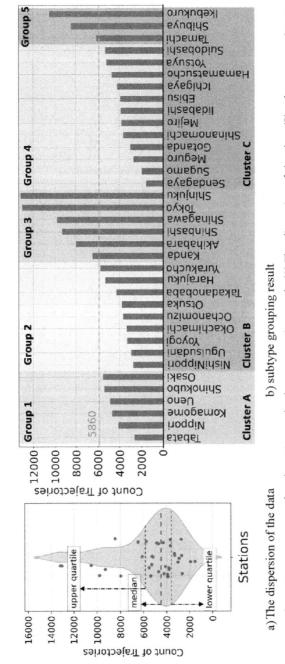

a) The dispersion of the data

b) subtype grouping result

Figure 5.7 The trajectory counts of each station and subtype grouping result. (A) The dispersion of the data (B) subtype grouping result.

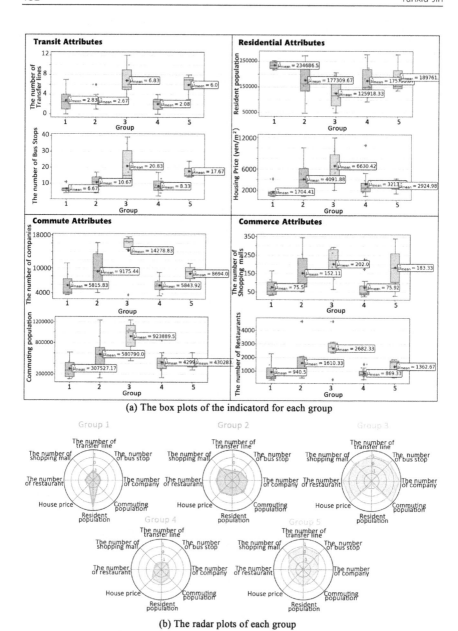

(a) The box plots of the indicatord for each group

(b) The radar plots of each group

Figure 5.8 Descriptive analysis of station built environment indicators. (A) The box plots of the indicators for each group. (B) The radar plot of each group.

Group 2—Balanced growth stations. The stations in Group 2 have more robust commute attributes and commerce attributes than the weakest transportation at-tributes. In general, there are relatively balanced across the attributes. Moreover, although housing prices in the areas are higher than those in Group 4 and 5, their resident populations are essentially the same as those in Group 4 and 5.

Group 3—Highly developed stations. Most of these stations in Group 3 are located in the city center (Tokyo station), subcenter (Shinjuku station), or important junction center (Shinagawa station). The areas near these stations concentrate on financial, trade, and intermediary services, which are well equipped with municipal transportation and commercial and recreational facilities. However, the house prices of the areas near such stations are so overpriced that they have a low population of long-term residents.

Group 4—Less developed stations. The stations in Group 4 are relatively balanced among the attributes, but it is in a weak state in all attributes compared to the other groups. Both the commuting and resident populations are deficient in this group. In addition, the average number of transfer lines, the average number of shopping malls, and the average number of restaurants are the lowest among the five groups.

Group 5—Livable stations. Group 5 contains two crucial subcenters of Tokyo (Ikebukuro and Shibuya), whose commerce attributes and transit attributes are slightly inferior to those of stations in group 2. Due to its relatively low housing prices, the areas around these stations have a high residential population. Since residents living near these stations enjoy convenient transportation and commercial services as well as a low cost of living, these stations are popular as livable stations.

5. Discussion and conclusions

Rail transit is closely related to daily commuting and travel as an important essential public transportation. The study of factors affecting passenger behavior has become a hot topic in the related field. Although there is a significant amount of literature on passenger travel behavior in past surveys, it is often analyzed from traditional Origin-destination (OD) survey or smart card data. GPS data are available with passenger location data, and our results can show passenger usage at different station buffers, which is difficult to obtain from survey data and smart card data.

Exploring station usage behavior through human GPS trajectory data reveals the imbalance of station development. Although the stations studied in this paper are located on two of the most important railway lines in Tokyo, their attractiveness to passengers and their surrounding environment's development varies greatly. As shown by the ridership of Group 3 and Group 5 (Fig. 5.7) and built environment indicators (Fig. 5.8), the convenience of transfers and the richness of commerce are the reasons for attracting many passengers. Stations with a single well-developed attribute, such as Group1, or stations with weak attributes, such as Group 4, do not attract many passengers. Similarly, the contribution of different stations to the railway network is uneven. For example, the JR Chuo Line, a transit route that crosses the JR Yamanote Line loop, attracts many passengers by the ease of interchange between its two stations that connect to the JR Yamanote Line. Although many people ride the JR Chuo Line, the stations along the JR Chuo Line in Group 4 do not attract many passengers, nor do they attract passengers far from the stations. One of the reasons for this situation is that the area surrounding these stations' resident population and working population is so small that the number of daily users is small. Another reason is that most of these stations are located along with tourist attractions such as Sotobori, Akasaka, Shinjuku Gyoen, Meiji Jingu Gyoen, where the lands are primarily used for the development of scenic spots at the expense of other functions.

In addition, our results have benefits for TOD development policies and are suitable for proposing improvements in the built environment that are tailored to specific station types. This work helps inform transportation and urban planners to better anticipate needs for mobility, future urban and transit-related infrastructure planning, service improvements, and policy development for humane and sustainable urban development.

References

[1] S. Riffat, R. Powell, D. Aydin, Future cities and environmental sustainability, Future Cities and Environment 2 (0) (2016) 1, https://doi.org/10.1186/s40984-016-0014-2.

[2] H. Dadashpoor, Z. Yousefi, Centralization or decentralization? A review on the effects of information and communication technology on urban spatial structure, Cities 78 (September 2017) (2018) 194–205, https://doi.org/10.1016/j.cities.2018.02.013.

[3] L. Fusco Girard, The role of cultural urban landscape towards a new urban economics: new structural assets for increasing economic productivity through hybrid processes, Housing Policies and Urban Economics 1 (1) (2014) 3–27.

[4] X. Liu, M. Wang, W. Qiang, K. Wu, X. Wang, Urban form, shrinking cities, and residential carbon emissions: evidence from Chinese city-regions, Applied Energy 261 (August 2019) (2020) 114409, https://doi.org/10.1016/j.apenergy.2019.114409.

[5]   Y. Zhang, R. Song, R. van Nes, S. He, W. Yin, Identifying Urban structure based on transit-oriented development, Sustainability (Switzerland) 11 (24) (2019), https://doi.org/10.3390/SU11247241.

[6]   X. Liu, L. Gong, Y. Gong, Y. Liu, Revealing travel patterns and city structure with taxi trip data, Journal of Transport Geography 43 (2015) 78−90, https://doi.org/10.1016/j.jtrangeo.2015.01.016.

[7]   K. Sasaki, Transportation system change and urban structure in two-transport mode setting, Journal of Urban Economics 25 (3) (1989) 346−367, https://doi.org/10.1016/0094-1190(89)90055-7.

[8]   G. Spadon, G. Gimenes, J.F. Rodrigues-Jr., Identifying urban inconsistencies via street networks, Procedia Computer Science 108 (2017) 18−27, https://doi.org/10.1016/j.procs.2017.05.103.

[9]   T. Cattaneo, Study on Architecture and Urban Spatial Structure in China's Mega-Cities Suburbs, Universitas studiorum, 2016.

[10] J. Zhu, Y. Sun, Building an urban spatial structure from urban land use data: an example using automated recognition of the city centre, ISPRS International Journal of Geo-Information 6 (4) (2017), https://doi.org/10.3390/ijgi6040122.

[11] S. Jiang, J. Ferreira, M.C. Gonzalez, Discovering urban spatial-temporal structure from human activity patterns, in: Proceedings of the ACM SIGKDD International Conference on Knowledge Discovery and Data Mining, 2012, pp. 95−102, https://doi.org/10.1145/2346496.2346512.

[12] C. Zhong, M. Schläpfer, S. Müller Arisona, M. Batty, C. Ratti, G. Schmitt, Revealing centrality in the spatial structure of cities from human activity patterns, Urban Studies 54 (2) (2017) 437−455, https://doi.org/10.1177/0042098015601599.

[13] R. Cervero, K. Kockelman, Travel demand and the 3Ds: density, diversity, and design, Transportation Research Part D: Transport and Environment 2 (3) (1997) 199−219, https://doi.org/10.1016/S1361-9209(97)00009-6.

[14] N.B. Hurst, S.E. West, Public transit and urban redevelopment: the effect of light rail transit on land use in Minneapolis, Minnesota, Regional Science and Urban Economics 46 (2014) 57−72.

[15] A. Galelo, A. Ribeiro, L.M. Martinez, Measuring and evaluating the impacts of TOD measures − searching for evidence of TOD characteristics in azambuja train line, Procedia - Social and Behavioral Sciences 111 (2014) 899−908, https://doi.org/10.1016/j.sbspro.2014.01.124.

[16] P. Mees, TOD and multi-modal public transport, Planning Practice and Research 29 (5) (2014) 461−470, https://doi.org/10.1080/02697459.2014.977633.

[17] M. Zhang, The role of land use in travel mode choice: evidence from boston and Hong Kong, Journal of the American Planning Association 70 (3) (2004) 344−360, https://doi.org/10.1080/01944360408976383.

[18] C. Lim, K.-J. Kim, P.P. Maglio, Smart cities with big data: reference models, challenges, and considerations, Cities 82 (2018) 86−99.

[19] X. Kong, F. Xia, K. Ma, J. Li, Q. Yang, Discovering transit-oriented development regions of megacities using heterogeneous urban data, IEEE Transactions on Computational Social Systems 6 (5) (2019) 943−955, https://doi.org/10.1109/TCSS.2019.2919960.

[20] Z. Gan, M. Yang, T. Feng, H.J.P. Timmermans, Examining the relationship between built environment and metro ridership at station-to-station level, Transportation Research Part D: Transport and Environment 82 (2020) 102332.

[21] R. Cervero, Alternative approaches to modeling the travel-demand impacts of smart growth, Journal of the American Planning Association 72 (3) (2006) 285−295, https://doi.org/10.1080/01944360608976751.

[22] M. Austin, D. Belzer, A. Benedict, P. Esling, P. Haas, G. Miknaitis, E. Wampler, J. Wood, L. Young, S. Zimbabwe, Performance-based Transit-Oriented Development Typology Guidebook, 2010.

[23] L. Bertolini, Spatial development patterns and public transport: the application of an analytical model in The Netherlands, Planning Practice and Research 14 (2) (1999) 199—210.

[24] Z. Cao, Y. Asakura, Z. Tan, Coordination between node, place, and ridership: comparing three transit operators in Tokyo, Transportation Research Part D: Transport and Environment 87 (September) (2020) 102518, https://doi.org/10.1016/j.trd.2020.102518.

[25] Y. Chen, M. Yao, Z. Cai, Research on the classification of urban rail transit stations-taking Shanghai metro as an example, in: 2018 15th International Conference on Service Systems and Service Management (ICSSSM), 2018, pp. 1—6.

[26] J. Zhou, Y. Yang, C. Webster, Using big and open data to analyze transit-oriented development: new outcomes and improved attributes, Journal of the American Planning Association 86 (3) (2020) 364—376, https://doi.org/10.1080/01944363.2020.1737182.

[27] J. Yang, P.C. Zegras, S. Mehndiratta, Walk the line: Station context, corridor type and bus rapid transit walk access in Jinan, China, Journal of Transport Geography 20 (1) (2012) 1—14.

[28] J. Gutiérrez, O.D. Cardozo, J.C. García-Palomares, Transit ridership forecasting at station level: an approach based on distance-decay weighted regression, Journal of Transport Geography 19 (6) (2011) 1081—1092, https://doi.org/10.1016/j.jtrangeo.2011.05.004.

[29] M.J. Jun, K. Choi, J.E. Jeong, K.H. Kwon, H.J. Kim, Land use characteristics of subway catchment areas and their influence on subway ridership in Seoul, Journal of Transport Geography 48 (2015) 30—40, https://doi.org/10.1016/j.jtrangeo.2015.08.002.

[30] H. Zhang, X. Song, T. Xia, M. Yuan, Z. Fan, R. Shibasaki, Y. Liang, Battery electric vehicles in Japan: human mobile behavior based adoption potential analysis and policy target response, Applied Energy 220 (March) (2018) 527—535, https://doi.org/10.1016/j.apenergy.2018.03.105.

[31] S. Ikezawa, H. Kanasugi, G. Matsubara, Y. Akiyama, R. Adachi, R. Shibasaki, Estimation of the number of railway passengers based on individual movement trajectories, in: 6th International Conference on Cartography and Gis, Vols 1 and 2, 2016, pp. 249—258, i(June).

[32] Y. Li, H. Wu, A clustering method based on K-means algorithm, Physics Procedia 25 (2012) 1104—1109, https://doi.org/10.1016/j.phpro.2012.03.206.

[33] C.D. Higgins, P.S. Kanaroglou, A latent class method for classifying and evaluating the performance of station area transit-oriented development in the Toronto region, Journal of Transport Geography 52 (2016) 61—72, https://doi.org/10.1016/j.jtrangeo.2016.02.012.

[34] S. Li, D. Lyu, X. Liu, Z. Tan, F. Gao, G. Huang, Z. Wu, The varying patterns of rail transit ridership and their relationships with fine-scale built environment factors: big data analytics from Guangzhou, Cities 99 (November 2019) (2020) 102580, https://doi.org/10.1016/j.cities.2019.102580.

[35] D.S. Vale, Transit-oriented development, integration of land use and transport, and pedestrian accessibility: combining node-place model with pedestrian shed ratio to evaluate and classify station areas in Lisbon, Journal of Transport Geography 45 (2015) 70—80, https://doi.org/10.1016/j.jtrangeo.2015.04.009.

[36] X. Li, Y. Liu, Z. Gao, D. Liu, Linkage between passenger demand and surrounding land-use patterns at urban rail transit stations: a canonical correlation analysis method and case study in Chongqing, International Journal of Transportation Science and Technology 5 (1) (2016) 10—16, https://doi.org/10.1016/j.ijtst.2016.06.002.

CHAPTER SIX

An Origin-Destination matrix prediction-based road dynamic pricing optimization system

Wenxiao Jiang
Center for Spatial Information Science, The University of Tokyo, Kashiwa-shi, Chiba, Japan

1. Introduction

Congestion pricing is designed to find the marginal social cost of a trip to the driver on each road in the network [1]. This pricing strategy is aimed at regulating travel demand on the roads to reduce congestion without increasing road capacity. In other words, the idea is to reduce travel demand on a certain road by pricing and distributing the travel demand on several other roads. It is believed that congestion pricing can control travel demand distribution and minimize traffic congestion.

The concept of congestion pricing was first proposed by Pigou [2]; and an optimal price on a congested road is suggested. Based on this theory, a method [3] is proposed to evaluate an efficient system of taxation of highway transport in the U.S. The results indicate that the price should be higher than the present levels on congested roads. In 1975, the Singapore Area Licensing Scheme, which is the first urban traffic congestion pricing scheme in the world, was successfully implemented [4]. Afterward, Singapore was also the first city in the world to adopt the Electronic Road Pricing system, which is an electronic toll collection scheme, in 1988. A study [5] for the Electronic Road Pricing system shows that the expressways are relatively less congested. During peak hours, travel speeds in the Central Business District were smoother, while on the expressways, the travel speeds improved from 45 to 65 km/h. Besides, there are many studies on congestion pricing in countries other than Singapore. Stefanello et al. [6] proposed a method to assign tolls to roads to induce drivers to take better alternative routes, and this method is evaluated in six synthetic instances and 11 real-world instances. A comparative study of congestion pricing [7] performs an evaluation of different congestion pricing strategies in London, Stockholm, and Milan.

The strategies are able to reduce negative externalities generated by traffic, such as accidents, congestion, and emissions, up to different levels.

Road dynamic pricing is one of the congestion pricing strategies that has received increasing attention in recent years. It is a method of having multiple prices based on different time periods, such as morning rush hour and evening rush hour. Rotaris et al. [8] illustrated the main features and impacts of a charging scheme in an area of the Milan city center. It is found that the scheme has been effective in curbing not only pollution emissions but also traffic congestion Schaller [9] proposed an assessment of the implications of New York's experience for pursuing congestion pricing and mileage-based taxes in the United States Stewart and Ge [10] present a dynamic congestion charging system to optimize a tolling scheme determined by travel time costs and delay costs. This optimization problem can be formulated as a bi-level mathematical program, in which the upper level is to optimize the objective, whereas the lower level is the dynamic user equilibrium (UE) traffic assignment model Han et al. [11] developed a more practical second-best dynamic road pricing scheme implemented on a subset of links for alleviating road congestion. It can drive the traffic evolution toward the desired second-best traffic UE state from any initial traffic state. Dynamic pricing is also used in High Occupancy Toll (HOT) lanes to estimate the route choice of drivers in a study [12]. The results show that a 10% increase in the price is a 1.6% reduction in usage of HOT lanes. Moreover, Pandey and Boyles [13] developed a formulation for determining optimal dynamic toll prices for managed lane networks with multiple entrances and exits. They formulate the problem as a deterministic Markov decision process and solve it using the value function approximation method for different initializations. A dynamic pricing strategy is proposed by Chen et al. [14] to price travelers' trips in intelligent transportation platforms. Como and Maggistro [15] study transportation networks controlled by dynamic pricing and focus on a multiscale model whereby the dynamics of the traffic flows are intertwined with those of the routing choices. However, most of these studies employ or simulate their road dynamic pricing strategies in a small area or an assumed road network. There are rare studies focused on a large real study area.

Since Wardrop [16] proposed UE and system optimism (SO), the two principles immediately became the main basis of traffic assignment algorithms. For the relationship between UE and SO, there is an agreed opinion: UE reflects the true situation where multiple travelers make decisions independently, while SO is an ideal state under a unified direction. Generally, the discussion on the quantitative relationship between the two is based on their own solution models.

The UE model is that each user chooses the best route in the road network, which is all travelers are minimizing their own travel costs. When no user can optimize his cost through unilateral action, then the equilibrium is reached. In this situation, travel times are equal on all used routes and lower than on any unused route. There is a general form of UE model, as shown in Eq. (6.1).

$$Minimize \sum_{e \in E} \int_0^{x_e} t_e(x) dx$$

$$x_e = \sum_s \sum_t \sum_p f_e^{st},$$

$$x_e \geq 0, f_p^{st} \geq 0 \tag{6.1}$$

where E is a road network and e is a road in it, x_e is the flow on the road e, f_p^{st} is the people with source s and target t on the route p.

The system optimum is an ideal situation in that travelers cooperate in order to reduce the total travel time. Although some travelers might cost more travel time compared with the UE, the total travel time is less than the UE. The system optimum model can be represented by Eq. (6.2).

$$Minimize \sum_{e \in E} x_e t_e(x) \tag{6.2}$$

$$s.t. \sum_p f_p^{st} = f^{st},$$

$$x_e = \sum_s \sum_t \sum_p f_e^{st},$$

$$x_e \geq 0, f_p^{st} \geq 0$$

In this study, a road dynamic pricing system is proposed for a large area. Based on the UE and SO two principles, a bi-level optimization model is designed for dynamic pricing. Without changing travel demands, the dynamic pricing system can reduce traffic congestion by setting optimal prices on toll roads of a road network. Also, the embedded grid-based Origin-Destination (OD) prediction model mentioned in the previous chapter can support the dynamic pricing system to provide optimal prices for the future.

A diagram of the dynamic pricing system is shown in Fig. 6.1. At first, the dynamic pricing system generates OD data and trajectory data by preprocessing GPS data. Secondly, the link travel time functions for describing the relationship between travel time and the number of vehicles are built on every road, and travel route data are collected by using trajectory data and road networks. Then, the OD prediction model is trained based on the OD data. Finally, depending on the model and data mentioned above, the road dynamic pricing system can provide dynamic pricing results, which are optimal prices in road segments for traffic congestion reduction.

2. Methodology

2.1 Karush–Kuhn–Tucker conditions

One classical approach to derive necessary optimality conditions for bi-level programming problems is proposed by Kuhn and Tucker [17], which is to replace the lower-level problem with its Karush–Kuhn–Tucker (KKT) conditions, and the problem of constraint qualification is usually solved. KKT method of nonlinear programming is a generalization of the Lagrange multiplier method, which only allows equality constraints. For example, the minimize problem can be formulated as Eq. (6.3).

$$Minimize\, f(x) \qquad (6.3)$$

$$s.t.\ h_i(x) = 0,\ \forall\, i = 1, \ldots, m$$

$$g_i(x) \leq 0,\ \forall\, i = 1, \ldots, n$$

where $g_i(x)$ are inequality constraints, and $h_i(x)$ are equality constraints. And then, the KKT conditions can be formulated as Eq. (6.4).

$$\nabla_x f(x) + \sum_{i=1}^{m} \nabla_x \lambda_i h_i(x) + \sum_{i=1}^{n} \nabla_x \mu_i g_i(x) = 0 \qquad (6.4)$$

$$h_i(x) = 0,\ \forall\, i = 1, .., m$$

$$\mu_i g_i(x) = 0,\ \forall\, i = 1, .., n$$

$$\mu_i \geq 0,\ \forall\, i = 1, .., n$$

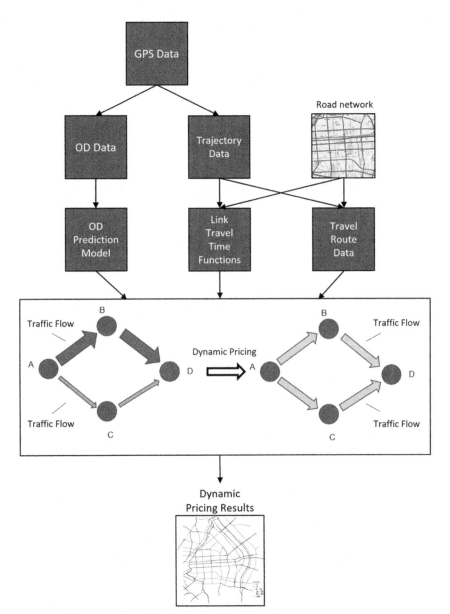

Figure 6.1 The diagram of the dynamic pricing system.

It is worth noting that the KKT conditions are the necessary conditions for optimality, in general, constrained problems but not the sufficient and necessary conditions. Only when the problems are the ones where the functions $f(x)$ and $g_i(x)$ are continuously differentiable and convex, and the functions $h_i(x)$ Are linear, these conditions also sufficient.

In the road dynamic pricing optimization problem from this study, the requirements of sufficient and necessary conditions are satisfied. Therefore, the lower-level optimization problem can be transformed into KKT conditions. And the bi-level optimization becomes a single objective optimization that is solvable.

2.2 Link travel time function

Since the link travel time functions in this study are used for building the dynamic pricing model, which is based on UE traffic assignment, and the KKT conditions are introduced into the model to solve the bilevel optimization problem, it is impossible to calculate if the link travel time functions are complicated. Like most related studies, the link travel time functions can be expressed as linear functions, as shown in Eq. (6.5).

$$T = \alpha + \beta q \tag{6.5}$$

where T is the travel time in a link. q is the traffic volume on the link. α is the intercept parameter. β are, the slope parameter of the line.

To obtain the link travel time functions that are used in the dynamic pricing model, the linear regression model is adopted. There are two types of input data that are extracted from the trajectory data to find the parameters for every link: travel time data and traffic volume data. The travel time data is used to show the average travel time of every link at different time steps. And the traffic volume data is used to present how many vehicles pass the links at different time steps. The process of the data generation is shown in Fig. 6.2. First, the trajectory data are divided by the links of the road network. Every link in a trajectory contains a start time and end time. Then, for each link in every trajectory, calculate the travel time by using the start time and the end time, and locate which time step it belongs to by using the start time. Finally, calculate the average travel time of every link at different time steps to generate the travel time data, and count the traffic volume of every link at different time steps to build the traffic volume data.

Fig. 6.3 is an example of the link travel time functions that are calculated by using the linear regression model. The blue points are the input data for

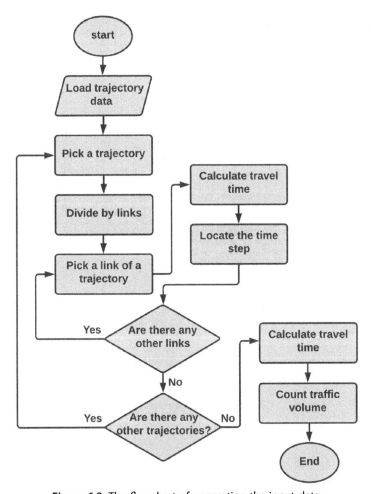

Figure 6.2 The flowchart of generating the input data.

determining the parameters. Each point represents a time step. The horizontal axis indicates the traffic volume of a certain link, and the vertical axis represents the average travel time of the link. After adopting the input data, the linear regression model generates the link travel time function as the red dotted line shown. The parameters α, and β, are 5.4129 and 0.2439, respectively.

2.3 Travel routes

There are many routes from one location to another for travelers, and the number of possible routes could be tremendous when there are a 1000

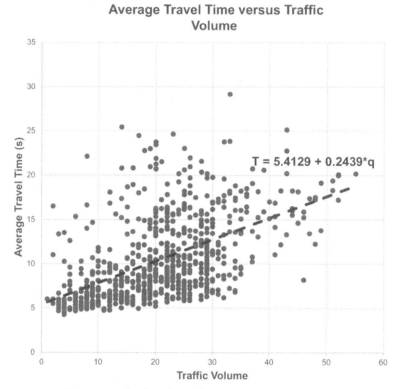

Figure 6.3 The flowchart of generating the input data.

road segments in the road network. In a metropolitan area, the number of road segments can easily exceed a 1000. Therefore, it is impossible to consider all routes from one location to another. To solve this problem, the routes are selected from trajectory data. Since the OD matrix prediction model is based on a grid, the travel routes are collected according to the same grids of origin and destination.

2.4 Bi-level optimization model

In this study, it is assumed that traffic flow is based on the UE condition. The effect of price is transformed to virtual time as parameters in the equation of the travel time model. Therefore, the optimal prices of toll roads are obtained by Eq. (6.6).

$$Minimize\ C = \sum_{e \in E} x_e t_e(x_e) \tag{6.6}$$

$$s.t.\ Minimize \sum_{e \in E} \int_0^{x_e} t_e(x_e, v_e)dx$$

$$s.t. \sum_p f_p^{st} = f^{st},$$

$$x_e = \sum_s \sum_t \sum_p f_p^{st} \delta^{st}(p, e),$$

$$x_e \geq 0,\ f_p^{st} \geq 0.$$

where C refers to the total time cost, x_e refers to the flow on road e, $t_e(x_e)$ represents the travel time t observed on road e for the flow x_e. f_p^{st} is the flow between the source s and target t on route p, and $\gamma^{st}(p, e) = 1$ when road e lies on route p. $t_e(x_e, v_e)$ represents $t_e(x_e)$ plus the virtual travel time t obtained on road e caused by the price value v_e. The lower-level optimization function is used to keep traffic flow under the UE condition. The upper-level optimization function is adopted to obtain the minimum total travel time. The dynamic price can add a virtual time v_e on the toll road to change the traffic flow. And these constraint functions can ensure that the UE conditions are not broken. Since the target of the optimization is to minimize the total time cost C, based on the constraint functions, the optimal price of every road can be found when the total time cost C is minimized.

To solve this bi-level optimization model, the KKT condition is used to transform the lower-level optimization function into equivalent constraints. Therefore, Eq. (6.6) transforms into Eq. (6.7).

$$Minimize\ C = \sum_{e \in E} x_e t_e(x_e) \tag{6.7}$$

$$s.t.\ \nabla_x \sum_{e \in E} \int_0^{x_e} t_e(x_e, v_e)dx + \sum_{i=1}^m \nabla_x \lambda_i \left(\sum_p f_p^{st} - f^{st} \right) + \sum_{e \in E}^n \nabla_x \mu_e x_e = 0$$

$$\sum_p f_p^{st} - f^{st} = 0$$

$$\mu_e x_e = 0$$

$$\mu_e \geq 0$$

Based on the OD data extracted from trajectory data and the bi-level optimization model, the traffic flow in every road segment and the optimal virtual time parameter can be obtained. The virtual time is used to represent the price on the toll roads due to the lack of data to convert the virtual time to the real price.

3. Study case

In this study, the used dataset is trajectory data provided by NTT Docomo from August 1st, 2012, to August 31st, 2012, in the center of Tokyo, and road network data provided by OpenStreetMap as shown in Fig. 6.4. The data from August 1, 2012, to August 25, 2012, are employed to train the grid-based OD matrix prediction model, and the data from

Figure 6.4 The road network data in the center of Tokyo.

August 26, 2012, to August 31, 2012, are adopted as test data. The number of road segments is 752, and the pairs of OD data are 8698 in the entire period. The time step is 1 h, which means the OD data are collected, and the function of the relationship between travel time and traffic flow on every road is calculated every hour as input data for the dynamic pricing system.

Fig. 6.5 is an example result of the price distribution of the dynamic pricing model. The black lines in which the virtual time equals −1 mean that these roads are normal roads. They are not toll roads. The green lines in which the virtual time equals 0 indicate that there is no price change on these roads. And the lines with other colors mean that these roads should increase the price equivalent to the virtual time, respectively.

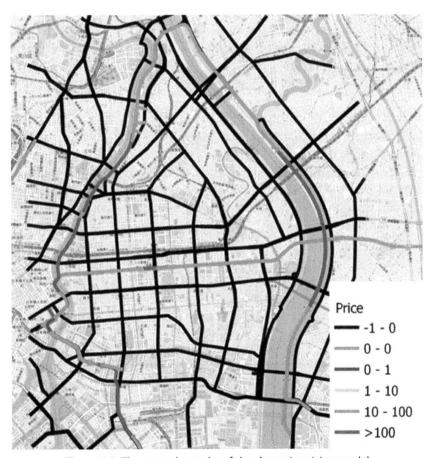

Figure 6.5 The example results of the dynamic pricing model.

4. Result and discussion

To show the performance of the proposed road dynamic pricing system, four scenarios are built to calculate the traffic flow results. The first one is calculated by using the UE model. This is the traffic flow results without any dynamic pricing. It can be employed as the baseline. The second one is based on the SO model. This traffic flow results save the total travel time compared with the first one. Therefore, it can be used as the upper bound of the traffic flow results. The traffic flow results of the third one are calculated by the proposed road dynamic pricing system with a grid-based OD prediction model. And the last one adopts the proposed road dynamic pricing system with perfect prediction results to generate the traffic flow results. It is used to show the traffic flow results when the error of the prediction model is zero.

Furthermore, an index called relative performance is proposed for the road dynamic pricing system evaluation, and it is represented by Eq. (6.8).

$$R_p = \frac{T_{ue} - T_{dp}}{T_{ue} - T_{so}} \qquad (6.8)$$

where R_p is the relative performance. T_{dp}, T_{so}, and T_{ue} are the total travel time provided by the road dynamic pricing system, SO model, and UE model.

Fig. 6.6 demonstrates the temporal distribution of the total travel time difference between the UE and the other three scenarios. The total travel time difference indicates how much time the other three scenarios can save, respectively. Prediction means the proposed road dynamic pricing

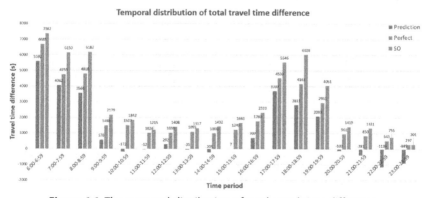

Figure 6.6 The temporal distribution of total travel time difference.

system with a grid-based OD prediction model. Perfect means the proposed road dynamic pricing system with perfect prediction results. SO means the SO model. There is no time period from 00:00 to 05:59 in this figure because the traffic flow is sparse during this time period. It is meaningless to compare the difference between UE and the other three scenarios. The results show that during the time period from 06:00 to 08:59, the road dynamic pricing system can save 5592, 4062, and 3566 s respectively. And from 17:00 to 19:59, the saving total travel time is 3707, 2811, and 2093 s respectively. It means that the road dynamic pricing system has a significant result, especially in the morning. It means that the proposed road dynamic pricing system has a better performance of saving total travel time in the morning than in the evening. During the time period from 06:00 to 08:59, the relative performances of the proposed road dynamic pricing system are 75.96%, 66.05%, and 57.64%, respectively, but the relative performances of the dynamic pricing system with perfect prediction results can reach 90.80%, 77.38%, and 77.74%, respectively. It shows that the OD prediction model still has some room for improvement. The relative performance of the dynamic pricing system cannot reach the results in the SO model, even with the perfect prediction results, due to the limitation that only the prices on toll roads are changed.

However, during the time period from 10:00 to 15:59 and from 20:00 to 23:59, the performance of the road dynamic pricing system is poor and even has a negative effect on saving total travel time. Since the upper bound of saving total travel time is relatively low during these time periods, the error of the prediction model can have a large impact on the road dynamic pricing system.

Fig. 6.7 indicates the percentage of total saved travel time in total travel time to further explain the total travel time difference between the UE and the other three scenarios. The negative values are deleted to show the figure more clearly. It shows that the results of the percentage of total saved travel time have the same trend as the results of the total travel time difference. And it also proves that the time period from 06:00 to 08:59 is the morning rush hours, and the time period from 17:00 to 19:59 is the evening rush hours, according to the input data. Therefore, the proposed road dynamic pricing system has a good performance during the rush hours.

The speed difference of road segments between the proposed road dynamic pricing system, and the UE is also counted to show the performance.

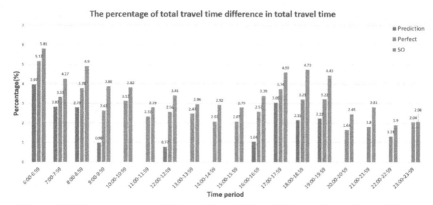

Figure 6.7 The percentage of the total travel time difference in total travel time.

For example, on August 31, 2012, from 8:00 to 8:59, among these 752 road segments, the speed of 475 road segments is increased, and 205 road segments are decreased. Most of the road segments have a speed change between 0 and 1 km/h. The road segments with a speed increase greater than 1 km/h are shown in Fig. 6.8. The values on the horizontal axis indicate that, for example, 1 means the speed increase of 1−2 km/h and so on. It is noticed that some road segments are increased by 1−3 km/h using the road dynamic pricing system, and a road segment is increased significantly by 7 km/h.

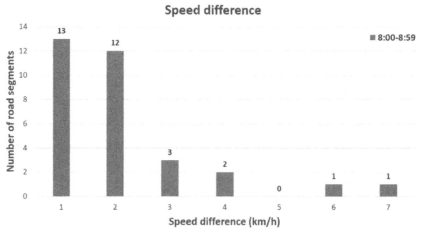

Figure 6.8 The speed difference of road segments between the proposed road dynamic pricing system and the UE.

5. Conclusion

In this study, based on the UE model and SO model, a bi-level optimization model is designed for dynamic pricing. Combining this optimization model with the OD matrix prediction model, a road dynamic pricing system is proposed. Without changing travel demands, the dynamic pricing system can reduce traffic congestion by setting optimal prices on toll roads of a road network, and the OD prediction model can support the dynamic pricing system to provide optimal prices for the future.

To show the performance of the proposed road dynamic pricing system, trajectory data provided by NTT Docomo from August 1, 2012, to August 31, 2012, in the center of Tokyo, and the corresponding road network data provided by OpenStreetMap are used as input data.

Moreover, four scenarios are built to calculate the traffic flow results for the road dynamic pricing system evaluation. The first one is calculated by using the UE model. The second one is based on the SO model. The third one is calculated by the proposed road dynamic pricing system with a grid-based OD prediction model. And the last one adopts the proposed road dynamic pricing system with perfect prediction results to generate the traffic flow results.

The results indicate that the proposed road dynamic pricing system has a good performance during the morning and evening rush hours. However, during other time periods, the performance of the road dynamic pricing system is poor and even has a negative effect on saving total travel time. Also, the results show that the OD prediction model still has some room for improvement compared with other scenarios. Moreover, the speed difference of road segments shows that more than half of the road segments have a speed increase by using the road dynamic pricing system.

References

[1] M. Winkler, W. Fan, Z. Gurmu, Congestion pricing and optimal tolling: the importance of both locations and levels, in: Cyber Technology in Automation, Control and Intelligent Systems (CYBER), 2013 IEEE 3rd Annual International Conference on, 2013, 2013, pp. 331–336.
[2] A.C. Pigou, The Economics of Welfare, MacMillan, London, 1920.
[3] A.A. Walters, The theory and measurement of private and social cost of highway congestion, Econometrica 29 (4) (1961) 676–699.
[4] L. Chen, H. Yang, Managing congestion and emissions in road networks with tolls and rebates, Transportation Research Part B: Methodological 46 (8) (2012) 933–948.
[5] M. Goh, Congestion management and electronic road pricing in Singapore, Journal of Transport Geography 10 (1) (2002) 29–38.

[6] F. Stefanello, L. Buriol, M. Hirsch, P. Pardalos, T. Querido, M. Resende, M. Ritt, On the Minimization of Traffic Congestion in Road Networks with Tolls, 2013.

[7] E. Croci, Urban road pricing: a comparative study on the experiences of London, Stockholm and Milan, Transportation Research Procedia 14 (2016) 253−262.

[8] L. Rotaris, R. Danielis, E. Marcucci, J. Massiani, The urban road pricing scheme to curb pollution in Milan, Italy: description, impacts and preliminary cost-benefit analysis assessment, Transportation Research Part 1050 A: Policy and Practice 44 (5) (2010) 359−375.

[9] B. Schaller, New York city's congestion pricing experience and implications for road pricing acceptance in the United States, Transport Policy 17 (4) (2010) 266−273.

[10] K. Stewart, Y. Ge, Optimising time-varying network flows by low-revenue tolling under dynamic user equilibrium, European Journal of Transport and Infrastructure Research 14 (1) (2014) 30−45.

[11] L. Han, D.Z.W. Wang, C. Zhu, The discrete-time second-best dynamic road pricing scheme, Transportation Research Procedia 23 (2017) 322−340.

[12] A.D. Brent, A. Gross, Dynamic road pricing and the value of time and reliability, Journal of Regional Science 58 (2) (2018) 330−349.

[13] V. Pandey, S.D. Boyles, Dynamic pricing for managed lanes with multiple entrances and exits[J], Transportation Research 96 (NOV) (2018) 304−320, 2018.

[14] L. Chen, S. Shang, B. Yao, J. Li, Pay your trip for traffic congestion: dynamic pricing in traffic-aware road networks, in: AAAI, 2020, 2020.

[15] G. Como, R. Maggistro, Distributed dynamic pricing of multiscale transportation networks, IEEE Transactions on Automatic Control (2021) 1625−1638.

[16] J.G. Wardrop, Some theoretical aspects of road traffic research, Proceedings of the Institute of Civil Engineers, Part II (1952) 325−378.

[17] H. Kuhn, A. Tucker, Nonlinear programming, 2nd Berkeley Symposium on Mathematical Statistics and Probability (1951) 481−492.

CHAPTER SEVEN

Blockchain for location-based big data-driven services

Guixu Lin[1], Haoran Zhang[3], Xuan Song[2], Ryosuke Shibasaki[1]

[1]Center for Spatial Information Science, The University of Tokyo, Kashiwa-shi, Chiba, Japan
[2]SUSTech-UTokyo Joint Research Center on Super Smart City, Department of Computer Science and Engineering, Southern University of Science and Technology (SUSTech), Shenzhen, China
[3]School of Urban Planning and Design, Peking University, Shenzhen, China

1. Introduction

1.1 Smart city

With the urbanization process all over the world, the urban population is showing an increasing trend. According to relevant statistics, by 2050, 70% of the world's population will live in cities [1]. Huge populations and limited resources pose urgent challenges to urban management in areas such as healthcare, environment, energy, and transportation. To cope with the challenges brought by urbanization, various solutions including hardware expansion, infrastructure construction, and software solutions have been implemented successively [2]. Among them, the smart city is regarded as a promising solution [3]. The concept of the smart city is proposed to address growing difficulties and complexities by balancing urban and economic growth with environmental and social concerns [4]. The development of the smart city is built on the comprehensive use of technologies such as network infrastructure, big data, Internet applications, IoT (Internet of Things), AI, cloud computing, and mobile applications [5]. Through the strategic use of various technologies, the smart city can improve the level of urban management, promote life quality, and protect the urban environment.

1.2 Location-based big data-driven services

Thanks to the infrastructure development of the smart city, massively connected devices in the city fuel the rapid growth of data. There are more and more data generated every day in cities, including traffic data, environment data, human social data, logistics data, etc. These kinds of smart city data can reflect ubiquitous aspects of the city. By mining the smart city data, city

Handbook of Mobility Data Mining, Volume 3
ISBN: 978-0-323-95892-9
https://doi.org/10.1016/B978-0-323-95892-9.00009-7

managers can understand the city, improve the quality of urban management, and enterprises can provide consumers with more efficient services. A certain proportion of smart city data has location information. These data are generated and collected by sensors capable of positioning functions, including mobile phone network data, GPS data, location-based social media data, smart card travel data, beacon log data, camera imagery data, etc [6]. This kind of data contains spatial-temporal information about the city, which is called location-based big data herein. Location-based big data has become a critical component in many scenarios of the smart city, including the epidemic spread analysis [7], urban planning [8,9], disaster evacuation [10], and intelligent transportation [11]. For instance, mining location-based big data can analyze the spread of the epidemic and help fight the spread of infectious diseases [12]. Location-based big data mining helps the urban planner to understand the city, understanding the daily flow pattern [13] and the distribution of commercial areas and residential areas [14]. Moreover, location-based big data is playing an essential role in predicting the traffic flow [15] and decreasing traffic congestion [16], which is helpful for the transportation of the city.

The development of tools and methods, including machine learning, geographic information system (GIS) technology, and visualization technology, has enabled a more efficient and meaningful location-based big data analysis. Advances in location-based big data technologies have facilitated a variety of location-based big data-driven services. Location-based big data-driven service means that service providers collect user data and adopt data mining methods to generate reliable knowledge to aid urban management, environmental protection, and traffic scheduling, and provide users with relevant and timely services, increasing customer satisfaction and engagement. Location-based big data-driven services can be categorized by administrative functions such as transportation, facility management, tourism services, and healthcare.

1.3 Challenges in location-based big data-driven services

Currently, location-based big data-driven services face some challenges. In location-based big data-driven services, data collection, sharing, and analysis are important steps to integrate all disparate resources into effective and efficient services. On the one hand, location-based big data driven services rely on data (majorly personal data), which raises concerns about the risk of private data being dissected, stolen, and out of control. On the other hand, the further development and innovation of services require a more transparent and trustworthy platform.

In terms of privacy security, location-based big data is sensitive, containing spatial and temporal attributes. For individual users, data mining can reveal their daily activities and life patterns based on their location data, which is undoubtedly very private [17]. Also, sharing location-based data with service providers is risky. In common situations, service providers utilize the central system to collect and store the user's location-based data and identity information. The centralized cloud architecture has the risk of information leakage because the centralized organization of data storage is vulnerable to a single point of failure, internal and external attacks, putting users in danger of their personal information being stolen and posing a major data privacy hazard [18].

A transparent and trustworthy ecosystem or platform is essential for the development of location-based big data-driven services. Transparency and synchronization of demand are essential to integrate optimal resources for a better service for service providers [19]. Customers also benefit from a transparent platform, because they can get more convenient and cheaper services. For example, in car sharing services, an efficient and transparent information sharing mechanism can allow service providers to know the distribution of vehicles around the passenger and then quickly select the most suitable vehicle. For the passenger, his/her waiting time is shortened, while the fee is more affordable and reasonable. A transparent platform can make the use of data more legitimate and the decision-making process more fair and reasonable. In traditional location-based big data-driven services, the analysis of user data lacks transparency. Data mining based on user's location data may lead to the phenomenon of "big data-enabled price discrimination against existing customers" [20,21]. Therefore, price discrimination based on personal data analysis raises concern [22], which not only damages the legitimate rights and interests of users [23] but also further affects user's trust in location-based big data-driven services.

In terms of trustworthiness, as more public and private service providers participate in location-based big data-driven services, there is an urgent need for a trusted platform for both service providers and customers. For service providers, a trustworthy platform is important to obtain more comprehensive and real information on supply and demand, so that they can provide an efficient service and obtain a higher income. Furthermore, a trustworthy platform can enable deeper cooperation between service providers, thereby creating more service forms and bringing more business opportunities. For customers, a trustworthy platform ensures that the services they choose are legal and reassuring. After all, the process of location-based big data-driven services consists of user information, if customers choose a dishonest service provider, the consequences can be horrible. That is, customers will be more willing to use the service only if the service is supported by a credible and transparent platform to eliminate their worries.

1.4 Blockchain for location-based big data-driven services

To address the two major challenges in location-based big data-driven services, advanced privacy-enhancing solutions are needed to protect users' private data, and new technologies need to be developed to build a transparent, reliable service environment. With the advent of Bitcoin [24], blockchain has shown disruptive potential in many fields. Not only does blockchain promise to enhance the security, integrity, and transparency of data [25–27], but also the blockchain is naturally suitable for building trustworthy and transparent ecosystems. Therefore, blockchain technology is considered as a promising solution to the above two challenges.

For privacy-preserving challenges, blockchain allows network users to use wallet addresses to transact without revealing their real identities. A common way to protect identity privacy in blockchain is to change addresses frequently. Additionally, identity privacy can be effectively protected by using more cryptographic techniques in combination with blockchain, such as mixing services [28], ring signatures [29], and noninteractive zero-knowledge (NIZK) proof [30]. Blockchain can protect transaction privacy. The data sharing from users or the necessary information exchange between users and service providers can be protected by cryptography technology on blockchain platform [31]. The common privacy protection methods for transaction privacy include NIZK proof and homomorphic encryption [32].

For trust and transparency, blockchain provides a platform of trust without third parties because of its natural properties such as decentralization, traceability, and immutability. All nodes in the blockchain system hold a copy of the ledger. All data recorded in the blockchain in the form of blocks need to be agreed upon by distributed consensus nodes, which is the process of consensus mechanism. After the consensus mechanism is completed, the confirmed block will be updated by each node to their respective ledgers, such distributed ledger technology ensures that modifications to the local ledger copy will not affect the public ledger. Additionally, the use of hash functions enables transactions in the blockchain to be easily traced. On this basis of blockchain, the smart contract of blockchain can achieve transparent transactions for location-based big data-driven services [27].

In sum, blockchain can play an essential role in privacy information protection and address the trust crisis in the location-based big data-driven service. Hence, more and more research about location-based big data-driven services begin to adopt blockchain in their work. This chapter introduces the application of blockchain for location-based big data-driven services, including shared mobility services, EV charging services, and smart logistics services.

2. Background of blockchain

2.1 Blockchain

By definition, blockchain is a distributed database solution that maintains a continuously growing list of data records confirmed by participating nodes [33]. Blockchain isn't a brand-new technology that sprung up out of nowhere. Blockchain is the integration of Peer-to-Peer (P2P) communication, distributed storage technology, consensus mechanism, and the cryptography technology. The key properties of decentralization, integrity, immutability, and transparency make blockchain play important role in different industries, such as including insurance [34,35], medicine [36,37], economics [38,39], Internet of things [40,41], supply chain [42,43], software engineering [44,45].

The essential reason for the popularity of blockchain comes from its natural characteristics: decentralization, traceability, and immutability. Decentralization refers to the decentralized shared public ledger of blockchain [46]. In a blockchain network, the public ledger is distributed among various nodes in the form of replicas. Nodes perform independently the process including ledger verification, storage, maintenance, and transmission, which creates the trust between distributed nodes and removes the third party. Traceability means that the data stored in the blockchain is traceable. In a blockchain system, blocks consisting of recorded data are connected in chronological order by uni-directional cryptographic hash. Every network user can check for themselves if transactions are valid by examing the block information linked by hash key values [47]. Immutability means that the confirmed data cannot be changed or modified in the blockchain. Once a node has tampered with its ledger replica, as nodes share and update their ledger, other nodes will verify the fake ledger and spot the tampering. Additionally, the uni-directional cryptographic hash used in blockchain makes the verification process easy [48] because any slight data modification can change the hash key values of the current block and subsequent blocks. Therefore, data stored in the blockchain is difficult to tamper with unless someone controls a majority of nodes.

Network users and validators (consensus nodes) are the two types of users that typically make up a blockchain system. Network users on the network can send and receive transactions and maintain ledger replicas, whereas consensus nodes not only have read access but are also in charge of the consensus process. According to the way that users access the ledger and participate in consensus, blockchains can be categorized as permissionless or permissioned. A permissionless blockchain is also known as a public blockchain. In a public blockchain, everyone is allowed to access the consensus process by joining the network as a consensus node. Permissioned blockchain only allows authenticated nodes to participate in the consensus process. The number of nodes is limited and the behavior of nodes is controllable in a permissioned blockchain.

2.2 Smart contract

With the evolution of blockchain, smart contracts are emerging as the key concept of blockchain 2.0, which aims to simplify business and trade between both anonymous and identified parties, sometimes without the need for a middleman. A smart contract is a set of programs that are self-verifying,self-executing, and tamper-resistant [49]. In other words, smart contracts are the small computer programs that "live" in the blockchain, and they can be executed automatically just like other computer programs.

The integration of blockchain technology and smart contracts greatly broadens the application scenarios of blockchain as it provides P2P transactions and databases that can be publicly maintained in a trusted environment in a secure manner. In location–based big data–driven services, smart contracts can balance data sources, implement multiple functions and provide a trusted environment [50]. Therefore, smart contracts have broad utility in location–based big data–driven services [51,52].

2.3 Consensus mechanism

Consensus mechanism originates in the field of distributed systems. Since a distributed system with multiple components needs to act as a whole to realize reliable functions in many cases [53], it utilizes consensus protocols to achieve the agreement on a piece of data through cooperative computation among components despite the failure of a limited number of components. The core algorithm of consensus protocols is consensus algorithms (also known as consensus mechanisms). Failures that a component may suffer include crash failure and Byzantine failure: crash failure is a kind of failure caused by failed hardware, crashed process, broken network, or software bugs, while Byzantine failure is caused by the arbitrary and malicious behavior of a component.

As a realization of a distributed system, blockchain is inseparable from the consensus mechanism. In a distributed blockchain network where all nodes hold their respective ledger replicas, the consensus mechanism is a mechanism that enables nodes to agree on the valid state of the ledger even if some nodes have crash failures or Byzantine failures. The consensus mechanism in the blockchain ensures the normal operation of the blockchain and the high security of the smart contract system.

3. Location-based big data-driven services

There are many location-based big data-driven services in the smart city, including the online taxi hailing services, vehicle sharing services, smart logistics, location-based services, etc. The following section will detail introduce three services: shared mobility services, charging services, and smart logistics services.

3.1 Shared mobility services

With the emergence of information and communication technology (ICT), APP, big data and GIS, shared mobility has emerged in the era of the smart city. Shared mobility is described as the shared use of a vehicle, motorcycle, scooter, bicycle, or other travel mode [54,55]. As shown in Fig. 7.1, the options of shared mobility services include car sharing, e-scooters, bike sharing, ride pooling, and personal vehicle sharing [59,60].

Shared mobility services can bring economic, environmental, and travel behavior benefits [58].

1. The first motivation of shared mobility services is economics [60]. The basic idea behind is simple, by sharing an expensive resource so that many people can use it without anyone having to bear the full financial burden themselves [61]. If the vehicle occupancy increases, travel service providers can earn higher revenue while paying less per passenger. Moreover, the emergence of various shared mobility services brings economic opportunities to urban development by creating new profit and employment space [62].

2. In terms of environment protection, reducing private vehicle commuting is necessary for the decarbonization and sustainable development of smart cities. The rise of shared mobility can alleviate the heavy burden of transportation on the environment. Vehicle resources are allocated precisely matching demand based on online supply and demand matching, which enhances vehicle utilization efficiency and reduce

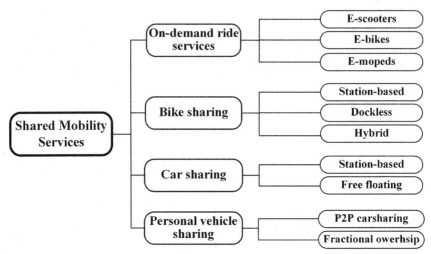

Figure 7.1 Shared mobility services. *(Based on Soares Machado, C.A. Patrick Marie de Salles Hue, N., Tobal Berssaneti, F. and Quintanilha, J.A., 2018. An overview of shared mobility. Sustainability, 10(12), 4342; Shaheen, S., Cohen, A., Chan, N. and Bansal, A., 2020. Sharing strategies: carsharing, shared micromobility (bikesharing and scooter sharing), transportation network companies, microtransit, and other innovative mobility modes. In Transportation, Land Use, and Environmental Planning, 237–262. Elsevier; Roukouni, A. and Homem de Almeida Correia, G., 2020. Evaluation methods for the impacts of shared mobility: Classification and critical review. Sustainability, 12(24), 10504).*

carbon dioxide (CO_2) and greenhouse gas (GHG) emissions [63]. Moreover, shared mobility can decrease traffic congestion and parking space requirements [64]. With shared mobility, fewer vehicles are needed to move the same number of users in the city [65].

3. Shared mobility services change travel behavior and become important and accessible mobility options [66]. Shared travel has been integrated into people's daily life and has become an indispensable part of transportation. For instance, by analyzing the 5-month trip data, authors in Ref. [67] conclude that shared bicycles have become an important means of transportation in commuting and daily life. For householders who do not own a car, car sharing plays an important role in their daily travel [68].

By combining various modes of transportation, and analyzing customers' mobility needs such as time and location, service providers can provide users with shared mobility services. To achieve smart shared mobility, location-based big data and artificial intelligence (AI) technologies are required to improve customer experience and simplify business. In the past 10 years, there are many studies about location-based big data and AI for transportation. For example, using deep learning methods can achieve good performance on tasks such as demand prediction [69,70] and travel time estimation [71,72]. These rapid advances in AI and location-based big data in transportation have also enabled shared transportation operators such as Uber and Didi to efficiently match passengers and drivers, plan routes and accurately estimate travel times, including pick-up and drop-off times.

3.2 Charging services

Due to the shortage of fossil fuel resources [73], major countries in the world start to decrease the consumption of fossil fuels. Electricity is considered as a cleaner energy as an alternative of gasoline. The increasing use of electricity can reduce the consumption of fossil fuels but also decrease GHG emissions [74]. Transportation is a major source of unsustainable energy use because it relies almost entirely on liquid fossil fuels. The development of EV technology has brought huge changes in the field of transportation [75]. The number of EVs in use is expected to increase to 1.25 million by 2030 [76]. The massive adoption of EVs can assist to reduce fossil fuel usage, and integrate different renewable energy sources into the existing electricity grid [77], and facilitate the long-term development of smart cities.

The growth of EVs raises the development of electric grids and charging stations, which provide the service for charging. EV charging infrastructure is deployed in buildings as well as in private or public charging stations according to customer needs. EV charging infrastructure is part of a complex ecosystem in which multiple entities exchange data often the personal user data. For a green intelligent transportation system in the smart city, location-based big data in charging services help users to find a suitable charging station to charge their cars, but also can schedule the charging assignment through optimization to ease the charging imbalance in the city [78]. There is increasing literature that start to research the charging services based on location-based big data analysis, including the determination of the charging station location, and the selection of an optimal charging station for EV drivers. Because the EV charging service includes not only the location of the charging station but also the service types, capacity options, the traditional method for the refueling station location problem cannot be directly used to address the selection of charging services. Therefore, authors in Ref. [79] proposed a biobjective model that balances cost and quality of service, in which real-world GPS trajectory data of Shenzhen, China, is used to estimate charging demand in urban areas.

3.3 Smart logistics services

Logistics management is a subset of supply chain management that coordinates the efficient flow and storage of goods and services between various origins and destinations in order to meet consumer demands [80]. With the progress of ICT technology, big data, and drone technologies, the smart logistics concept prevails. As an important concept of the smart city, smart logistics refers to the use of new intelligent technologies in the implementation of logistics tasks, understood as equipped with computer-supported intelligent systems that can fully automate processes [81]. Recently, drones and unmanned vehicles have begun to be used in logistics. Amazon launched the Prime Air [82] service in 2013, using multirotor drones to deliver the package to customers. The German logistics company Deutsche Post-DHL started its Parcelcopter project in 2014 [83]. Potential advantages of drones in logistics shorten delivery times, reduce transportation costs, increase the flexibility of logistics systems, and improveing the sustainability of logistics services [84]. With the continuous innovation and integration of new technologies, smart logistics will develop in the direction of high efficiency, environmental protection, safety and energy saving.

Historical location-based big data are increasingly used in smart logistics services to improve service efficiency. For instance, the work [85] proposed a data driven approach, the adaptive multi-phase approach based on GPS data to address the vehicle routing problem (VRP) in smart logistics. The work [86] proposed an algorithm for drone delivery scenarios to reach the "last mile" of the delivery effort. Based on the customer locations, the work [87] proposed an optimization algorithm that determines the optimal number of launch sites and locations by using K-means algorithms and genetic algorithms. For the parcel delivery of smart logistics, historical delivery data can be utilized to predict the future delivery result by using address intelligence [88]. Authors in Ref. [89] used mobile location data to predict the future location of customers, which helps delivery service providers understand the best delivery times and locations for customers to better implement delivery schedules.

4. Blockchain in location-based big data-driven services

4.1 Blockchian in shared mobility services

Shared mobility services require the cooperation of different entities in a city to integrate different modes of transportation. In a centralized platform for shared mobility services, decisions and data are invisible and opaque which raises concerns about service fairness and misuse of user data. For business partners, traditional service platforms do not provide an efficient trust mechanism for data sharing and cooperation, and often require the participation of a trusted third party for cooperation and collaboration. Trust is the cornerstone of shared mobility services. A transparent and trustworthy platform is essential to strengthen trust and collaboration between businesses, consumers, and vehicles [90,91], which is important for the sustainable development of shared mobility services. Blockchain, as a decentralized platform without a third party, can be a good choice to build a trustworthy and transparent platform for shared mobility services.

Privacy protection is another challenge in shared mobility services. In the traditional shared mobility services, the operation and the data storage rely on a central cloud system. Not only does the system become vulnerable to a single point of failure, but also the risk of privacy leakage caused by internal or external attacks is very serious. Shared mobility services can be processed through blockchain-based distributed algorithms, and only a small amount of necessary information needs to be exchanged to complete the service, thereby reducing the risk of data leakage under the traditional centralized computing framework. For the user data that must be transmitted and shared in the shared mobile service, cryptographic methods can be used to protect the security of the data. The work of [92] proposed a ride-sharing service based on the public blockchain, where riders send their request for trips and drivers submit their biddings through the smart contract. By conducting the spatial cloaking and temporal cloaking, all travel information is hidden from the exact location coordinate.

Blockchain can provide a variety of services for shared mobility services by customizing the content of smart contracts. For example, the smart contract of the blockchain provides token-based incentives. In the distributed blockchain system, the incentive mechanism can be launched based on smart contract to provide open opportunities for shared mobility services. That is, rewarding specific user behaviors through the smart contract designed in advance can change the behavior of users in shared mobility services. Common rewards include reward referrals, reward safe driving and reward data sharing [93]. For example, in Helbiz [94], a blockchain-based car sharing project, users can earn tokens by providing driving data to insurance companies via the smart contract. The current state of shared mobility services is that the entire market is dominated by a few large companies. The emergence of the blockchain may change this situation, because blockchain allows for a decentralized operation mode. The P2P service mode based on blockchain may bring new vitality to the entire market and bring new opportunities for small companies or individuals [95].

4.2 Blockchian in charging services

The realization of a smart charging service is inseparable from the mutual communication and data sharing between entities in the charging infrastructure. As the scale of charging services becomes larger in the world, data protection for charging services will become increasingly important. In the current standards of EV charging protocols such as OCPP and ISO 15,118, a trusted intermediary mobility operator is required for the storage of private information such as EV identity, location, charge state, charging parameter, and payment information [96,97]. It raises the concern that the privacy information leakage from mobility operators may lead to the risk for users with the rapid increment of charging service. The blockchain can be used for privacy protection in the charging services. As for the protection of requirement data of EV drivers, authors in Ref. [96] proposed a blockchain-based protocol to enable EVs to select the charging station efficiently. By solving the optimization model on the EV side, EVs can obtain the optimal charging station without sharing information with charging stations. The selection and reservation service are executed by the smart contract, the proposed protocol is proved to be scalable with low blockchain transaction and storage overhead.

A trustworthy and transparent platform is important for EV charging services. All the entities in the charging services need a trust relationship. In the traditional charging method, some service providers may overcharge users, and in many countries, the laws on illegal charging of EVs in this regard are not strictly enforced. Blockchain can build trust and transparent platforms for EV charging services [98]. Authors in Ref. [99] proposed the blockchain-based P2P energy trading and charging payment system to build the transparent environment for the charging services, in which the payment is completed via the smart contract.

Blockchain provides opportunities in EV charging services. Customized smart contracts of blockchain can achieve many functions, including payment services, decision-making, etc. For example, blockchain can achieve safe and autonomous payment of EV charging, which is very important for the development of EVs. Small transactions in EV charging services can be realized profitably through blockchain [90]. The selection of a suitable charging station can be done through the smart contract. The work [100] utilized the smart contract to launch an auction, in which the driver can select the appropriate charging station from the bids. The work of [100] also proposed a blockchain system in which the auction based on the smart contract is utilized to select a charging station based on pricing and the distance to the EV. Further, the consensus mechanism of blockchain provides new solutions to some pain points in traditional EV charging services. For example, reputation matters with service providers. In the traditional charging service system, some service providers may hire more fake customers to obtain higher reputation value, thereby attracting more customers. Blockchain-driven solutions can prevent such illegal operations and ensure the transparency and fairness of the credible evaluation mechanism [101].

4.3 Blockchian in smart logistics services

Privacy protection becomes more important in next-generation logistics. In particular, as more and more logistics companies use drones in logistics services, the risk of drones being attacked, such as physical attacks [102], will increase, so the risk of privacy leakage will also increase. Therefore, blockchain-based solutions have been proposed recently. The work [103] proposed a blockchain-based framework, called DeliveryCoin, to protect the drone-delivered services in a smart city, the hash functions and short signatures are utilized based on the blockchain platform to protect the sensitive information. Based on the classic PBFT consensus mechanism, the work proposed a UAV-aided forwarding mechanism to achieve the consensus in the blockchain-based delivery platform.

The information sharing with transparency between logistics entities enhances the relationship and trust between them, which also contribute to the efficiency of logistics services [104]. The tracking of goods and financial exchange in smart logistics is very important. In the traditional system, the status information of goods and the financial exchange process are not transparent enough. Blockchain provides the solution to manage the service and information in the logistics process. All data recorded in the blockchain can be traced back, which is meaningful for the decision-making and optimization of the logistics process. For example, by proposing a blockchain-based system for logistics systems to improve the quality of traceability data and reliable information sharing in the work [105], it allows us to see the huge potential of blockchain as a trusted data sharing platform for logistics and operational arrangements. For customers, the use of blockchain makes smart logistics services more transparent and visible, which allows them to easily monitor and evaluate products, services, and suppliers. Blockchain supports product traceability, which can reduce the risk of fraud and counterfeit products.

5. Future trend of blockchain

Blockchain technology has demonstrated its advantages in location-based big data-driven services and has the potential to revolutionize the business model of location-based big data-driven services. Different from the original centralized service management method, blockchain establishes trust between nodes via consensus mechanisms, processing services in a distributed manner, which reduces the possibility of data leakage to a certain extent and increases the reliability of services. By combining with encryption technology, blockchain shows better capacity in privacy data protection. Furthermore, by integrating with smart contracts, more and more services can be implemented on the blockchain.

It must be noted that there are still many challenges with blockchain, including issues of scalability, efficiency, and energy consumption. Although the application of blockchain in location-based big data-driven services is still in the research stage, there is no large-scale application of location-based big data-driven services. But with the growth of blockchain, these challenges will gradually be solved. Public blockchains and consortium blockchains will play different roles in the different scenarios of location-based big data-driven services.

References

[1] R. Paola Dameri, Comparing smart and digital city: initiatives and strategies in amsterdam and genoa. are they digital and/or smart?, in: Smart City Springer, 2014, pp. 45–88.

[2] J.H. Kim, Smart city trends: a focus on 5 countries and 15 companies, Cities 123 (2022) 103551.

[3] H. Kumar, M. Kumar Singh, M.P. Gupta, J. Madaan, Moving towards smart cities: solutions that lead to the smart city transformation framework, Technological Forecasting and Social Change 153 (April 2020).

[4] K.H. Law, J.P. Lynch, Smart city: technologies and challenges, IT Professional 21 (6) (2019) 46–51.

[5] M. Pańkowska, A. Sołtysik-Piorunkiewicz, Ict supported urban sustainability by example of silesian metropolis, Sustainability 14 (3) (2022) 1586.

[6] H. Huang, X. Angela Yao, J.M. Krisp, B. Jiang, Analytics of location-based big data for smart cities: opportunities, challenges, and future directions, Computers, Environment and Urban Systems 90 (2021) 101712.

[7] M. Zhang, S. Wang, T. Hu, X. Fu, X. Wang, Y. Hu, B. Halloran, Z. Li, Y. Cui, H. Liu, et al., Human mobility and covid-19 transmission: a systematic review and future directions, Annals of GIS (2022) 1–14.

[8] J. Wang, X. Kong, A. Rahim, F. Xia, A. Tolba, Z. Al-Makhadmeh, Is2fun: identification of subway station functions using massive urban data, IEEE Access 5 (2017) 27103–27113.

[9] X. Gao, J. Cai, Optimization analysis of urban function regional planning based on big data and gis technology, Boletin Tecnico/Technical Bulletin 55 (11) (2017) 344–351.

[10] X. Song, Q. Zhang, Y. Sekimoto, T. Horanont, S. Ueyama, R. Shibasaki, Modeling and probabilistic reasoning of population evacuation during large-scale disaster, in: Proceedings of the 19th ACM SIGKDD International Conference on Knowledge Discovery and Data Mining, 2013, pp. 1231–1239.

[11] X. Kong, Z. Xu, G. Shen, J. Wang, Q. Yang, B. Zhang, Urban traffic congestion estimation and prediction based on floating car trajectory data, Future Generation Computer Systems 61 (2016) 97–107.

[12] J. Huang, H. Wang, M. Fan, A. Zhuo, Y. Sun, Y. Li, Understanding the impact of the covid-19 pandemic on transportation-related behaviors with human mobility data, in: Proceedings of the 26th ACM SIGKDD International Conference on Knowledge Discovery & Data Mining, 2020, pp. 3443–3450.

[13] R.A. Becker, R. Caceres, K. Hanson, J. Meng Loh, S. Urbanek, A. Varshavsky, C. Volinsky, A tale of one city: using cellular network data for urban planning, IEEE Pervasive Computing 10 (4) (2011) 18–26.

[14] J. Yuan, Y. Zheng, X. Xie, Discovering regions of different functions in a city using human mobility and pois, in: Proceedings of the 18th ACM SIGKDD International Conference on Knowledge Discovery and Data Mining, 2012, pp. 186–194.

[15] Z. He, C.-Y. Chow, J.-D. Zhang, Stcnn: a spatio-temporal convolutional neural network for long-term traffic prediction, in: 2019 20th IEEE International Conference on Mobile Data Management (MDM), IEEE, 2019, pp. 226–233.

[16] N. Cárdenas-Benítez, R. Aquino-Santos, P. Magaña-Espinoza, J. Aguilar-Velazco, A. Edwards-Block, A.M. Cass, Traffic congestion detection system through connected vehicles and big data, Sensors 16 (5) (2016) 599.

[17] A. Gkoulalas-Divanis, Y. Saygin, D. Pedreschi, Privacy in mobility data mining, ACM SIGKDD Explorations Newsletter 13 (1) (2011) 4–5.

[18] Q. Dai, K. Xv, S. Guo, L. Dai, Z. Zhou, A private data protection scheme based on blockchain under pipeline model, in: 2018 1st IEEE International Conference on Hot Information-Centric Networking (HotICN), IEEE, 2018, pp. 37–45.

[19] J. Eckhardt, L. Nykänen, A. Aapaoja, P. Niemi, Maas in rural areas-case Finland, Research in Transportation Business & Management 27 (2018) 75–83.

[20] M. Qian, Analysis on the phenomenon of "big data-enabled price discrimination against existing customers" of Internet enterprises based on evolutionary game theory, in: 2021 2nd International Conference on Big Data Economy and Information Management (BDEIM), IEEE, 2021, pp. 371–374.

[21] Y. Chen, Oligopoly price discrimination by purchase history, The Pros and Cons of Price Discrimination (2005) 101–130.

[22] A. Hannak, G. Soeller, D. Lazer, A. Mislove, C. Wilson, Measuring price discrimination and steering on e-commerce web sites, in: Proceedings of the 2014 Conference on Internet Measurement Conference, 2014, pp. 305–318.

[23] J. Poort, F.J. Zuiderveen Borgesius, Does everyone have a price? understanding people's attitude towards online and offline price discrimination, Internet Policy Review 8 (1) (2019) 1–20.

[24] S. Nakamoto, Bitcoin: a peer-to-peer electronic cash system, Decentralized Business Review (2008) 21260.

[25] T. Dargahi, H. Ahmadvand, M. Naser Alraja, C.-M. Yu, Integration of blockchain with connected and autonomous vehicles: vision and challenge, ACM Journal of Data and Information Quality (JDIQ) 14 (1) (2021) 1–10.

[26] D. Lopez, B. Farooq, A blockchain framework for smart mobility, in: 2018 IEEE International Smart Cities Conference (ISC2), IEEE, 2018, pp. 1–7.

[27] A. Karinsalo, K. Halunen, Smart contracts for a mobility-as-a-service ecosystem, in: 2018 IEEE International Conference on Software Quality, Reliability and Security Companion (QRS-C), IEEE, 2018, pp. 135–138.

[28] D.L. Chaum, Untraceable electronic mail, return addresses, and digital pseudonyms, Communications of the ACM 24 (2) (1981) 84–90.

[29] R.L. Rivest, A. Shamir, Y. Tauman, How to leak a secret, in: International Conference on the Theory and Application of Cryptology and Information Security, Springer, 2001, pp. 552–565.

[30] M. Blum, P. Feldman, S. Micali, Non-interactive zero-knowledge and its applications, acm symp, Theory Comput. doi 10 (62212.62222) (1988).

[31] P. Zhong, Q. Zhong, H. Mi, S. Zhang, Y. Xiang, Privacy-protected blockchain system, in: 2019 20th IEEE International Conference on Mobile Data Management (MDM), IEEE, 2019, pp. 457–461.

[32] R.L. Rivest, L. Adleman, M.L. Dertouzos, et al., On data banks and privacy homomorphisms, Foundations of secure computation 4 (11) (1978) 169–180.

[33] J. Yli-Huumo, D. Ko, S. Choi, S. Park, K. Smolander, Where is current research on blockchain technology?—a systematic review, PLoS One 10 (2016) e0163477, 11.

[34] R. Brophy, Blockchain and insurance: a review for operations and regulation, Journal of Financial Regulation and Compliance 28 (2) (2019) 215–234, https://doi.org/10.1108/JFRC-09-2018-0127.

[35] V. Gatteschi, F. Lamberti, C. Demartini, C. Pranteda, V. Santamaría, Blockchain and smart contracts for insurance: is the technology mature enough? Future Internet 10 (2) (2018) 20.

[36] A. Ali Siyal, A. Zahid Junejo, M. Zawish, K. Ahmed, A. Khalil, G. Soursou, Applications of blockchain technology in medicine and healthcare: challenges and future perspectives, Cryptography 3 (1) (2019) 3.

[37] I. Radanović, R. Likić, Opportunities for use of blockchain technology in medicine, Applied Health Economics and Health Policy 16 (5) (2018) 583–590.

[38] S. Huckle, R. Bhattacharya, M. White, N. Beloff, Internet of things, blockchain and shared economy applications, Procedia Computer Science 98 (2016) 461–466.

[39] P. Hurich, The virtual is real: an argument for characterizing bitcoins as private property, Banking & Finance Law Review 31 (3) (2016) 573.

[40] A. Dhar Dwivedi, G. Srivastava, S. Dhar, R. Singh, A decentralized privacy-preserving healthcare blockchain for iot, Sensors 19 (2) (2019) 326.

[41] Y. Po Tsang, K. Lun Choy, C.H. Wu, G. To Sum Ho, H. Yan Lam, Blockchain-driven iot for food traceability with an integrated consensus mechanism, IEEE Access 7 (2019) 129000–129017.

[42] K. Francisco, D. Swanson, The supply chain has no clothes: technology adoption of blockchain for supply chain transparency, Logistics 2 (1) (2018) 2.

[43] R. Azzi, R. Kilany Chamoun, M. Sokhn, The power of a blockchain-based supply chain, Computers & Industrial Engineering 135 (2019) 582–592.

[44] S. Porru, A. Pinna, M. Marchesi, R. Tonelli, Blockchain-oriented software engineering: challenges and new directions, in: 2017 IEEE/ACM 39th International Conference on Software Engineering Companion (ICSE-C), IEEE, 2017, pp. 169–171.

[45] F. Tariq, R. Colomo-Palacios, Use of blockchain smart contracts in software engineering: a systematic mapping, in: International Conference on Computational Science and its Applications, Springer, 2019, pp. 327–337.

[46] H. Yumna, M. Murad Khan, M. Ikram, S. Ilyas, Use of blockchain in education: a systematic literature review, in: Asian Conference on Intelligent Information and Database Systems, Springer, 2019, pp. 191–202.

[47] G. Chen, B. Xu, M. Lu, N.-S. Chen, Exploring blockchain technology and its potential applications for education, Smart Learning Environments 5 (1) (2018) 1–10.

[48] G. Srivastava, S. Dhar, A. Dhar Dwivedi, J. Crichigno, Blockchain education, in: 2019 IEEE Canadian Conference of Electrical and Computer Engineering (CCECE), 2019, pp. 1—5.

[49] B. Kumar Mohanta, S.S. Panda, D. Jena, An overview of smart contract and use cases in blockchain technology, in: 2018 9th International Conference on Computing, Communication and Networking Technologies (ICCCNT), IEEE, 2018, pp. 1—4.

[50] K. Gai, J. Guo, L. Zhu, S. Yu, Blockchain meets cloud computing: a survey, IEEE Communications Surveys & Tutorials 22 (3) (2020) 2009—2030.

[51] S. Ernest Chang, Y.-C. Chen, M.-F. Lu, Supply chain re-engineering using blockchain technology: a case of smart contract based tracking process, Technological Forecasting and Social Change 144 (2019) 1—11.

[52] F. Victor, S. Zickau, Geofences on the blockchain: enabling decentralized location-based services, in: 2018 IEEE International Conference on Data Mining Workshops (ICDMW), IEEE, 2018, pp. 97—104.

[53] M.J. Fischer, The consensus problem in unreliable distributed systems (a brief survey), in: International Conference on Fundamentals of Computation Theory, Springer, 1983, pp. 127—140.

[54] A. Cohen, S. Shaheen, Planning for Shared Mobility, 2018.

[55] SAE International, Taxonomy and definitions for terms related to shared mobility and enabling technologies, Warrendale, Pennsylvania, USA: SAE International. (2018).

[56] C.A. Soares Machado, N. Patrick Marie de Salles Hue, F. Tobal Berssaneti, J.A. Quintanilha, An overview of shared mobility, Sustainability 10 (12) (2018) 4342.

[57] S. Shaheen, A. Cohen, N. Chan, A. Bansal, Sharing strategies: carsharing, shared micromobility (bikesharing and scooter sharing), transportation network companies, microtransit, and other innovative mobility modes, in: Transportation, Land Use, and Environmental Planning, Elsevier, 2020, pp. 237—262.

[58] A. Roukouni, G. Homem de Almeida Correia, Evaluation methods for the impacts of shared mobility: classification and critical review, Sustainability 12 (24) (2020) 10504.

[59] F. Creutzig, From smart city to digital urban commons: institutional considerations for governing shared mobility data, Environmental Research: Infrastructure and Sustainability 1 (2) (2021) 025004.

[60] S. Shaheen, Shared mobility: the potential of ridehailing and pooling, in: Three Revolutions, Springer, 2018, pp. 55—76.

[61] L. Sioui, C. Morency, M. Trépanier, How carsharing affects the travel behavior of households: a case study of montréal, Canada, International Journal of Sustainable Transportation 7 (1) (2013) 52—69.

[62] C.E. Cherry, N.F. Pidgeon, Is sharing the solution? exploring public acceptability of the sharing economy, Journal of Cleaner Production 195 (2018) 939—948.

[63] J.-W. Hu, F. Creutzig, A systematic review on shared mobility in China, International Journal of Sustainable Transportation 16 (4) (2022) 374—389.

[64] M. Drut, Urban mobility and degrowth strategies: a note on the role of shared transportation modes, in: 5. International Degrowth Conference, 2016 page np.

[65] M. Drut, Spatial issues revisited: the role of shared transportation modes, Transport Policy 66 (2018) 85—95.

[66] A. Durand, L. Harms, S. Hoogendoorn-Lanser, T. Zijlstra, Mobility-as-a-service and Changes in Travel Preferences and Travel Behaviour: A Literature Review, 2018.

[67] Y. Zhang, M.J.G. Brussel, T. Thomas, M.F.A.M. van Maarseveen, Mining bike-sharing travel behavior data: an investigation into trip chains and transition activities, Computers, Environment and Urban Systems 69 (2018) 39—50.

[68] A. Millard-Ball, Car-sharing: Where and How it Succeeds vol. 60, Transportation Research Board, 2005.

[69]   S. Woo Ham, J.-H. Cho, S. Park, D.-K. Kim, Spatiotemporal demand prediction model for e-scooter sharing services with latent feature and deep learning, Transportation Research Record 2675 (11) (2021) 34–43.

[70]   S. Kim, S. Choo, G. Lee, S. Kim, Predicting demand for shared e-scooter using community structure and deep learning method, Sustainability 14 (5) (2022) 2564.

[71]   Y. Li, K. Fu, Z. Wang, C. Shahabi, J. Ye, Y. Liu, Multi-task representation learning for travel time estimation, in: Proceedings of the 24th ACM SIGKDD International Conference on Knowledge Discovery & Data Mining, 2018, pp. 1695–1704.

[72]   H. Yuan, G. Li, Z. Bao, L. Feng, Effective travel time estimation: when historical trajectories over road networks matter, in: Proceedings of the 2020 Acm Sigmod International Conference on Management of Data, 2020, pp. 2135–2149.

[73]   D. Abbott, Keeping the energy debate clean: how do we supply the world's energy needs? Proceedings of the IEEE 98 (1) (2009) 42–66.

[74]   H.A.J.I. Zakaria, M.O.U.N.I.R. Hamid, E.L. MARJANI Abdellatif, A.M.A.R.I.R. Imane, Recent advancements and developments for electric vehicle technology, in: 2019 International Conference of Computer Science and Renewable Energies (ICCSRE), 2019, pp. 1–6.

[75]   S. Campanari, G. Manzolini, F. Garcia De la Iglesia, Energy analysis of electric vehicles using batteries or fuel cells through well-to-wheel driving cycle simulations, Journal of Power Sources 186 (2) (2009) 464–477.

[76]   T. Bunsen, P. Cazzola, M. Gorner, L. Paoli, S. Scheffer, R. Schuitmaker, J. Tattini, J. Teter, Global Ev Outlook 2018: Towards Cross-Modal Electrification, 2018.

[77]   D.B. Richardson, Electric vehicles and the electric grid: a review of modeling approaches, impacts, and renewable energy integration, Renewable and Sustainable Energy Reviews 19 (2013) 247–254.

[78]   A.Y.S. Lam, Y.-W. Leung, X. Chu, Electric vehicle charging station placement: formulation, complexity, and solutions, IEEE Transactions on Smart Grid 5 (6) (2014) 2846–2856.

[79]   X. Bai, K.-S. Chin, Z. Zhou, A bi-objective model for location planning of electric vehicle charging stations with gps trajectory data, Computers & Industrial Engineering 128 (2019) 591–604.

[80]   K. Nowicka, Smart city logistics on cloud computing model, Procedia-Social and Behavioral Sciences 151 (2014) 266–281.

[81]   S. Kauf, Smart logistics as a basis for the development of the smart city, Transportation Research Procedia 39 (2019) 143–149.

[82]   Amazon.com, Inc. Amazon Prime Air. [Online]. Available: http://www.amazon.com/primeair.

[83]   DHL (2014). Press Release DHL parcelcopter launches initial operations for research purposes. [Online]. Available: [https://www.reutersevents.com/supplychain/3pl/dhl-parcelcopter-launches-initial-operations-research-purposes, access May 30, 2022].

[84]   A. Rejeb, K. Rejeb, S.J. Simske, H. Treiblmaier, Drones for supply chain management and logistics: a review and research agenda, International Journal of Logistics Research and Applications (2021) 1–24.

[85]   E. Žunić, S. Delalić, D. Donko, Adaptive multi-phase approach for solving the realistic vehicle routing problems in logistics with innovative comparison method for evaluation based on real gps data, Transportation Letters 14 (2) (2022) 143–156.

[86]   K. Dorling, J. Heinrichs, G.G. Messier, S. Magierowski, Vehicle routing problems for drone delivery, IEEE Transactions on Systems, Man, and Cybernetics: Systems 47 (1) (2016) 70–85.

[87]   S. Mourelo Ferrandez, T. Harbison, T. Weber, R. Sturges, R. Rich, Optimization of a truck-drone in tandem delivery network using k-means and genetic algorithm, Journal of Industrial Engineering and Management (JIEM) 9 (2) (2016) 374–388.

[88]   J.H.R. Van Duin, W.de Goffau, B. Wiegmans, L.A. Tavasszy, M. Saes, Improving home delivery efficiency by using principles of address intelligence for b2c deliveries, Transportation Research Procedia 12 (2016) 14–25.

[89]   S. Praet, D. Martens, Efficient parcel delivery by predicting customers' locations, Decision Sciences 51 (5) (2020) 1202—1231.

[90]   M. Gösele, P. Sandner, Analysis of blockchain technology in the mobility sector, Forschung im Ingenieurwesen 83 (4) (2019) 809—816.

[91]   S. Auer, S. Nagler, S. Mazumdar, R.R. Mukkamala, Towards blockchain-iot based shared mobility: car-sharing and leasing as a case study, Journal of Network and Computer Applications (2022) 103316.

[92]   M. Baza, M. Mahmoud, G. Srivastava, W. Alasmary, M. Younis, A light blockchain-powered privacy-preserving organization scheme for ride sharing services, in: 2020 IEEE 91st Vehicular Technology Conference (VTC2020-Spring), IEEE, 2020, pp. 1—6.

[93]   E. Bothos, B. Magoutas, K. Arnaoutaki, G. Mentzas, Leveraging blockchain for open mobility-as-a-service ecosystems, in: IEEE/WIC/ACM International Conference on Web Intelligence-Companion Volume, 2019, pp. 292—296.

[94]   Helbiz. Helbiz Mobility System: Blockchain P2P Car Sharing. [Online]. Available: [https://www.amazix.com/blog/helbiz-mobility-system-blockchain-p2p-car-sharing/, access June 08, 2022].

[95]   S. Shaheen, E. Martin, M. Hoffman-Stapleton, Shared mobility and urban form impacts: a case study of peer-to-peer (p2p) carsharing in the us, Journal of Urban Design 26 (2) (2021) 141—158.

[96]   S. Muhammad Danish, K. Zhang, H.-A. Jacobsen, N. Ashraf, H. Khaliq Qureshi, Blockev: efficient and secure charging station selection for electric vehicles, IEEE Transactions on Intelligent Transportation Systems 22 (7) (2020) 4194—4211.

[97]   J. Antoun, M. Ekramul Kabir, B. Moussa, R. Atallah, C. Assi, A detailed security assessment of the ev charging ecosystem, IEEE Network 34 (3) (2020) 200—207.

[98]   Z. Dong, F. Luo, G. Liang, Blockchain: a secure, decentralized, trusted cyber infrastructure solution for future energy systems, Journal of Modern Power Systems and Clean Energy 6 (5) (2018) 958—967.

[99]   P. Waqas Khan, Y.-C. Byun, Blockchain-based peer-to-peer energy trading and charging payment system for electric vehicles, Sustainability 13 (14) (2021) 7962.

[100] M. Pustišek, A. Kos, U. Sedlar, Blockchain based autonomous selection of electric vehicle charging station, in: 2016 International Conference on Identification, Information and Knowledge in the Internet of Things (IIKI), IEEE, 2016, pp. 217—222.

[101] D. Huang, Z.-Y. Tang, W.-Y. Hu, Q.-Z. Wu, Blockchain-based electric vehicle charging reputation management mechanism, in: 2021 International Conference on Artificial Intelligence, Big Data and Algorithms (CAIBDA), IEEE, 2021, pp. 58—61.

[102] S. Hoon Chung, B. Sah, J. Lee, Optimization for drone and drone-truck combined operations: a review of the state of the art and future directions, Computers & Operations Research 123 (2020) 105004.

[103] M. Amine Ferrag, L. Maglaras, Deliverycoin: an ids and blockchain-based delivery framework for drone-delivered services, Computers 8 (3) (2019) 58.

[104] A. Sivula, A. Shamsuzzoha, P. Helo, Blockchain in logistics: mapping the opportunities in con-struction industry, in: International Conference on Industrial Engineering and Operations Management, 2018.

[105] G.T.S. Ho, Y. Ming Tang, K. Yat Tsang, V. Tang, K.Y. Chau, A blockchain-based system to enhance aircraft parts traceability and trackability for inventory management, Expert Systems with Applications 179 (2021) 115101.

CHAPTER EIGHT

Mobility data in urban road emission mitigation

Shikun Qi[1], Meng Yuan[2], Haoran Zhang[3], Yongtu Liang[1], Jinyu Chen[3]
[1]National Engineering Laboratory for Pipeline Safety/MOE Key Laboratory of Petroleum Engineering/ Beijing Key Laboratory of Urban Oil and Gas Distribution Technology, China University of Petroleum-Beijing, Beijing, China
[2]Department of Planning, Aalborg University, Aalborg, Denmark
[3]School of Urban Planning and Design, Peking University, Shenzhen, China

1. Introduction

The rapidly increasing greenhouse gas (GHG) emissions pose a huge challenge to the global ecological environment and human health [1]. Urban road emissions are found to contribute a major part to air pollution in traffic-related microenvironments [2]. Transportation is responsible for approximately 16% of GHG emissions, with a growth of 71% during recent decades [3]. It is also found that there are a high proportion of transportation-related emissions in the air pollution [4]. Reducing transportation-related emissions is urgent on a global scale. Road transportation accounts for about 47% of CO, 42% of NOx, and 18.4% of PM emissions, respectively, in Europe [5]. In China, it is estimated that transportation-related activities account for approximately 78% of CO, 46% NOx, and 83% of HC in metropolises [6].

Identifying the emission behavior of road transport emissions helps to provide the theoretical basis for emission mitigation. Most previous studies used portable emission measurement (PEM) systems to collect real-time exhaust pipe emission data and arrange the crew to manually record the number of passengers. These methods are practical, but their application is limited by the financial resources and labor required for the collection of emission data and passenger data [7]. Therefore, the traditional method mainly focuses on several vehicles running in a limited area and in a short time. In metropolitan areas, the temporal and spatial characteristics of vehicle emission patterns with different real-time passenger volumes and locations are still unclear to a great extent.

Handbook of Mobility Data Mining, Volume 3
ISBN: 978-0-323-95892-9
https://doi.org/10.1016/B978-0-323-95892-9.00004-8

Mobility data mining technology is becoming an emerging and strong decision support tool in the transportation area in recent years. The emission behavior of urban roads can be identified by leveraging types of mobility data. Vehicle trajectory data is one of the mobility data involving in traffic prediction. In the urban area, a large number of public vehicles (such as taxis and buses) are equipped with GPS, and their status can be reported regularly, including current position, driving speed, direction, etc. These data show vehicle trajectories that contain measurements of road traffic conditions. GPS data have been adopted in many studies to support empirical analyses for emerging transportation modes and show their superiorities in accuracy and practicability [8].

This paper aims to provide a guideline for employing mobility data in analyzing urban road emissions. We show four case studies on the following topics: different emission behavior of ride-hailing and taxi; potential changes in bus emissions caused by reducing passenger volume; emission behavior of particulate matter produced by vehicle braking; and the relationship between travel attraction and urban vehicle emissions.

The remainder of the paper is organized as follows: Section 2 provides an overview of the related work of this research. Section 3 introduces the datasets, and the analysis approaches are described. Empirical results and discussions are given, and we discuss our findings in this section. Finally, Section 4 provides the conclusion of this study.

2. Literature review

Thanks to the popularity of ubiquitous sensing and Intelligent Transportation Systems in recent years, we can gather unprecedented mobility data by exploiting a variety of mobile devices (e.g., smartphones and onboard GPS devices) and automatic fare collection devices widely deployed by urban transit systems (e.g., subways, buses, and taxis). Mobility data are highly related to urban road emission, and thus GPS trajectory data of the vehicle is used to study urban road emission in various ways.

Caulfield [9] estimated the environmental benefits of traditional ride-sharing in Dublin based on the 2006 Census of Ireland and found that 12,674t of CO_2 emissions were saved by individual ride-sharing. Martin and Shaheen [10] surveyed a sample of 6281 households around North America and found that car-sharing can reduce GHG emissions. Since data were observed from surveys and Censuses, the above literature cannot fully investigate the emission patterns of private car-sharing and taxis. Li et al.

[11] studied how ride-sharing services affected traffic congestion and carbon emissions. However, influencing mechanisms of private car-hailing on emissions had not been studied. In addition, since study data came from Uber, whether the emission patterns of Uber are similar to China is worth a further investigation. Ma et al. [12] used Didi's regional network car Hailing data to study travel characteristics and evaluate environmental impact. Spatial heterogeneity and travel characteristics. Different from their study, 1 month GPS trajectory datasets of Didi Chuxing vehicles and taxis in Chengdu, China are adopted to explore the mechanism behind their difference and provide suggestions to improve and upgrade traditional taxi efficiency in terms of fuel consumption (FC) and emissions.

The existing research on the emissions of transit buses focuses on estimating bus emissions and understanding their relationship with driving operation (speed [13], acceleration/deceleration [14], road, air conditioner on/off [15,16]), fuel types (conventional diesel, compressed natural gas, liquefied natural gas, and electricity [17]). However, most literature studied emissions at a microlevel, that is, bus, route, and corridor level. Emissions across a network of 200 bus lines in the city of Montreal, Canada, were studied [18]. However, ridership data used in their study were simulated, which cannot reveal real passenger load. Spatio-temporal characteristics of bus emissions in combination with real ridership during different periods and locations at a metropolitan-wide scale remain uncovered. With the negative impact of COVID-19, potential ridership reduction poses a significant challenge to the decarburization capacity of buses. Existing studies emphasize the estimation of emissions and analysis of influencing factors based on limited bus data sets but do not discuss the impact of potential passenger reduction caused by personal travel behavior changes in the future after COVID-19 on bus emission reduction capacity.

Among the various emissions of traffic sections, braking behavior emissions have not been fully studied by estimating the CO_2 emissions in real-time using inertial information gathered from mobile phone sensors. Partheeban et al. [19] monitored vehicular emission using internet GIS, GPS, and sensors data. Gately et al. [20] quantified vehicle congestion and air pollution emissions using mobile phone GPS data. Zhang et al. [21] proposed a bike-sharing layout optimization and emission reduction potential analysis structure based on smartphone GPS data. In addition, there is also some research focusing on GPS-based braking event detection. Dang et al. [22] proposed a method to estimate incident locations that interfered with smooth driving by using smartphones, but the method just works for the cases of vehicle stops. Dang et al. [23] proposed a model which can detect the location of sudden braking for vehicle stop and nonstop based on vehicle speed, the movement distance, and GPS locations, but this model can only work in incident cases. The previous studies analyzed the emission behavior and braking from many aspects. Some strengthened our understanding of brake-wearing emission impact. Some proposed good suggestions for determining the factors which influence the emission from braking behavior and evaluating methods. Some gave us inspiration for estimating emission performance on an urban scale with urban computing. However, there is no direct evidence of the impact of the on-road braking events on on-road transportation emissions. Only a few studies evaluate the emission from braking behavior on a large urban scale. Under the precondition that on-road driving events can be detected by GPS trajectory [24], the emission performance of braking behavior based on specific records of individual trajectories of large urban scales can be studied further.

The construction of transportation infrastructure is closely related to traffic behavior. Many studies focus on the construction environment and transportation sustainability. Dorina et al. [25] reviewed the potential impacts of sustainable transportation infrastructures from the road and public transportation in developing countries and revealed the significance of sustainable transportation infrastructures in small and medium-sized cities. The system dynamics model was applied to analyze the impact of various transport policies on the urban scale [1] and the future scenarios was used to monitor sustainable indicators as well as to determine effective urban transport policies. Subsequently, Mansourianfara et al. [26] modeled urban street networks by using Trans Cad 5.0 software and selected three dimensions (environmental, social, and economic) related to urban transport to evaluate the sustainability of urban transport infrastructure projects. Despite that the studies on urban transportation infrastructures have provided a lot of decision support for the transportation policy, there are still less involved in urban development and resource allocation. In this study, the unbalance between urban development and transportation facilities development is proposed to be investigated through the travel attraction, and their internal relations are further explored on a microscale.

The conventional solutions cannot provide us with a sufficient understanding of urban traffics in real time. Besides, existing solutions often suffer from biased coverage or inaccurate samplings and may incur huge labor costs. The studies mentioned above are mainly focus on the interaction between urban development and transportation on a relatively macroscale, which are heavily constrained by the feasibility of the scale and corresponding data operability. In the urban cities, a large number of public vehicles (e.g., taxis and buses) have been equipped with GPS devices and thus can periodically report their status, including Driver ID, Order ID, Timestamp, Longitude, and Latitude, etc. This paper shows four examples of using vehicle GPS trajectory data to analyze the urban road emissions.

3. Case studies

This section presents four case studies on emission behavior analysis of urban road transportation based on GPS data, which provide references for mobile data mining technology in urban road emissions.

3.1 Case A: comparison between ride-hailing and taxi

Case A is summarized from the research conducted by Sui et al. [27]. This case investigates the travel mode differences between online car-hailing and traditional taxis based on GPS trajectory. The differences in FC and emission between the two travel modes are further studied.

3.1.1 Descriptions of the case study

Chengdu is taken as an example, which is the capital of Sichuan province in Southwest China. The population density in five central districts, Jinjiang, Qingyang, Jinniu, Wuhou, and Chenghua, reaches about 8460 persons per km^2 [28].

The taxi trajectories dataset of November 2016 in Chengdu was adopted, which is provided by Qingdao Hisense Network Technology Co., Ltd., covering about 13 1000 taxis in Chengdu, and the timestamp is automatically collected at an average time interval of the 30 s. The Didi Chuxing dataset is provided by Didi Chuxing GAIA Initiative. In this study, the trajectories data and order data of express vehicles are adopted. The trajectories data is sampled at a time interval of 3s. After preprocessing steps, there are average around 71,000 taxi vehicles with 0.3 million trips and 231,000 Didi vehicles with 0.1 million trips remaining each day. In addition, the statistical features of weekdays are very similar. For obtaining higher statistical power, this study only focuses on handling weekday datasets in this paper.

3.1.2 Results

Emissions are determined based on the COPERT model (Computer Program to calculate the Emissions from Road Transport), which can calculate the emissions of different pollutants (CO, NO$_x$, HC, PM, etc.) and FC by adopting regression analysis of speeds and traveling distance of vehicles. FC and emissions are divided into two parts: one from the idle trace and the other one from the delivery trace.

Fig. 8.1 shows the median FC and emissions per taxi trip and Didi trip. It can be observed that the Didi trip's FC and emissions from the idle trace are lower than the taxi trip, whereas those from the delivery trace are higher than the taxi trip. According to the COPART model, FC and emissions

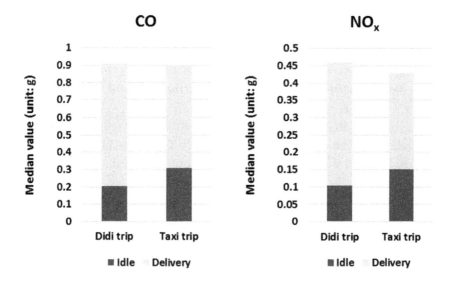

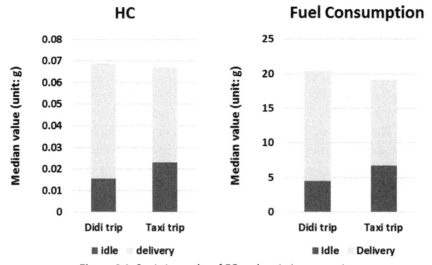

Figure 8.1 Statistic results of FC and emissions per trip.

are associated with velocity and traveling distance. Didi trip contributes to lowering FC and emissions from the idle trace, while the longer delivery distance of the Didi trip leads to more FC and emissions from delivery traces. Overall, Didi idle trip's CO, NOx, HC, and FC account for around 22.60%, 22.46%, 22.48%, 22.08% of its total emissions, and FC. These indicate that short idle distance plays an important role in saving FC and reducing emissions from the idle trace.

Fig. 8.2 illustrates the distributions of passengers on FC and emissions. It can be observed that the median R_{CO}, R_{NOX}, R_{HC}, and R_{FC} of Didi trips are much smaller than those of taxi trips. This study uses the Kruskal−Wallis

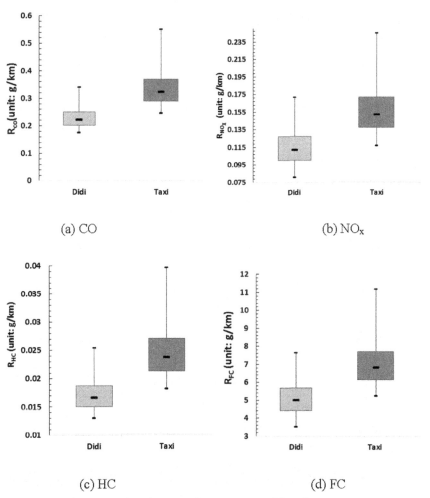

(a) CO   (b) NO$_x$

(c) HC   (d) FC

Figure 8.2 Distributions of passenger-on FC and emissions.

test to confirm that there is a statistically significant difference between Didi travel and taxi travel. Results show that the median R_{CO}, R_{NOX}, R_{HC}, and R_{FC} of Didi trips present a significant difference from those of taxi trips, in which *P*-values are much less than the significance level of 0.05. The results suggest that, in contrast with taxi mode, the online ride-hailing mode has the advantage of saving fuel and reducing emissions sourced from empty cruising.

3.2 Case B: emission potential analysis of urban transit buses post-COVID-19

Case B is based on the work by Sui et al. [29], which investigates the spatial and temporal emission characteristics of buses in Qingdao using GPS trajectory data and smart card passenger flow data. The focus is put on the post-COVID-19.

3.2.1 Descriptions of the case study

Qingdao is a city located in the east coast of China. The downtown area owns a high population, in which peak population density reaches 18,153.95/km^2 in the Shinan district. The population density of the study area decreases from south to north, implying various ridership in spatial range. Therefore, the city is suitable for this study.

2056 CNG buses from 278 routes with an average of 1.5 million passengers' trip data and 7589 taxis with 0.2 million passengers' trip data per day in Qingdao was adopted in this study to investigate the patio-temporal emissions characteristics of buses. Results of this case are regarded as the normal case before COVID-19. Based on that, 224 online survey data are used to study potential ridership reduction in the post-COVID-19 future, and several comparative analyses are given to explore emission benefits change of buses between the normal case and the post-COVID- 19 case.

GPS trajectory data of buses and taxis and Smart Card data of buses used in this study were collected from March 14, 2017 (Tuesday) to March 18, 2017 (Saturday). GPS trajectory data and Smart Card data of buses are provided by Qingdao Public Transport Group. GPS sensors record real-time trajectory information at an average time interval of the 30s. Taxi trajectories data is provided by Qingdao Hisense Network Technology Co., Ltd., covering a total of 8513 taxis in the study area. Information on each taxicab's driver ID, longitude, latitude, status (i.e., 'occupied' or 'vacant'), speed, and timestamp is automatically collected at an average time interval of the 30s. In this study, taxi trips with passengers occupied are used to represent passenger car trips, and idle trips with no passengers are omitted. Considering the real driving condition of buses, unreasonable records of buses are filtered out. Unreasonable trips by taxis are also removed [27]. For obtaining higher statistical power, this study focuses on handling the weekday dataset.

3.2.2 Methodology

The framework of the methodology is shown in Fig. 8.3.

The departure destination (OD) travel of passengers is inferred by using GPS track data, bus smart card passenger volume data, and line GIS information. The OD inference method was proposed in the previous work [30,31]. After this step, the real-time passenger volume of each bus can be obtained. Based on the emission model, the per capita emission of buses per kilometer is calculated. The temporal and spatial emission characteristics of the overall urban route and each route are analyzed by a power law and normalized entropy. To understand the emission benefits of buses, this study use taxi trips with passengers to represent passenger car trips and compares their emission differences with buses. In addition, Tencent survey collected 224 complete social surveys on changes in personal travel behavior after the 2019 coronavirus disease. Based on these investigations, the normal cases and the -post-COVID-19 cases were compared and analyzed. The emission changes that may reduce the number of passengers and the impact on buses was discussed by calculating the exhaust CO_2 emissions of buses and cars.

3.2.3 Results

The spatial distribution of per capita CO_2 emissions per kilometer around the city is shown in Fig. 8.4. The results show that during peak hours (7:00−8:59 and 17:00−18:59), most bus lines are related to low emissions,

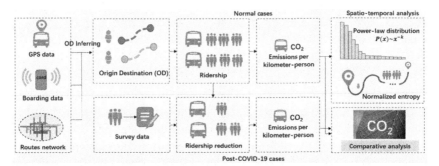

Figure 8.3 Analysis framework of spatio-temporal emission patterns of buses and potential emission changes affected by COVID-19.

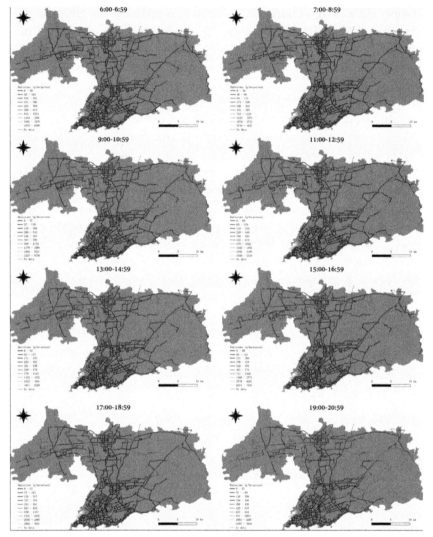

Figure 8.4 Spatial distribution of per kilometer-person CO2s (for interpretation of the references to color in this figure legend, the reader is referred to Ref. [29]).

while few bus lines are related to high emissions in the suburbs (Jiaozhou Bay North Park, Qingdao high tech Zone). During off-peak hours, the number of bus lines with high per capita carbon dioxide emissions per kilometer will increase. Unbalanced distribution of per capita carbon dioxide emissions per kilometer after 19:00. The difference in emissions between the north and the south is due to the heterogeneous spatial characteristics of passengers around the city. This finding shows that investing in bus lines with low travel demand has little help in reducing per capita carbon dioxide emissions per kilometer.

As shown in Fig. 8.5, when the number of passengers is reduced by 40%, 50%, or 60%, the bus may be as polluted as the car or even produce more emissions than the car, which indicates that the emission benefit of the bus after COVID-19 may be uncertain. To illustrate which route connections emit more than taxis when passenger volume decreases, Fig. 8.6 gives a simple comparison between peak and off-peak hours. The number of passengers on buses will be reduced by 10%–50%. During off-peak hours, more links related to high emissions can be observed, and links with emissions higher than the median taxi emissions are concentrated in the suburbs (north of the map).

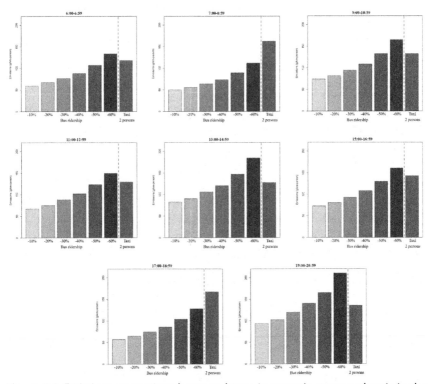

Figure 8.5 Emissions comparison between buses in scenario cases and taxis in the normal case.

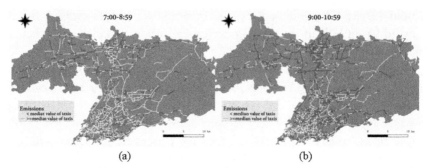

Figure 8.6 Spatial distribution comparison of emissions between buses with ridership reduced by 50% and taxis in normal case. (A) Morning rush hours; (B) Nonrush period.

3.3 Case C: spatio-temporal analysis on on-road braking emission

Based on a large number of GPS track records at short time intervals in Tokyo, a comprehensive spatio-temporal analysis of the emission performance of braking behavior is carried out. This case is based on the previous study by Chen et al. [32].

3.3.1 Descriptions of the case study

This study uses a large number of vehicle trajectories at short intervals in Tokyo as a database to compute the number of PM emissions and give an analysis of the emission behavior of on-road braking events. The vehicle type is distinguished by light-duty vehicles (LDV) and heavy-duty vehicles (HDV). The original track contains 2,342,331 GPS points in 24,846 original track records. This data set was collected in October 2015 by a navigation application called NAVITIME. The average driving distance of each trajectory is 6.02 km. The time interval of two neighboring GPS point records is 1 s. Due to the bad connection of cell phones to the internet during the driving procedure, there are large record vacancies, where the time interval between the latter GPS record and the former one is very large. In these vacancies, it is very hard to determine the exact location as well as the acceleration and deceleration situation of the vehicle. Thus, this situation is ignored in this study.

3.3.2 Methodology

The research framework of this study is shown in Fig. 8.7.

The framework consists of three parts: (1) extraction of on-road driving events from raw trajectory data. It includes road network topology, map

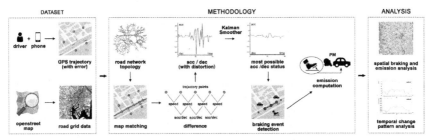

Figure 8.7 The framework used in this case.

matching, and Kalman Smoothing; (2) detection of on-road braking event from driving event as well as driving distance during the braking event; and (3) computation of particle matter emission from the driving distance during the braking event.

Firstly, the road grid data from the open street map is downloaded, and the road network topology is carried out to provide the logical connection and geographical location of the road grid. Then, the map matching algorithm is applied to the original trajectory data and matched with the road network. To solve the problem that the deceleration information in the matching trajectory is always distorted, this case chooses to use Kalman smoothing method to optimize the calculation of road deceleration change mode.

Secondly, we use a reliable indicator to detect road braking events from driving events [33]. According to the braking event detection index, we found 729,743 braking events from all matched vehicles trajectories of 24,846 independent navigation identities. At the same time, by determining the braking interval on the GPS track, the driving distance during the braking event can also be determined.

Lastly, the driving distance in the braking process is linked with the particulate emission in the braking process. The emission coefficient is taken as one of the main calculation tools for particulate emission.

3.3.3 Results

Results of the map matching track is shown in Fig. 8.8. As can be seen from the figure, the driving track is mainly located in hot areas and downtown, such as Tokyo Station, Ikebukuro, Shinjuku, and some expressways. These areas are hot and crowded business centers with heavy traffic, which means that these areas are usually plagued by serious traffic-related emissions.

(a) All matched trajectory records

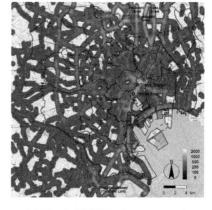

(b) Matched LDV trajectory records   (c) Matched HDV trajectory records

Figure 8.8 (A) The spatial distribution of trajectory records (B) LDV trajectory records (C) HDV trajectory records.

The braking behavior is investigated from two aspects: space and time mode. The spatial pattern analysis will focus on the spatial distribution of road braking events. The spatial distribution of all braking events is shown in Fig. 8.9. Braking incidents usually occur in the city center, crowded areas, and main highways, such as the Shibuya line, Shinjuku line, and Ikebukuro line. These roads connect the crowded commercial center with the outside world and play an important role in the busy traffic roads. These sections are also common areas of braking and high traffic emissions.

The distribution of braking events is different, and so does the distribution of emissions. The PM10 emission distribution of each track is shown in

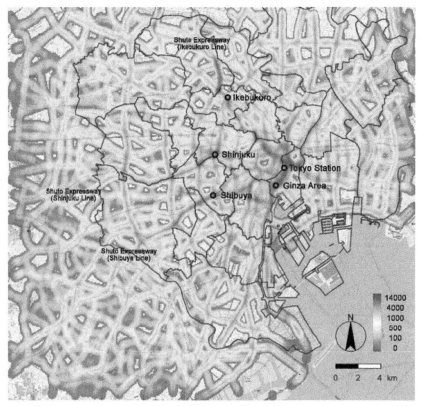

Figure 8.9 The spatial distribution of braking events.

Fig. 8.10. In the four regions, the emission of each vehicle is close, and only in a few cases the emission is very high. Generally speaking, in four crowded areas, the braking emission is at least 1.99 mg and at most 4.91 mg. The average value is 3.50 mg. Compared with the result that the average PM10 emission of each track in the whole study area is 14.09 mg, the average PM10 emission of the four crowded areas accounts for 24.84% of the average PM10 emission of the whole study area. However, these four areas account for only 1.67% of the total study area.

The time pattern within 2 days is shown in Fig. 8.11. From the figure, we can see that the time change pattern between weekdays and weekends is completely different. On weekdays, brake emissions and traffic volumes remain high during the day but low at night and late at night. The total amount of braking emissions on weekends is less than that on weekdays, and the variation law remains at a stable level during the active period of the city. PM 10 emissions from braking events remain at a certain value.

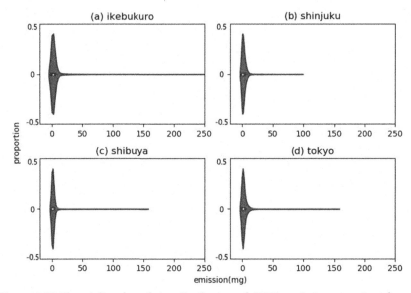

Figure 8.10 The violin plot of the distribution of PM10 emission quantity of each trajectory.

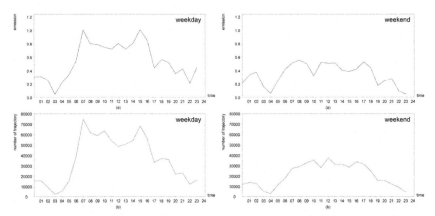

Figure 8.11 The temporal change of emission and quantity of trajectory record in the study area (unit: kg).

3.4 Case D: travel attraction and urban vehicle emissions in Japan

The application of GPS data to urban event analysis, travel mode detection, and traffic emissions helps to understand urban activities and human mobility [27,34] and serves as a reference for measuring vehicle emissions in Tokyo. This case is based on the study carried out by Song et al. [35].

3.4.1 Descriptions of the case study

Tokyo is an international city with a high population density and highly developed transportation. It is also one of the most representative cities with coordinated development of urban function and transportation [36]. In 2014, the proportion of built-up areas occupied by roads in the Tokyo expansion area was 25%, higher than the world average.

Ebisu situated in Shibuya, western Tokyo, is selected as the study case, as shown in Fig. 8.12. This region has outperformed other places with extremely top popularity almost every year since 2016. In this study, 15—45 min were set to represent the potential long trip demands according to the average travel time in Tokyo.

In this case, an indicator of potential traffic attraction (PTA) is proposed to measure the performance of urban sustainable development and generate the correlation between traffic attraction and high emission traffic through GPS trajectory, to ensure the reliability of high emission travel mode in the correlation model. According to the obtained urban sustainable development performance, this study analyzes the development status of Ebisu and determines which areas have the potential for further sustainable redevelopment.

3.4.2 Methodology

As shown in Fig. 8.13, the method concerns four steps. Firstly, the study area shed is identified by the road network. Secondly, a metric named PTA is proposed to measure the urban sustainable performance based on the

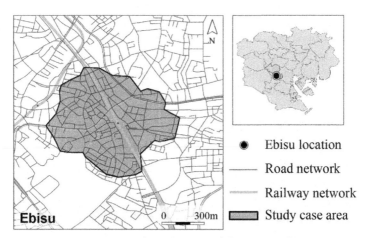

Figure 8.12 Selected region of the case study.

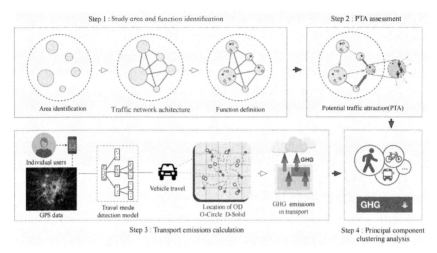

Figure 8.13 The research framework of this case study.

improved gravitational model. Then, the trajectories of vehicle traffic are detected and extracted using an emission model. After that, the principal component of the impact on vehicle emission is confirmed by the correlation analysis. Finally, a cluster analysis of the PTA is proposed to identify the status of the integrated development. Although the selection criteria of the central activities zones (CAZs) could vary according to the development state of each city, the procedure mentioned above could be a general technique and apply to various cities.

3.4.3 Results
The GPS data as a reference are used for measuring vehicle emissions rather than measurement data, which ensures the credibility of the high emission driving mode of the relevant model. Three gases: CO, NO_x, and HC [27] are selected and calculated in three aspects with the covert model, namely, invalid emission proportion, invalid emission, total emission, and other results.

The spatial distribution, which represents the GHG emissions from vehicular travel at the ward level, is presented in Fig. 8.14. In general, emissions increase gradually as the CAZs network radiates outward from the Tokyo, and the highest emission wards are Kita and Ota, located separately in the north and south of Tokyo. The wards with a high density of CAZs network (such as Taito, Chuo, and Minato) possess lower emissions surrounding the center. In reality, these wards are supporting much more urban

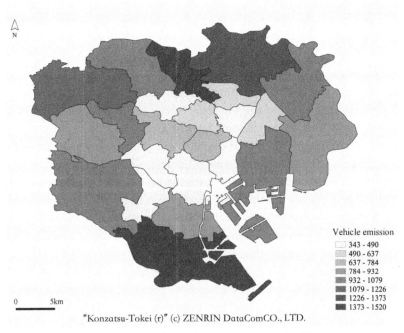

"Konzatsu-Tokei (r)" (c) ZENRIN DataComCO., LTD.

Figure 8.14 Vehicular emission in each ward of Tokyo.

activities than the wards with high emissions. Especially, different from the above low-emission wards which are situated adjacently and consecutively, Toshima is surrounded by the wards which have significantly increased emissions. It reveals that the difference in vehicle emissions among Toshima and its adjacent wards might be caused by the distinction of urban development levels.

4. Conclusion

Under the pressure of global climate change, how to reduce urban road transportation emissions is becoming a research interest. The use of data mining technology has greatly enriched the research on the temporal and spatial patterns of emissions from the transportation sector and can reveal the pollutant emissions in different periods and places in the metropolitan area. In this study, we have mainly summarized four cases to provide guidelines for stakeholders in related fields.

In case A, 1-month GPS trajectory and order data set of Chengdu taxi and Didi travel in China are used to identify whether there are significant differences in FC and emission patterns between taxis and ride-hailing. This study shows that compared with the taxi mode, the online taxi model has great advantages in reducing FC passengers and emissions.

Case B proposes a methodological framework to study the spatio-temporal emission characteristics of buses and analyzes the potential changes in bus emissions caused by reducing the number of passengers. Based on the bus trajectory data of Qingdao, the results show that buses cannot travel in a "greener" way than private cars in the post-COVID-19.

Case C attempts to uncover the particulate emission behavior from road braking events through data mining of large-scale vehicle trajectory data. This study detected 713,676 braking events on 24,846 vehicle trajectories in Tokyo. It is found that braking events usually occurr in urban central areas, densely populated areas, and highway trunk roads. From the time change of braking events and emissions, the total amount of braking events and emissions on working days is greater than that on weekends.

Case D proposes a performance evaluation model of urban sustainable development to reveal the relationship between potential travel attractions and urban vehicle emissions, and the Tokyo, Japan is taken as the research area. Results show that from the central area outward, the regional vehicle emissions increase radially.

References

[1] N.B. Grimm, S.H. Faeth, N.E. Golubiewski, C.L. Redman, J.G. Wu, X.M. Bai, et al., Global change and the ecology of cities, Science 319 (5864) (2008) 756−760.

[2] P. Pant, R.M. Harrison, Estimation of the contribution of road traffic emissions to particulate matter concentrations from field measurements: a review, Atmospheric Environment 77 (Oct) (2013) 78−97.

[3] IEA, CO2 Emissions Statistics, 2018.

[4] E.E. Agency, National Emissions Reported to the Convention on Long-Range Transboundary Air Pollution, LRTAP Convention, 2018.

[5] M. Kousoulidou, L. Ntziachristos, G. Mellios, Z. Samaras, Road-transport emission projections to 2020 in European urban environments, Atmospheric Environment 42 (32) (2008) 7465−7475.

[6] H. Wang, C. Chen, H. Cheng, L. Fu, On-road vehicle emission inventory and its uncertainty analysis for Shanghai, China, Science of the Total Environment 398 (1−3) (2008) 60−67.

[7] X. Shan, X. Chen, W. Jia, J. Ye, Evaluating urban bus emission characteristics based on localized MOVES using sparse GPS data in shanghai, China, Sustainability 11 (2019).

[8] H. Zhang, X. Song, T. Xia, et al., Battery electric vehicles in Japan: human mobile behavior based adoption potential analysis and policy target response, Applied Energy 220 (2018) 527−535.

[9] B. Caulfield, Estimating the environmental benefits of ride-sharing: a case study of Dublin, Transportation Research Part D-Transport and Environment 14 (7) (2009) 527−531.

[10] E.W. Martin, S.A. Shaheen, Greenhouse gas emission impacts of carsharing in North America, Ieee Transactions on Intelligent Transportation Systems 12 (4) (2011) 1074−1086.

[11] Z. Li, Y. Hong, Z. Zhang, Do On-Demand Ride-Sharing Services Affect Traffic Congestion? Evidence from Uber Entry, Social Science Electronic Publishing, 2016.

[12] Y. Ma, B. Yu, M. Xue, Spatial heterogeneous characteristics of ridesharing in Beijing-Tianjin-Hebei region of China, Energies 11 (11) (2018).

[13] A. Wang, Y. Ge, J. Tan, M. Fu, A.N. Shah, Y. Ding, et al., On-road pollutant emission and fuel consumption characteristics of buses in Beijing, Journal of Environmental Sciences 23 (3) (2011) 419−426.

[14] H. Zhai, H.C. Frey, N.M. Rouphail, A vehicle-specific power approach to speed- and facility-specific emissions estimates for diesel transit buses, Environmental Science & Technology 42 (21) (2008) 7985.

[15] S. Zhang, W. Ye, J. Hu, R. Huang, Z. Yu, X. Bao, et al., Can Euro V heavy-duty diesel engines, diesel hybrid and alternative fuel technologies mitigate NOX emissions? New evidence from on-road tests of buses in China, Applied Energy 132 (nov.1) (2014) 118−126.

[16] A. Hy, A. Ml, A. Jl, L.A. Yu, L.A. He, B. Km, Real-road NOx emission and fuel consumption characteristics of China IV public transit buses, Energy Procedia 158 (2019) 4623−4628.

[17] M. Hatzopoulou, A. Alam, Investigating the Isolated and Combined Effects of Congestion, Roadway Grade, Passenger Load, and Alternative Fuels on Transit Bus Emissions, Transportation research, Part D Transport and environment, 2014.

[18] Waraich AS, Anowar S, Tenaglia T, Sider T, Eluru N. Disaggregate Level Simulation of Bus Transit Emissions in a Large Urban Region. Conference Disaggregate Level Simulation of Bus Transit Emissions in a Large Urban Region.

[19] P. Partheeban, R.R. Hemamalini, H.P. Raju, Vehicular Emission Monitoring Using Internet GIS, GPS and Sensors, 2012.

[20] C.K. Gately, L.R. Hutyra, S. Peterson, I.S. Wing, Urban emissions hotspots: quantifying vehicle congestion and air pollution using mobile phone GPS data, Environmental Pollution 229 (oct) (2017) 496−504.

[21] H. Zhang, X. Song, T. Xi, J. Zheng, D. Haung, R. Shibasaki, et al., MaaS in bike-sharing: smart phone GPS data based layout optimization and emission reduction potential analysis, in: Conference MaaS in Bike-Sharing: Smart Phone GPS Data Based Layout Optimization and Emission Reduction Potential Analysis, Shanghai, PEOPLES R CHINA vol. 152, 2018, pp. 649−654.

[22] V.C. Dang, M. Kubo, H. Sato, T. Shirakawa, A. Namatame, Occupancy grid map of semi-static objects by mobile observer, Artificial Life and Robotics 20 (1) (2015) 7−12.

[23] Dang VC, Kubo M, Sato H, Yamaguchi A, Namatame A. A Simple Braking Model for Detecting Incidents Locations by Smartphones. Conference A Simple Braking Model for Detecting Incidents Locations by Smartphones.

[24] Q. He, K.L. Head, Pseudo-Lane-Level, Low-Cost GPS Positioning with Vehicle-To-Infrastructure Communication and Driving Event Detection, 2010.

[25] P. Dorina, S. Dominic, Sustainable urban transport in the developing world: beyond megacities, Sustainability 7 (7) (2015) 7784−7805.

[26] M.H. Mansourianfara, H. Haghshenasb, Micro-scale sustainability assessment of infrastructure projects on urban transportation systems: case study of Azadi district, Isfahan, Iran, Cities 72 (2018) 149−159.

[27] Y. Sui, H. Zhang, X. Song, F. Shao, X. Yu, R. Shibasaki, et al., GPS data in urban online ride-hailing: a comparative analysis on fuel consumption and emissions, Journal of Cleaner Production 227 (2019) 495−505.

[28] C. SBo, Chengdu Statistical Yearbook, 2018.

[29] Y. Sui, H. Zhang, W. Shang, R. Sun, C. Wang, J. Ji, et al., Mining urban sustainable performance: spatio-temporal emission potential changes of urban transit buses in post-COVID-19 future, Applied Energy 280 (2020) 115966.

[30] Yu X, Shao F, Sun R, Sui Y. Boarding stations inferring based on bus GPS and IC data. Conference Boarding Stations Inferring Based on Bus GPS and IC Data.

[31] Y. Sui, F. Shao, X. Yu, R. Sun, S. Li, Public transport network model based on layer operations, Physica A: Statistical Mechanics and Its Applications 523 (2019) 984—995.

[32] J. Chen, W. Li, H. Zhang, W. Jiang, W. Li, Y. Sui, et al., Mining urban sustainable performance: GPS data-based spatio-temporal analysis on on-road braking emission, Journal of Cleaner Production 270 (2020) 122489.

[33] Mohan P, Padmanabhan VN, Ramjee R. Nericell: rich monitoring of road and traffic conditions using mobile smartphones. Conference Nericell: Rich Monitoring of Road and Traffic Conditions Using Mobile Smartphones.

[34] H. Zhang, M. Yuan, Y. Liang, B. Wang, W. Zhang, J. Zheng, A risk assessment based optimization method for route selection of hazardous liquid railway network, Safety Science 110 (2018) 217—229.

[35] X. Song, R. Guo, T. Xia, Z. Guo, Y. Long, H. Zhang, et al., Mining urban sustainable performance: millions of GPS data reveal high-emission travel attraction in Tokyo, Journal of Cleaner Production 242 (2020) 118396.

[36] P. Chorus, L. Bertolini, An application of the node-place model to explore the spatial development dynamics of station areas in Tokyo, Journal of Transport & Land Use 4 (1) (2011) 45—58.

CHAPTER NINE

Living environment inequity analyses based on mobile phone big data

Chen Zhiheng
Center for Spatial Information Science, The University of Tokyo, Kashiwa-shi, Chiba, Japan

1. Introduction
1.1 Background
1.1.1 Environmental justice

Environmental justice (EJ) means that no one, regardless of race, nationality, income, age, or gender, should bear a disproportionate share of the negative environmental consequences [1]. Since the concept of EJ was proposed in the 1980s, scholars have conducted a lot of EJ research and expanded its content. The initial research focused on the unequal exposure of ethnic minorities and people with low socioeconomic status to toxic pollution [2–5]. Then the field was extended to other types of pollution and environmental disasters, including air pollution [6–10], noise exposure [11], and flooding [12]. In the past 10 years, researchers have expanded the scope of EJ by exploring the convenience of access to environmental resources and the social injustices exposed to a wider range of environmental disasters. In terms of environmental convenience, the researchers analyzed the social inequity of the accessibility of green spaces and beaches [13,14]. In terms of environmental disasters, research has found that ethnic minorities and people with low socioeconomic status are related to higher urban high-temperature exposure [15,16].

1.1.2 Artificial light at night

Excessive artificial light at night (ALAN) is one of the fastest-growing and most common hazards [17,18]. A study of satellite imagery by Ref. [19] shows that 83% of the world's population lives under light-polluted skies. Several recent studies at the individual and group levels have revealed a statistical association between some human diseases and ALAN exposure. Most

Handbook of Mobility Data Mining, Volume 3
ISBN: 978-0-323-95892-9
https://doi.org/10.1016/B978-0-323-95892-9.00001-2

of these studies have used the Defense Meteorological Satellite Program (DMSP) imagery or the Visible Infrared Imaging Radiometer Suite (VIIRS) Day/Night band (DNB) imagery to measure ALAN [20,21]. (using DMSP imagery) found that women exposed to higher levels of ALAN had an increased risk of breast cancer [22]. (using VIIRS imagery) found that exposure to ALAN during adolescence may contribute to a higher risk of atopic diseases in young adulthood through a study of Chinese college students. Other studies have also revealed associations between ALAN and non-Hodgkin lymphoma [23], sleep disturbances [24], depression [25], and obesity [26]. Notably, this association may not be linear [27]. found that when air pollution was taken into account, the significant association between ALAN and mental health was not observed anymore.

1.1.3 TOD usage in the context of aging
Transit-oriented development (TOD) is an urban development strategy that aims at developing multiple land use functions such as residential, working, and space for daily activities within the catchment area of public transit [28]. Typical TOD models include two characteristics, namely, efficient and accessible transportation services and the potential for users to obtain various land functions.

Tokyo is one of the cities most reliant on public transportation [29]. Although TOD was first proposed and implemented in the United States and European countries, Japan began to advocate the development of a combination of public transportation systems and land use [30]. After years of development, Tokyo has been regarded as a leading city for TOD practice [31]. However, in recent years, some studies have found that TOD can lead to an unequal phenomenon that is often overlooked. Low-income families and minority families living in the surrounding areas of TOD often face high rents, which makes life extremely difficult [32–36]. The problem that scholars worry about is that although TOD can indeed improve the accessibility of public transportation, reduce transportation costs, improve the environment of community facilities, etc., these benefits may not have a major effect on those who rely on public transportation [37,38]. In a superaging society such as Tokyo, whether the elderly as an EJ population [39,40] can obtain equal transportation and livable opportunities as other population is an issue that cannot be ignored. Due to the differences in characteristics between TODs, it is difficult to formulate and implement policies to optimize the inequity of TOD usage without understanding the current status of TODs [41]. Therefore, quantitative assessment and classification of TOD station levels based on land use, transportation supply, and user attributes are particularly important for development strategy.

1.2 Literature review
1.2.1 EJ research on ALAN
Despite the evidence that ALAN may be harmful to human health, there are few studies on the inequity of ALAN exposure in the field of EJ so far. Until 2020 [5], conducted the first EJ study of unequal exposure to night light pollution in the United States using VIIRS imagery and census data. They found that the population-weighted average light pollution exposure rate in Asian, Hispanic, or black communities was approximately twice that of whites [5]. However, using census data may ignore the mobility of people due to the lack of information on travel behavior [42–48]. Studies have shown that due to the spatial heterogeneity of some pollution, exposure may be incorrectly estimated without considering population mobility [49–52]. Recently [49], used GPS data to estimate the exposure of 5452 people in Montreal, Canada, to NO_2, $PM_{2.5}$, and UFPs at home and on the move. By tracking an individual's daily trajectory and calculating multiple activity locations, misclassifications can be avoided [49,53–55]. In the context of evidence that personal mobility may affect exposure estimates, no studies have been conducted on ALAN exposure and its inequity using trajectory data.

1.2.2 TOD typology and its extension
According to the value of each indicator, different TODs are reflected in a two-dimensional or three-dimensional distribution coordinate map—called TOD typology [30].

The node-place model [41] is the most popular TOD classification method in the literature. The model provides an analytical framework to describe the relationship between transportation (node) and urban development (place). The node-place model distinguishes five typical TOD forms (Fig. 9.1). The first is the "balance" form: transport and land use are coordinated and integrated. The second is the "dependency" form: transportation and land use are both underdeveloped. Conversely, the third category is the "stress" form: both transportation and land use are highly developed. The last category is the "unbalance" form: "unbalance nodes" (transportation far outweighs land use development) and "unbalance places" (land use development far outweighs transportation).

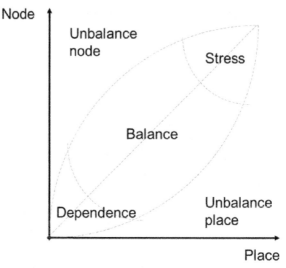

Figure 9.1 Five typical TOD forms.

The node-place model is useful for understanding transportation and land use development in subway station areas; however, it cannot reveal the morphological and functional interrelationships between transportation and land use. Therefore, an improvement to the node-place model in recent years is to add an "oriented" dimension to quantify the degree of interaction between transportation and development [56]. used an extended node-place model to classify TOD into eight categories, including the "integrated" form, "morphologically double-developed" form, and so on.

The essence of TOD is to realize the potential of human interaction in and around public transport nodes [41]. However, there has been little mention of humans or human behavior in previous applications of the node-place model.

According to the above literature, we have proposed the research ideas for this chapter:

For ALAN inequity, based on the quantification results of ALAN in Tokyo, Japan, using remote sensing images combined with mobile phone positioning big data, we analyzed the ALAN exposure and its inequity in different demographic groups. We have explored three questions: (1) How does ALAN exposure differ between individuals and between different population groups in Tokyo? (2) How does travel behavior affect ALAN exposure and inequity? (3) Are there geographic differences in the impact mechanism of travel behavior on ALAN exposure and inequity estimates?

For TOD inequity, we proposed a research framework that correlates TOD performance evaluation and user attributes for evaluating TOD inequity in traffic-oriented, high-density metropolises. We collected user age and built environment information in 36 TOD catchment areas on the Tokyo Yamanote Line using mobile phone positioning data and ground feature data and examined the correlation between them. Afterward, we integrated the user's age attribute into the node-place model, used k-means to classify TOD, and explored the inequity of TOD usage from the aspects of traffic and land use, etc.

2. Framework and dataset

2.1 Framework for ALAN inequity analysis

Fig. 9.2 shows the framework of ALAN inequity analysis. We extracted the average pixel brightness value of the VIIRS imagery in each grid boundary of the mobile phone positioning big data as nighttime light (NTL) intensity. Then we divided the mobile phone location data into two time periods (dynamic and static) for analysis. We first measured individual ALAN exposure inequity in Tokyo at dynamic and static periods separately using the Gini coefficient. Then we calculated and compared the difference between the two periods in average ALAN exposure for demographic groups of different ages and places of residence. Finally, we

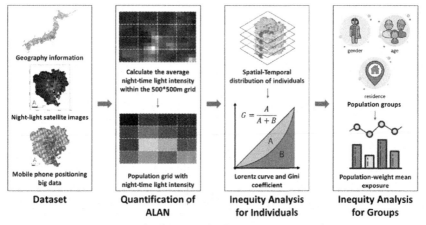

Figure 9.2 The framework of ALAN inequity analysis.

aggregated the grid data to the district level to examine whether there are geographic differences in ALAN exposure inequity and the impact of travel behavior on it.

2.2 Framework for TOD inequity analysis

Shown as in Fig. 9.3 we quantified the various TOD indicators within the defined station catchment area and calculated the average age of users by counting the stay points within the catchment area and using the stay time as the weight. Then we analyzed the correlation between the average age of users and other indicators and analyzed the inequity of TOD from the two dimensions of node value and place value. Finally, using the node value, place value, and average age of users as feature vectors, cluster analysis of stations is carried out, and the relationship between user age and built environment characteristics of different clusters is discussed.

2.3 Case study

The case study of ALAN inequity analysis is the 23 districts of Tokyo, Japan, and the 36 TOD stations and their surrounding area on the Yamanote line are the cases of TOD inequity analysis (Fig. 9.4).

As the largest metropolitan area in the world [57], Tokyo is still bright even at night. In Tokyo, the popularity of light-emitting diode (LED) lighting may cause excessive brightness and glare, which may also become light damage to the environment, people, flora and fauna, and the night sky [58]. Observing the change in the intensity of light emitted to the sky from the

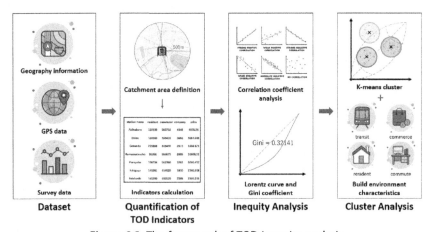

Figure 9.3 The framework of TOD inequity analysis.

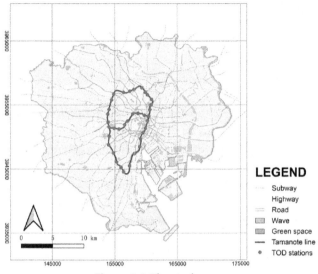

Figure 9.4 The study area.

area (approximately 400 km^2) centered on the Yamanote Line area in Tokyo, it can be seen that it is increasing at an average of 2%—3% per year [58]. As the busiest line in Tokyo, the development around the transit node on the Yamanote Line is a typical TOD strategy.

2.4 Data description

The data used in this study mainly includes three categories: mobile phone positioning big data, night-light satellite imagery, and geographic information data. During processing, we uniformly use an Albers Equal Area Conic Projection with the central meridian 138°E and the standard parallels 34°N and 40°N for spatial layers.

(1) Mobile phone positioning big data: We mainly use Mobaku data coming from Mobaku Inc. The Mobaku data is a dynamic population grid data estimated from location data covering 80 million of the 126 million mobile phone users in Japan [59], which is obtained after the location data of mobile phone users goes through three processing procedures of De-identification, aggregation, and concealment [60]. In addition to hourly population distribution across Japan, Mobaku data also includes demographic information such as age, gender, and place of residence [61]. This chapter selects Mobaku data of Tokyo from 2019/12/01 to 2019/12/07 (7 days of data for December 2019) for research.

As shown in Fig. 9.5, each grid (500m × 500m) contains population of different demographic groups: male/female with age falling into eight groups (>0—15, >15—20, >20—30, >30—40, >40—50, >50—60, >60—70, >70—80) and place of residence (district level). For ALAN exposure analysis, we filtered the data from 6 p.m. to 6 a.m. To explore how travel behavior affects estimates of ALAN exposure and its inequity, we split Mobaku data into two groups by time. The period of the first group is from 18:00 to 24:00, during which time people still travel normally. The second group is from 0:00 to 6:00, during which time most people are resting, and it can be approximately considered that there is no travel behavior.

(2) NPP/VIIRS night-light satellite imagery: The Suomi National Polar-orbiting Partnership (Suomi-NPP) satellite launched in 2011 uses the day-night band (DNB) of the Airborne Visible Infrared Imaging Radiometer Suite (VIIRS) for night imaging technology. Compared with its predecessor Defense Meteorological Satellite Program-Operational Linescan System (DMSP-OLS), DNB has made great progress in radiation accuracy, spatial resolution, and geometric quality [62]; P [63]. The NPP/VIIRS DNB cloud-free composite night light imagery released by NOAA (National Oceanic and Atmospheric Administration) is the most commonly used data type for NPP/VIIRS.

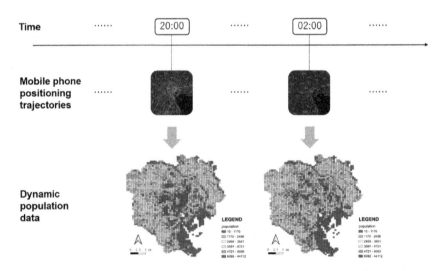

Figure 9.5 Illustration of mobile phone positioning big data (mobile phone enables instant fine-scale population tracking).

These imageries are monthly composite data that have been post-processed to remove clouds and correct for stray light, with a spatial resolution of 15 arc seconds, which is approximately 462.5 m [64]. Each pixel of the satellite imagery records its night-time light (NTL) value of it in $nW/cm^2/sr$. In this chapter, we used the first version of VIIRS Day/Night Band Nighttime Lights of October 2013 as the data source for ALAN.

(3) Geographic information data: This dataset comes from the open geographic data of Open Street Map, the National Land Information Department and the Ministry of Land, Infrastructure, Transport, and Tourism. The administrative area data of Tokyo collected in 2021 is used in ALAN inequity analysis. The raw data uses JGD2011 (EPSG: 6668) as the coordinate reference system, and each polygon contains the code attribute of the administration in which it is located. For TOD study, we counted various ground features in the station catchment area, such as land use, population, etc., as indicators of TOD.

3. Methodology

3.1 Methodology for ALAN inequity analysis

3.1.1 Quantification of NTL intensity

The pixel brightness values of the NPP/VIIRS imagery we used ranged from $3.02 \, nW/cm^2/sr$ to $528.86 \, nW/cm^2/sr$. To measure the NTL intensity of each grid in the dynamic population data, we used ArcGIS to overlay night-light satellite imagery onto the grid boundaries of the Mobaku data. Since the grid size of Mobaku data is not aligned with that of the night-light satellite imagery, using zonal statistics may result in missing output. So we first convert the VIIRS raster imagery to point vector features using the raster to point function. The number of points is the same as the number of cells, and the cell value is inherited. We then calculated the average NTL intensity of all points contained within each grid boundary using the "join the attributes of features by their location" function. Units for the NTL intensity are reported in $nW/cm^2/sr$.

3.1.2 Inequity analysis of population groups

Dynamic population data include the gender and age groups, but the residence information only records the registered residence of the user. To distinguish residents and nonresidents in the grid, we overlayed the administrative boundary data on the grid of dynamic population data and used the join function of ArcGIS to add a location attribute to the grid. We then compared the residence information and location information of the populations in the grid, if they matched, the populations were identified as residents, otherwise as nonresidents. To address our second question, we calculated hourly population-weighted mean exposure to ALAN for each group over two time periods. We first sliced the dynamic population data by hour, multiplying the population of each group $P_{n,i,g}$ within each grid by the NTL intensity L_n. These values within each grid are then summed and divided by the total population for each group in Tokyo. Finally, the hourly population-weighted exposure to ALAN of each group E_g in each time period was obtained by calculating the average ALAN exposure of the group over t hours in the time period. The equation for E_g is as follows:

$$E_g = \frac{1}{t} * \sum_{i=1}^{t} \frac{\sum_n L_n * P_{n,i,g}}{\sum_n P_{n,i,g}}$$

where E_g is the hourly population-weighted exposure to ALAN of a population group; L_n is the NTL intensity in grid n; $P_{n,i,g}$ is the population of group g in grid n in the i hour of a time period; t is the 6 h of a time period.

3.2 Methodology for TOD inequity analysis

3.2.1 TOD indicators

We used a variety of data to measure 13 variables that represent the value of TOD (Table 9.1). Most of the data are summarized within 500 m of the subway station, and the commuting population, residential population, land use, and land price are summarized within 2 km of the subway station. For node value, we measured four indicators related to traffic. Among them, the average daily passenger flow of the station and the number of transfer lines indicate the traffic service level of the station, and the number of bus stops and bicycle parking lots within 500 m indicates the design level around the station.

For place value, we measured the commuting population and residential population within 2 km. Secondly, we counted the number of commercial and entertainment points of interest within 500 m, such as companies, entertainment facilities, restaurants, shopping malls, etc. The value of the land is measured by the average land price, which is expressed by the average land price within 2 km of the station. Land use diversity is measured using

Table 9.1 Variables and definitions.

Dimension	Indicators	Description
Node	Volume	N1-Mean of passenger flow/per day
	Transfer	N2-The number of transfer lines in the target station
	Bus stop	N3-Number of bus stops within 500m
	Bic parking	N4-Number of bicycle parking lots within 500m
Place	Commuter	P1-Number of commuters within 2 km
	Resident	P2-Number of residents within 2 km
	Company	P3-Number of companies within 500m
	Entertainment	P4-Number of entertainment facilities within 500m
	Restaurant	P5-Number of restaurants within 500m
	Shopping_mall	P6-Number of shopping malls within 500m
	Entropy	P7-Land use entropy within 2 km $$E = 1 - \sum_{i=1}^{n} (a_i/A)^2,$$ where a_i represents the area of each type of land, and A is the total land area
	Price	P8-average land price within 2 km
User	Average_age	U1-Average age of users

the following formula of the Simpson Diversity Index, where higher values represent more land-use diversity (values range from 0 to 1):

$$\text{Land use diversity} = 1 - \sum_{i=1}^{n} (a_i/A)^2$$

where a_i represents the area of a certain type of land in the station is the buffer zone, and A is the total area of all types of land in the buffer zone. In this study, referring to the Japanese urban land classification, 12 types of land use were considered.

We use the average age of users to represent the age structure of the station user group. For the average age of users, this study uses data from 23 wards of Tokyo to obtain user information for each station by separating the stay points. In order to distinguish the importance of users, we use the length of stay time as the weight to calculate the weighted average age of the user groups at each station.

After calculating all the indicators, the indicators need to be aggregated into nodes and placed values. Because the numerical difference between different indicators may be very large, we normalized all indicators from 0 to 1 before aggregation. Finally, calculate the average value of each indicator in each dimension as the node and place value.

3.2.2 Inequity analysis: correlation coefficient analysis
In order to investigate whether the resource allocation of TOD is unfair among users of different age groups or not, we first draw a correlation coefficient heat map to see whether there is a correlation between the average age of users and the variable representing the value of TOD. Here we use Pearson's correlation coefficient to express the relationship between variables. The value range of Pearson's correlation coefficient is between -1 and 1. If the correlation coefficient is positive, there is a positive correlation between the variables, and if the correlation coefficient is negative, there is a negative correlation. The larger the absolute value, the stronger the correlation.

$$r(X, Y) = \frac{Cov(X, Y)}{\sqrt{Var[X]\,Var[Y]}}$$

where $Cov(X, Y)$ is the covariance of X and Y, $Var[X]$ is the variance of X, and $Var[Y]$ is the variance of Y.

3.2.3 Validation of inequity: cluster analysis

In order to verify the inequity of the distribution of TOD resources among users of different age groups, and to explore how the inequity is reflected, we conducted a cluster analysis on these stations. We use the three factors of node value, place value, and the average age of users to perform k-means cluster analysis on stations. This part is mainly divided into three steps:

- Step 1: Before clustering, we use the elbow method to select the best number of clusters. The core of the elbow method is SSE (Sum of Squared Errors). As the number of clusters k increases, the sample division will be more refined, and the degree of aggregation of each cluster will gradually increase, so the error squared sum SSE will gradually become smaller. When k is less than the true number of clusters since the increase of k will greatly increase the degree of aggregation of each cluster, the SSE will decrease greatly, and when k reaches the number of true clusters, The return obtained from the aggregation level will decrease rapidly as k increases. So the decline of SSE will decrease sharply, and then it will flatten out as the value of k continues to increase. That is to say, the relationship between SSE and k is in the shape of an elbow, and the k value corresponds to this elbow is the true number of clusters of the data.

- Step 2: Use the selected best k value as the number of clusters of k-means clustering, and classify 36 stations. Here we have selected three factors node value, place value, and the average age of users, so the result will be a three-dimensional clustering. Then we refer to the classic N-P model in TOD classification research, project the clustering results onto the node–place two-dimensional coordinate system, and explore its relationship with five typical TOD types(Unsustained Node, Dependency, Balance, Stress, and Unsustained Place).

- Step 3: Perform index statistics and visualization on the clustering results. In order to explore how the inequity of TOD resource allocation is reflected, we selected seven indicators of commuting population, residential population, commercial index, land use diversity, node value, place value, and the average age of users, and performed the chart visualization and spatial visualization. The commercial index is the average of the three indicators of entertainment facilities, restaurants, and shopping malls. In addition, we also selected 1 or 2 typical stations from each cluster for further discussion.

4. Results

4.1 Result of ALAN inequity analysis

4.1.1 Descriptive analysis

Fig. 9.6 depicts the spatial distribution of ALAN in Tokyo on a 500 × 500m grid. Because the numerical distribution of NTL intensity is not uniform, for visual comparison, we use natural discontinuity (Jenks) classification in QGIS. ALAN is most obvious in the highly urbanized central region. Moreover, the distribution of high-light pollution areas is basically along the subway, with the circular Yamanote line as the center, and radially distributed outward along each line. The brightest areas are also the most densely populated places in the dynamic population data, such as Shinjuku, Ikebukuro, Shibuya, Ginza, and Ueno. These places are often very popular shopping streets, and there are still many people visiting at night. In contrast, ALAN in other areas is not so strong.

4.1.2 ALAN exposure among different age groups

Fig. 9.7 reports the population-weighted mean exposure to ALAN of different age groups in two time periods. It shows that population-weighted mean exposure to ALAN is negatively correlated with the age of the user group, and younger people are exposed to higher intensity of ALAN. During the period from 18:00 to 24:00, the >15−20 years old group has the highest ALAN exposure level, with an average level of 76.6 nW/cm^2/sr per hour; while the >70−80 years old group has the

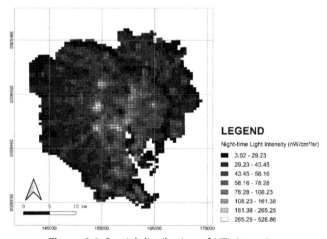

Figure 9.6 Spatial distribution of NTL intensity.

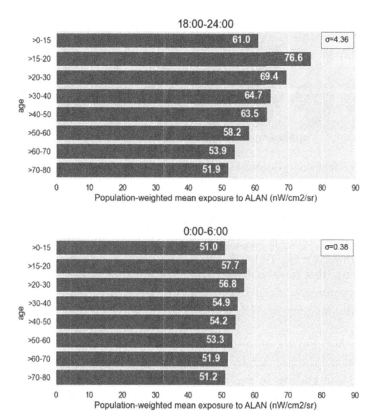

Figure 9.7 Population-weighted mean exposure to ALAN for different age groups in two time periods.

lowest exposure level, with an average level of 51.9 nW/cm²/sr per hour. From >15 to 20 years old to >70– to 80-year-old, as the age increases, the ALAN exposure level decreases successively. But the >0–15-year-old group is an exception. Although it is the youngest group, the mean ALAN exposure of it is not the highest but close to that of people aged >50–60. From 0:00 to 6:00, ALAN exposure decreased in different magnitudes across all age groups. Groups with higher ALAN exposure intensity also have a greater reduction. For example, ALAN exposure decreased by 18.9 for >15–20 years old, while only 0.7 for >70–80 years old. This makes the inequity of ALAN exposure among different age groups less notable at late night.

Fig. 9.8 shows the visual results of population-weighted mean exposure to ALAN of different age groups in the 23 wards of Tokyo during two time

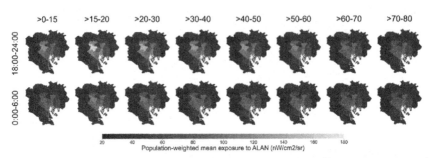

Figure 9.8 Population-weighted mean exposure to ALAN for different age groups of each district in two time periods.

periods. During the same time period, it can be found that the difference in ALAN exposure among age groups in central Tokyo is greater than that in the marginal areas of Tokyo. A similar phenomenon can also be found in a single group, that travel behavior will have a greater impact on changes in ALAN exposure in central Tokyo. This shows that there are regional differences in the inequity of ALAN among different age groups.

4.1.3 ALAN exposure among different residence groups

Fig. 9.9 shows the population-weighted mean exposure to ALAN of residents and nonresidents in two time periods. In comparison, it is significant that the population-weighted mean exposure to ALAN of nonresidents is higher than that of residents. During the period from 18:00 to 24:00, the average ALAN exposure of nonresidents reaches 100.7, which is 87.2% higher than the 53.8 of residents. From 0:00 to 6:00, there is little change in the average ALAN exposure of the residents, while the average ALAN exposure of nonresidents has experienced a substantial reduction of 32.9, and the difference between them also reduced to 28%. In general, nonresidents experience higher ALAN exposure than residents, but the inequity will decrease late at night.

Fig. 9.10 shows the spatial distribution of the population-weighted mean exposure to ALAN of residents and nonresidents in each district of Tokyo during two time periods. It can be seen that the ALAN exposure of residents and nonresidents in the marginal area of Tokyo is relatively close, and the difference between them is mainly concentrated in the urban center. In the center of Tokyo, even in the same district, nonresidents' ALAN exposure is much higher than that of residents. This shows that nonresidents in the central area are highly concentrated in places with high-intensity ALAN.

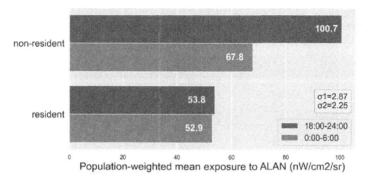

Figure 9.9 Population-weighted mean exposure to ALAN for different residence groups in two time periods.

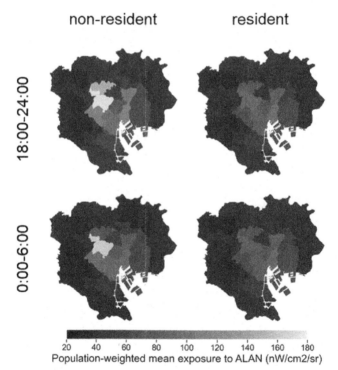

Figure 9.10 Population-weighted mean exposure to ALAN for different residence groups of each district in two time periods.

4.2 Result of TOD inequity analysis

4.2.1 Correlation coefficient analysis

After calculating the indicators for each station, a correlation coefficient analysis of average age and other variables was carried out (Fig. 9.11). It

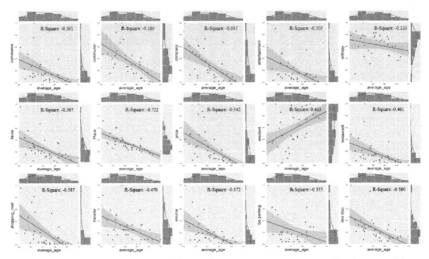

Figure 9.11 The correlation coefficient between average age and other variables.

can be seen that the "average age" variable has a positive correlation with the "resident population" variable and has strong negative correlations with other variables. Therefore, we can determine that the resource allocation of TOD is related to the age of users, and there is inequity in the allocation of users of different age groups, which will be verified by cluster analysis later.

4.2.2 Clusters of TODs

The K-means cluster analysis generates three clusters (Fig. 9.12), the projection of clustering results on N-P coordinate system is shown in Fig. 9.13. The corresponding indicator value distribution is shown in Fig. 9.14.

- **Cluster 0—Dependent balanced residence-oriented node**: The characteristic of cluster 0 is that the "average age" of users is relatively high, but the value of "Node" and "Place" are extremely low, and the value of "Place" is slightly higher than that of "node" These stations are generally distributed in areas with higher residential density, with the largest residential population and the minimal commuting population, and the consumption density is relatively low. This shows that the potential traffic demand at these stations is limited and matches the intensity of traffic development. Therefore, we designate cluster 0 as a "dependent balanced residence-oriented node."

- **Cluster 1—Commuter-oriented nodes with balanced potential**: The characteristic of cluster 1 is that the "average age" of users is higher

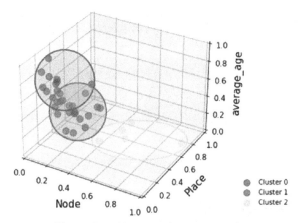

Figure 9.12 K-means clustering results.

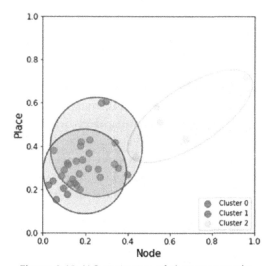

Figure 9.13 N-P projection of clustering results.

than cluster 0 and lower than cluster 2. The value of "Node" and "Place" tends to be moderate and balanced, and the value of "Place" is slightly higher than the value of "Node" So, it is described as "commuter-oriented nodes with balanced potential" because these stations have the largest commuter population, the lowest residential population and moderate consumption density. However, in terms of spatial distribution, stations close to the city center tend to have a large commuter

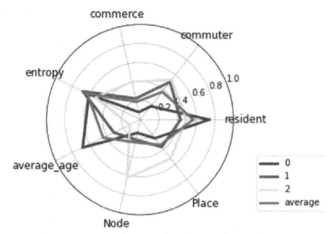

Figure 9.14 Distribution of indicators for each cluster.

population but a small residential population and high consumption density. Stations far away from the city center are the opposite. Therefore, they have high traffic demand, and there will be several peaks of demand during the working day, and the value of "Node" is slightly lower than the value of "Place" indicating that these stations may be difficult to cope with peak demand and have the potential to balance.

- **Cluster 2—Stress-balanced consumption-oriented node**: The stations included in cluster 2 are generally located in the city center or at the intersection of multiple lines, such as Tokyo Station, Ikebukuro Station, Shinjuku Station, and Shibuya Station. They are characterized by extremely high "Node" and "Place" values, and "Node" value is higher than the value of "place", which makes these stations can effectively deal with the moment when the passenger flow is overloaded. In addition, the "average age" of users is relatively young, the commuting population is slightly less than cluster 1, the residential population is moderate, and the consumption density is high. Therefore, we describe cluster 2 as a "stress-balanced consumption-oriented node".

5. Conclusion and limitation

5.1 Conclusion of ALAN equity

Based on other researchers, this study used mobile phone positioning data for the first time to conduct an EJ study of ALAN. Considering the temporal changes of the population, this study uses night-light remote sensing to estimate ALAN and discusses whether the ALAN in Tokyo, Japan is unequal among different groups from the aspects of age, gender, and place of residence. The results show that there is indeed a considerable degree of inequity in ALAN in Tokyo. Among user groups of different ages, people aged 15—20 have suffered the most exposure to ALAN. The elder groups are exposed to weaker ALAN, and children and the elderly under 15 are not affected by the inequity of ALAN. There is almost no inequality in ALAN between user groups of different genders. The average ALAN exposure of nonresidents and residents showed obvious inequity, and the nonresidents were significantly higher than the residents. In addition, we also found that there are regional differences in the inequities among different groups. Central Tokyo tends to be more unequal than marginal areas, and its inequity is more affected by time.

In further discussion, we found that over time at night, the decrease in ALAN exposure and inequity is related to the decrease in travel behavior. Because the destination of night travel and places with high-intensity ALAN are highly overlapped, the per capita ALAN exposure increases with the increase in travel behavior. The difference in travel patterns between different groups of people makes their average ALAN exposure increase or decrease differently, so the iniquity of ALAN will also change accordingly.

Because of the impact of travel behavior on ALAN exposure and the inequity of ALAN, the government should consider controlling the outdoor lighting of high-frequency destinations for night travel when taking policy actions. For example, by controlling the light distribution of light shields, hoods, etc., light leakage and glare from street lamps, billboards, etc. can be reduced. Relevant regulations have also appeared in the lighting control guidelines of "Lighting Up Tokyo" [65]. This shows that the purpose of research based on EJ is being combined with the environmental protection movement, which aims to protect everyone from environmental pollution. To achieve this goal, it is necessary to recognize and understand the differences in exposure of different populations to ALAN. We hope that this research can help scholars and the government better solve the problem of inequity in ALAN exposure.

5.2 Conclusion of TOD equity

In the process of TOD planning and construction, unequal resource allocation will inevitably occur. To explore whether TOD service level is unequal among users of different ages, this research attempts to establish a social equity performance evaluation and analysis method for urban TOD. Correlation coefficient analysis, Gini coefficient and cluster analysis are used to measure the equity of TOD development level among people of different ages, and to propose corresponding strategies for TOD future development. The result shows:

The Lorentz curve and the Gini coefficient reveal that the inequity of resource allocation in TOD is universal among all users, and the inequity of node value is greater than the inequity of place value. The Gini coefficient of the node value is close to the warning line of 0.4, which requires the attention of researchers. The Gini coefficient of place value is close to 0.2, which is relatively reasonable, but there is still room for optimization.

The analysis of the correlation coefficient between the variables representing the value of TOD reveals that among users of different age groups, TOD does indeed have inequity in resource allocation. Except for the commuting population, the average age of users and other value indicators of TOD are obviously negatively correlated, which means that stations with a higher proportion of elderly users have fewer resources.

Cluster analysis and visualization further illustrate how the inequity of TOD is reflected. The clustering results are divided into three categories, which are basically similar to the classification of the classic node–place model. Among them, stations with older users are described as "dependent balanced residence-oriented nodes" which are characterized by a large residential population, a small commuting population, and low node and venue values.

Stations with a moderate average user age are described as "commuter-oriented nodes with balanced potential," which are characterized by a small population and a large population, nodes and venue values are close to average, and the node value is lower than the venue value, which has the potential for balance.

Stations with a relatively small average user age are described as "stress-balanced consumption-oriented nodes" which are characterized by a relatively balanced residential population and commuting population, and high node value and place value.

The correlation between the various indicators and the average age of users is basically consistent with the results of the correlation coefficient analysis, except that the commuting population and residential population are found to be not simply linearly related to the average age of users. In an attempt to establish a social equity performance evaluation and analysis method for urban TOD, to measure the equity of TOD development level among people of different ages, the study also proposes a method and framework for using mobile big data to isolate and understand the TOD usage among different age groups. The study can be transferred to other TOD locations to support strategies for the future development of TOD.

References

[1] US Environmental Protection Agency, Learn about Environmental Justice, 2020. https://www.epa.gov/environmentaljustice/learn-about-environmental-justice.
[2] N. Aksaker, S.K. Yerli, Z. Kurt, M. Bayazit, A. Aktay, M.A. Erdoğan, A case study of light pollution in France, Astrophysics and Space Science 365 (9) (2020) 1—9, https://doi.org/10.1007/s10509-020-03869-4.
[3] P. Brown, RACE, class, and environmental-health—A review and systematization of the literature, Environmental Research 69 (1) (1995) 15—30, https://doi.org/10.1006/enrs.1995.1021.
[4] R.J. Brulle, D.N. Pellow, Environmental justice: human health and environmental inequalities, Annual Review of Public Health 27 (2006) 103—124, https://doi.org/10.1146/annurev.publhealth.27.021405.102124.
[5] S.M. Nadybal, T.W. Collins, S.E. Grineski, Light pollution inequities in the continental United States: a distributive environmental justice analysis, Environmental Research 189 (April) (2020), https://doi.org/10.1016/j.envres.2020.109959.
[6] K. Ard, Trends in exposure to industrial air toxins for different racial and socioeconomic groups: a spatial and temporal examination of environmental inequality in the US from 1995 to 2004, Social Science Research 53 (2015) 375—390, https://doi.org/10.1016/j.ssresearch.2015.06.019.
[7] J. Chakraborty, Convergence of COVID-19 and chronic air pollution risks: racial/ethnic and socioeconomic inequities in the U.S, Environmental Research 193 (August 2020) (2021) 110586, https://doi.org/10.1016/j.envres.2020.110586.
[8] T.W. Collins, S.E. Grineski, J. Chakraborty, Household-level disparities in cancer risks from vehicular air pollution in Miami, Environmental Research Letters 10 (9) (2015), https://doi.org/10.1088/1748-9326/10/9/095008.
[9] S. Grineski, B. Bolin, C. Boone, Criteria air pollution and marginalized populations: environmental inequity in metropolitan Phoenix, Arizona, Social Science Quarterly 88 (2) (2007) 535—554, https://doi.org/10.1111/j.1540-6237.2007.00470.x.
[10] J. Maantay, Asthma and air pollution in the Bronx: methodological and data considerations in using GIS for environmental justice and health research, in: HEALTH & PLACE, 13(Workshop on New Approaches to Researching Environmental Justice), 2007, pp. 32—56, https://doi.org/10.1016/j.healthplace.2005.09.009.
[11] R. Lagonigro, J.C. Martori, P. Apparicio, Environmental noise inequity in the city of Barcelona, Transportation Research Part D: Transport and Environment 63 (2018) 309—319, https://doi.org/10.1016/j.trd.2018.06.007.
[12] T.W. Collins, S.E. Grineski, J. Chakraborty, A.B. Flores, Environmental injustice and Hurricane Harvey: a household-level study of socially disparate flood exposures in Greater Houston, Texas, USA, Environmental Research 179 (September) (2019) 108772, https://doi.org/10.1016/j.envres.2019.108772.
[13] N. Dahmann, J. Wolch, P. Joassart-Marcelli, K. Reynolds, M. Jerrett, The active city? Disparities in provision of urban public recreation resources, Health & Place 16 (3) (2010) 431—445, https://doi.org/10.1016/j.healthplace.2009.11.005.

[14] M.C. Montgomery, J. Chakraborty, S.E. Grineski, T.W. Collins, An environmental justice assessment of public beach access in Miami, Florida, Applied Geography 62 (2015) 147−156, https://doi.org/10.1016/j.apgeog.2015.04.016.

[15] S.L. Harlan, A.J. Brazel, G.D. Jenerette, N.S. Jones, L. Larsen, L. Prashad, W.L. Stefanov, The shade of affluence: the inequitable distribution of the urban heat island, in: R.C. Wilkinson, W.R. Freudenburg (Eds.), Equity and the Environment, vol. 15, 2007, pp. 173−202, https://doi.org/10.1016/S0196-1152(07)15005-5.

[16] J. Voelkel, D. Hellman, R. Sakuma, V. Shandas, Assessing vulnerability to urban heat: a study of disproportionate heat exposure and access to refuge by socio-demographic status in portland, Oregon, International Journal of Environmental Research and Public Health 15 (4) (2018), https://doi.org/10.3390/ijerph15040640.

[17] R. Chepesiuk, Missing the dark: health effects of light pollution, Environmental Health Perspectives 117 (1) (2009), https://doi.org/10.1289/EHP.117-A20.

[18] C.C.M. Kyba, T. Kuester, A.S. de Miguel, K. Baugh, A. Jechow, F. Holker, J. Bennie, C.D. Elvidge, K.J. Gaston, L. Guanter, Artificially lit surface of Earth at night increasing in radiance and extent, Science Advances 3 (11) (2017), https://doi.org/10.1126/sciadv.1701528.

[19] F. Falchi, P. Cinzano, D. Duriscoe, C.C.M. Kyba, C.D. Elvidge, K. Baugh, B.A. Portnov, N.A. Rybnikova, R. Furgoni, The new world atlas of artificial night sky brightness, Science Advances 2 (6) (2016), https://doi.org/10.1126/sciadv.1600377.

[20] P. James, K.A. Bertrand, J.E. Hart, E.S. Schernhammer, R.M. Tamimi, F. Laden, Outdoor light at night and breast cancer incidence in the nurses' health study II, Environmental Health Perspectives 125 (8) (2017), https://doi.org/10.1289/EHP935.

[21] B.A. Portnov, R.G. Stevens, H. Samociuk, D. Wakefield, D.I. Gregorio, Light at night and breast cancer incidence in Connecticut: an ecological study of age group effects, Science of the Total Environment 572 (2016) 1020−1024, https://doi.org/10.1016/J.SCITOTENV.2016.08.006.

[22] Z. Tang, S. Li, M. Shen, Y. Xiao, J. Su, J. Tao, X. Wang, S. Shan, X. Kang, B. Wu, B. Zou, X. Chen, Association of exposure to artificial light at night with atopic diseases: a cross-sectional study in college students, International Journal of Hygiene and Environmental Health 241 (2022) 113932, https://doi.org/10.1016/J.IJHEH.2022.113932.

[23] C. Zhong, M. Franklin, J. Wiemels, R. McKean-Cowdin, N.T. Chung, J. Benbow, S.S. Wang, J.V. Lacey, T. Longcore, Outdoor artificial light at night and risk of non-Hodgkin lymphoma among women in the California Teachers Study cohort, Cancer Epidemiology 69 (2020) 101811, https://doi.org/10.1016/J.CANEP.2020.101811.

[24] Q. Xiao, G. Gee, R.R. Jones, P. Jia, P. James, L. Hale, Cross-sectional association between outdoor artificial light at night and sleep duration in middle-to-older aged adults: the NIH-AARP Diet and Health Study, Environmental Research 180 (2020) 108823, https://doi.org/10.1016/J.ENVRES.2019.108823.

[25] J. young Min, K. bok Min, Outdoor light at night and the prevalence of depressive symptoms and suicidal behaviors: a cross-sectional study in a nationally representative sample of Korean adults, Journal of Affective Disorders 227 (2018) 199−205, https://doi.org/10.1016/J.JAD.2017.10.039.

[26] Y.S. Koo, J.Y. Song, E.Y. Joo, H.J. Lee, E. Lee, S.K. Lee, K.Y. Jung, Outdoor artificial light at night, obesity, and sleep health: cross-sectional analysis in the KoGES study, Chronobiology International 33 (3) (2016) 301−314, https://doi.org/10.3109/07420528.2016.1143480, https://doi.org/10.3109/07420528.2016.1143480.

[27] Y. Lan, H. Roberts, M.-P. Kwan, M. Helbich, Daily space-time activities, multiple environmental exposures, and anxiety symptoms: a cross-sectional mobile phone-

based sensing study, Science of the Total Environment 834 (2022) 155276, https://doi.org/10.1016/J.SCITOTENV.2022.155276.

[28] Z. Yu, X. Zhu, X. Liu, Characterizing metro stations via urban function: thematic evidence from transit-oriented development (TOD) in Hong Kong, Journal of Transport Geography 99 (2022) 103299, https://doi.org/10.1016/J.JTRANGEO.2022.103299.

[29] P. Newman, J.R. Kenworthy, Cities and Automobile Dependence : A Sourcebook, 1989, p. 388.

[30] L. Ke, K. Furuya, S. Luo, Case comparison of typical transit-oriented-development stations in Tokyo district in the context of sustainability: spatial visualization analysis based on FAHP and GIS, Sustainable Cities and Society 68 (2021) 102788, https://doi.org/10.1016/J.SCS.2021.102788.

[31] R. Thomas, L. Bertolini, International Case Studies in TOD, Transit-Oriented Development, 2020, pp. 43−71, https://doi.org/10.1007/978-3-030-48470-5_3.

[32] D.M. Baker, B. Lee, How does light rail transit (LRT) impact gentrification? Evidence from fourteen US urbanized areas, Journal of Planning Education and Research 39 (1) (2017) 35−49, https://doi.org/10.1177/0739456X17713619.

[33] M.T. Clagett, If it's not mixed-income, it won't be transit-oriented: ensuring our future developments are equitable & promote transit, Transportation Law Journal 41 (2014). https://heinonline.org/HOL/Page?handle=hein.journals/tportl41&id=7&div=&collection=.

[34] H. Dong, Rail-transit-induced gentrification and the affordability paradox of TOD, Journal of Transport Geography 63 (2017) 1−10, https://doi.org/10.1016/J.JTRANGEO.2017.07.001.

[35] G.F. Sandoval, R. Herrera, Transit-Oriented Development and Equity in Latino Neighborhoods: A Comparative Case Study of MacArthur Park (Los Angeles) and Fruitvale (Oakland), 2015, https://doi.org/10.15760/trec.58.

[36] Sandoval, F. Gerardo, Making Transit-Oriented Development Work in Low-Income Latino Neighborhoods: A Comparative Case Study of Boyle Heights, Los Angeles and Logan Heights, San Diego. May, 2016.

[37] R. Bostic, M. Boarnet, E. Burinskiy, E. Andrew, S. Rodnyansky, R. Santiago-Bartolomei, H.-T.W. Jamme, Sustainable and Affordable Housing Near Rail Transit: Refining and Expanding a Scenario Planning Tool, 2018.

[38] K. Chapple, P. Waddell, D. Chatman, E. Org, Developing a New Methodology for Analyzing Potential Displacement, 2017. https://escholarship.org/uc/item/6xb465cq.

[39] G. Adorno, N. Fields, C. Cronley, R. Parekh, K. Magruder, Ageing in a low-density urban city: transportation mobility as a social equity issue, Ageing and Society 38 (2) (2018) 296−320, https://doi.org/10.1017/S0144686X16000994.

[40] A. of M.P. Organizations, More than Mobility Examining Impacts to Environmental Justice Populations, 2011.

[41] L. Bertolini, Spatial Development Patterns and Public Transport: The Application of an Analytical Model in the Netherlands, Planning Practice and Research 14 (2) (1999) 199−210, https://doi.org/10.1080/02697459915724. Http://Dx.Doi.Org/10.1080/02697459915724.

[42] B. Dong, Y. Liu, H. Fontenot, M. Ouf, M. Osman, A. Chong, S. Qin, F. Salim, H. Xue, D. Yan, Y. Jin, M. Han, X. Zhang, E. Azar, S. Carlucci, Occupant behavior modeling methods for resilient building design, operation and policy at urban scale: a review, Applied Energy 293 (2021) 116856, https://doi.org/10.1016/J.APENERGY.2021.116856.

[43] X. Kang, D. Yan, J. An, Y. Jin, H. Sun, Energy and Buildings 250 (2021) 111264, https://doi.org/10.1016/J.ENBUILD.2021.111264.

[44] P. Li, H. Zhang, W. Li, K. Yu, A.K. Bashir, A. Ali Al Zubi, J. Chen, X. Song, R. Shibasaki, IIoT based trustworthy demographic dynamics tracking with advanced

Bayesian learning, IEEE Transactions on Network Science and Engineering (2022), https://doi.org/10.1109/TNSE.2022.3145572.

[45] W. Li, H. Zhang, J. Chen, P. Li, Y. Yao, X. Shi, M. Shibasaki, H.H. Kobayashi, X. Song, R. Shibasaki, Metagraph-based life pattern clustering with big human mobility data, IEEE Transactions on Big Data (2022), https://doi.org/10.1109/TBDATA.2022.3155752, 1—1.

[46] Y. Song, B. Huang, J. Cai, B. Chen, Dynamic assessments of population exposure to urban greenspace using multi-source big data, in: Science of the Total Environment, vol. 634, 2018, https://doi.org/10.1016/j.scitotenv.2018.04.061.

[47] H. Zhang, J. Chen, Q. Chen, T. Xia, X. Wang, W. Li, X. Song, R. Shibasaki, A universal mobility-based indicator for regional health level, Cities 120 (2022) 103452, https://doi.org/10.1016/J.CITIES.2021.103452.

[48] H. Zhang, P. Li, Z. Zhang, W. Li, J. Chen, X. Song, R. Shibasaki, J. Yan, Epidemic versus economic performances of the COVID-19 lockdown: a big data driven analysis, Cities 120 (2022) 103502, https://doi.org/10.1016/J.CITIES.2021.103502.

[49] M. Fallah-Shorshani, M. Hatzopoulou, N.A. Ross, Z. Patterson, S. Weichenthal, Evaluating the impact of neighborhood characteristics on differences between residential and mobility-based exposures to outdoor air pollution, Environmental Science and Technology 52 (18) (2018a) 10777—10786, https://doi.org/10.1021/acs.est.8b02260.

[50] M. Shekarrizfard, A. Faghih-Imani, L.F. Tetreault, S. Yasmin, F. Reynaud, P. Morency, C. Plante, L. Drouin, A. Smargiassi, N. Eluru, M. Hatzopoulou, Modelling the spatio-temporal distribution of ambient nitrogen dioxide and investigating the effects of public transit policies on population exposure, Environmental Modelling & Software 91 (2017a) 186—198, https://doi.org/10.1016/j.envsoft.2017.02.007.

[51] M. Shekarrizfard, A. Faghih-Imani, L.F. Tetreault, S. Yasmin, F. Reynaud, P. Morency, C. Plante, L. Drouin, A. Smargiassi, N. Eluru, M. Hatzopoulou, Regional assessment of exposure to traffic-related air pollution: impacts of individual mobility and transit investment scenarios, Sustainable Cities and Society 29 (2017b) 68—76, https://doi.org/10.1016/j.scs.2016.12.002.

[52] Y. Song, B. Huang, Q. He, B. Chen, J. Wei, R. Mahmood, Dynamic assessment of PM2.5 exposure and health risk using remote sensing and geo-spatial big data, in: Environmental Pollution, vol. 253, 2019, https://doi.org/10.1016/j.envpol.2019.06.057.

[53] C. Perchoux, B. Chaix, S. Cummins, Y. Kestens, Conceptualization and measurement of environmental exposure in epidemiology: accounting for activity space related to daily mobility, Health & Place 21 (2013) 86—93, https://doi.org/10.1016/j.healthplace.2013.01.005.

[54] E. Setton, J.D. Marshall, M. Brauer, K.R. Lundquist, P. Hystad, P. Keller, D. Cloutier-Fisher, The impact of daily mobility on exposure to traffic-related air pollution and health effect estimates, Journal of Exposure Science and Environmental Epidemiology 21 (1) (2011) 42—48, https://doi.org/10.1038/jes.2010.14.

[55] S. Steinle, S. Reis, C.E. Sabel, Quantifying human exposure to air pollution-moving from static monitoring to spatio-temporally resolved personal exposure assessment, Science of the Total Environment 443 (2013) 184—193, https://doi.org/10.1016/j.scitotenv.2012.10.098.

[56] Z. Li, Z. Han, J. Xin, X. Luo, S. Su, M. Weng, Transit oriented development among metro station areas in Shanghai, China: variations, typology, optimization and implications for land use planning, Land Use Policy 82 (2019) 269—282, https://doi.org/10.1016/J.LANDUSEPOL.2018.12.003.

[57] Wendell Cox, Demographia World Urban Areas, 2021. http://www.demographia.com/db-worldua.pdf.

[58] The Ministry of the Environment, Guidelines for Countermeasures against Light Pollution, Revised Edition, 2021. https://www.env.go.jp/press/files/jp/115913.pdf.

[59] NTT DOCOMO, What is mobile spatial statistics?. https://mobaku.jp/about/, 2018c.

[60] NTT DOCOMO, Information about Mobile Spatial Statistics, 2018. https://www.docomo.ne.jp/corporate/disclosure/mobile_spatial_statistics/.

[61] NTT DOCOMO, Distribution Statistics (Domestic Occupants) | Mobile Spatial Statistics, 2018. https://mobaku.jp/service/jpn_distribution/.

[62] X. Jing, X. Shao, C. Cao, X. Fu, L. Yan, Comparison between the Suomi-NPP day-night band and DMSP-OLS for correlating socio-economic variables at the provincial level in China, Remote Sensing 8 (1) (2016), https://doi.org/10.3390/RS8010017.

[63] P. Li, H. Zhang, X. Wang, X. Song, R. Shibasaki, A spatial finer electric load estimation method based on night-light satellite image, Energy 209 (2020) 118475, https://doi.org/10.1016/j.energy.2020.118475.

[64] NOAA, Version 1 VIIRS Day/Night Band Nighttime Lights: Monthly Composites - Tile 2, 2017. https://ngdc.noaa.gov/eog/viirs/download_dnb_composites.html.

[65] Office of the Governor for Policy Planning, LIGHTING UP TOKYO (Basic Policy for Lighting up Public Facilities, 2018 etc.), https://www.seisakukikaku.metro.tokyo.lg.jp/cross-efforts/lightup/pdf/policy.pdf.

Further reading

[1] Y. Song, B. Chen, H.C. Ho, M.P. Kwan, D. Liu, F. Wang, J. Wang, J. Cai, X. Li, Y. Xu, Q. He, H. Wang, Q. Xu, Y. Song, Observed inequality in urban greenspace exposure in China, Environment International 156 (2021) 106778, https://doi.org/10.1016/J.ENVINT.2021.106778.

[2] X. Zhou, D. Yan, X. Feng, G. Deng, Y. Jian, Y. Jiang, Influence of household air-conditioning use modes on the energy performance of residential district cooling systems, Building Simulation 9 (4) (2016) 429—441, https://doi.org/10.1007/s12273-016-0280-9.

Index

Printed in the United States
by Baker & Taylor Publisher Services